MESTENGO

A Wild Mustang, a Writer on the Run,
and the Power of the Unexpected

MELINDA ROTH

LYONS PRESS
Guilford, Connecticut
An imprint of Globe Pequot Press

Lyons Press is an imprint of Globe Pequot Press.

All photographs from the personal collection of the author.

Project editor: Tracee Williams
Layout artist: Melissa Evarts

Library of Congress Cataloging-in-Publication Data

Roth, Melinda.
    Mestengo : a wild mustang, a writer on the run, and the power of the unexpected / Melinda Roth.
        pages cm
    Summary: "Exhausted by her job as a political press secretary, Melinda Roth found the courage to escape. Her goal: a simpler life in rural Illinois that would let her pursue her passion for writing. But then real life intervened. A fire at a neighboring farm and a misinterpreted gesture of kindness transformed her into the reluctant caretaker of a homeless menagerie of animals. Roth, coauthor of the New York Times-bestseller From Baghdad with Love, writes vividly, movingly, and often humorously of the chaos that descended into her life. One of her new tenants was a wild mustang, broken but not bowed, his restless spirit propelling him to escape the fences and pens that enclosed him—a far different life than before he was violently captured by a government-sponsored 'round-up.' Ultimately these two fiercely independent characters each provide the catalyst for the other's life-changing and life-affirming decisions. Mestengo is a captivating, emotional account that taps into readers' love of animals: Marley and Me meets The Horse Whisperer. An entertaining and delightful read, it is a cinematic, sometimes tense, but always beautiful story of the power of healing"— Provided by publisher.
    ISBN 978-0-7627-9019-7 (hardback)
    1. Mustang—Illinois. 2. Roth, Melinda. 3. Human-animal relationships—Illinois. 4. Farm life—Illinois. 5. Mental healing—Case studies. 6. Life change events—Case studies. 7. Career changes—Case studies. I. Title.
    SF293.M9R68 2013
    636.1'309773—dc23

                                                                                                    2013016669

Printed in the United States of America

10 9 8 7 6 5 4 3 2 1

Dedicated to Alicia, Jacob, Sarah, Adam, and Vivien, who may very well inherit all of the animals some day.

Prologue

The stallion paced through the snow in the front yard and snorted threats that jetted sulfuric clouds from his nostrils. At the end of each lap, which spanned the length of the front porch, he pawed the ground, arched his neck, and shook his head with the apparent intent of extracting revenge for every injustice done to any wild horse that ever roamed the plains and ended up stuck on a farm in the northern Midwest with a middle-aged woman who didn't like horses and was late for work.

I peered around the edge of the living room curtain and pulled it up to just below my eyes so he couldn't see my face. As the stallion carved his warpath through the snow, a gust of wind lifted his mane and exposed the government tattoo on his neck, which legally branded him my captive, and his eyes, which expressed independent notions to the contrary. On many occasions over the past several months I told him he was free to leave, "Take our road south to the next road, turn west, and keep going until you reach Montana." But for some reason, perhaps as part of his grand plan of vengeance against the Bureau of Land Management's Wild Mustang Relocation Program, or because there'd be no one to feed him along the way, the Mustang stayed.

"I have nothing to do with the Bureau of Land Management," I whispered to him after reading a book about horse whisperers. "I am innocent." But the Mustang curled his upper lip in disgust, and when he realized I had no peppermints, took a swipe at my scalp as well.

I lowered the curtain away from my eyes as another blast of wind roared in from across the northern fields and bullied an old metal bell once used to call in men for dinner that now clanged like a helpless idiot.

In the few short months I'd lived on the farm, I'd grown to hate the bell, which every visitor felt compelled to pull and, which when pulled sent sledgehammer-against-oil-drum clangs across the entire county. Just the week before, when the FedEx driver delivered two books, *Horses for Dummies* and *Why Bad Things Happen to Good People*, and pulled the bell's chain to announce his presence, I yanked a piece of paper out of the computer printer, grabbed a tube of lipstick, and scratched DO NOT TOUCH in big red letters followed by a gruesome smiley face with an upside-down, zigzagged smile. I duct-taped the sign to the bell's chain.

That might have solved at least one of my problems had not that morning's wind—the one that now blew cyclones of snow dust up and around the Mustang's pacing legs—ripped the sign off the chain, duct tape and all, and flung it straight onto the stallion's side rump, where it stuck: DO NOT TOUCH followed by a lurid smiley face. I didn't need *Secrets of the Horse Whisperers* to interpret his point.

Had I the luxury, I'd just wait it out, wait for a cat or a snowmobiler or a lost driver looking for directions upon whom he could vent his rage, but I'd clocked in late to my new job five of the twelve days I'd worked there and had no coherent excuses left. I was out of time.

I tiptoed to the front door window to scope things out from a different perspective, but when the Mustang saw my face through the glass, he trotted to the foot of the porch steps, where he stood and stared back up at me. Slowly, methodically, never taking his eyes from the door and apparently oblivious to the smiley face stuck to his butt, he pawed a hole in the snow with his hoof.

What did he want from me anyway?

Maybe he was just after Dustin, whom I'd turn over gladly. But my son's best friend—an aeronautical engineering student—was cocooned upstairs in a world of logarithms, correlations, and exponential probabilities (video poker) and wouldn't hear me if I called. Besides, even though he took thirty-minute showers, spent precious workable hours on the phone with his girlfriend, and had no apparent aptitude for shoveling snow, repairing fences, or hauling horse manure to the ever-growing muck pile, which he referred to as the "equine excrement mass," I couldn't very well sacrifice him to the animal on the lawn without guilt of the heavy scale-tipping type plaguing me for the rest of my life.

Through the frost on the glass I saw the garage where my car sat and the fifty yards of unplowed snow between it and me. Even if Dustin had cleared a path with the ergonomic, cushioned-grip snow shovel I bought at Farm & Fleet instead of sprinkling salt pellets (which he claimed worked just as well as shoveling, because they helped the snow reach its freezing point depression more quickly by changing its colligative properties but which in reality sank in the twelve inches of snow like lead bombs and did nothing), I still couldn't outrun the stallion to the garage.

I couldn't outrun him. I could, however, outthink him. At least that's what the complex and growing thickets of horse whispering, horse training, and horse management books—strewn across the kitchen table and living room floor like self-help books after a bad breakup—said. Horses have hooves, but people have brains. That's what they said. So all I had to do was . . . think of something.

"You'll never outthink a horse like that," Irene would tell me several months later, during the spring when she first visited the farm and shot me fairly continual looks of suspicion as she took in the scene—the holes in the barn walls splattered with dry blood, the dented metal stock gates held shut with barbed wire, the electric fences strung chaotically across the property like the poorly planned perimeter of a penal colony.

"He's not like other horses. He was born in the wild. He was raised in the wild. And then he's captured and beaten by people who don't understand why *he* can't understand what's happening to him . . ." Irene paused, shaded her eyes, and looked toward the driveway. "Are those . . .," she squinted, ". . . *goats* on my truck?"

They were, two pygmies bought after reading a book about controlling uncontrollable horses, which suggested that the poorly behaved horse might only need a few friends but didn't explain what to do with the friends if the poorly behaved horse tried to kill them.

The book also did little toward explaining what to do with all of the Mustang's other friends, the ones who came with him originally—the geese and chickens, the ewes, the two sets of triplet lambs, the rams, the pregnant mare, the dirty pony, the white stallion, and the two-year-old stallion, the "other stallion," as I called him—or how to explain to visiting dignitaries, such as Irene or the long string of veterinarians or the McHenry County Animal Control officers or the Woodstock Police, who they all were and how they all got there in the first place.

Eventually I would learn to wave my hand dismissively and say, "It's a long story." But in the beginning, back when the damage unfurled and the books piled up and the escape routes dwindled doing a real number on my logic, back then, I usually started out with, "I only moved here to write a novel . . ."

I rested my forehead against the cold glass of the front door window and let my breath fog a curtain between the Mustang and me. As my finger traced T-H-I-N-K in the condensation, half-formed sentences of any value from the books pushed through my brain at about the same velocity as escaped convicts through waist-high swamp water . . . *don't show your fear . . . assert your authority . . . be the herd leader . . .* all of which might have applied were I still a political press secretary facing skeptical media but none of which remotely applied to my current status as hostage to a horse.

I exhaled over T-H-I-N-K and wrote T-H-I-N-K-!-!-! . . . *learn their language . . . know what they're thinking . . . forge a partnership . . .* again, all foreign concepts to a would-be novelist who only wanted to get away from it all and ended up overseeing a bloodthirsty horse with unrestricted access to her lawn instead.

Bloodthirsty or otherwise, he *was* beautiful, and were he the subject of a Raphael portrait—a Baroque chiaroscuro of a dark bay horse contrasted against white snow, dramatically lit from an unseen, divine source and titled *Animal with Smiley Face*—I might have appreciated his form and so-called function a little more than I did as he stood there like a four-legged assassin blocking the way between me and a paycheck.

But there was more than that. More than the aggressive stance and muscled elegance of a wild stallion who disappeared from the mountains leaving no forwarding address. There were also . . . I rubbed a circle in the frost with my fingertips and looked out . . . the scars, the quarter moon bite marks from the competing stallions of his youth and the newer lines from ropes, twitches, chains, barbed wire, and rubber hoses caused by humans that crisscrossed his body like pick-up sticks.

And the tattoo. The strange white string of symbols branded on his neck by the BLM after his capture, which when interpreted meant EL FINAL to his life in the wild.

And the eyes. The haunted eyes. What they looked for, what they couldn't find, and reflections still in them of a herd he once knew.

Slowly, with the despondency of one condemned, I gave a final blow to the glass to blot it all out, and I wrote my final essay on the window, G-O A-W-A-Y, in reverse with hopes as plausible as anything else that had happened to me since I moved to the farm, that the Mustang could read.

That's when the smell of smoke returned again—as it would more than once that winter. It came in waves, in and out, here and gone, when things got tough and the scenery turned bad. Maybe I just imagined the smoke when I smelled it, and maybe I smelled it after the facts as a form of confirmation. But I almost believed then as I almost believe to this day, that I smelled the smoke before everything happened, like an omen or a premonition or an ongoing call to arms.

Chapter One

I first smelled the smoke as I stood in the driveway of the farmhouse on top of a hill in McHenry County in Northern Illinois that was, according to the man who leased it to me one month before, the highest point in all of Northern Illinois. As such, it took the brunt of the northwesterly winds that blew in off the pastures during autumn and brought with them dried corn husks, empty fertilizer bags, NO HUNTING signs, and the shorn remnants of store receipts and newspaper pages from as far away as the Arctic Circle that now whipped in eddies around my feet and flew up into my face.

I wondered where the smell of smoke came from as I watched a black pickup truck at the base of the hill rumble up the driveway toward me. It was huge, nearly the size of an armored tank, and the sound of a potent engine or broken muffler, I didn't know which, rolled its way up before the truck itself ever did.

As I held my breath and willed it away, Dustin called from the porch through cupped hands, "Who is it?" with the hope of an island castaway at the sighting of a ship.

I looked up at the porch and shrugged. Unlike my twenty-three-year-old boarder, I didn't want visitors. I especially didn't want visitors who were neighbors and would ask questions about who I was, where I came from, and why I was here in the first place.

The truck prowled toward me anyway, upward along a rotted wood fence surrounding a field of weeds, crumbling stone silos, and a dairy barn the size of an abandoned city cathedral whose wooden frame tilted from its stone foundation as if pushed by the finger of a god.

Like almost every building on the property, the barn was on life support. White paint peeled from the clapboards. The remnants of loose gutters banged along the roofline. Opaque plastic sheets that billowed in and out with the late-October wind covered gutted windows. To its north a dented metal machine shed butted up against an older wooden shed with a caved-in roof that butted up against an old outhouse with its door hanging loose on one hinge. To the west, a slatted corncrib filled with tractor parts and barbed wire moaned with every gust of wind, as did the skeletal remains of a long-abandoned chicken house. The only thing still breathing on its own was the house on top of the hill as big and white and square and solid as a head nurse with hands on hips. It looked down on everything, kept watch on everything.

The sound of the truck startled two crows out of a large cupola balanced precariously on the barn's roof, and when I looked up, I saw tight black tendrils of smoke that unwound in the distance like loose braids as they reached the sky. I couldn't tell how far away the smoke was, but it didn't matter because I judged the distance with satisfaction as I judged every other distance here on the farm: somewhere between me and everyone else.

When I first visited the farm, the estate agent dredged up every environmental hazard from the *Grapes of Wrath* to the *Wizard of Oz* to convince me how isolated it was. "Specially bad in winter," he said. "Lotta tree limbs down. Roof shingles fly off. Lose power at least once a month, and with the wind chills down below zero, well," he shook his head as if confirming a death, "it gets cold as hell when the power goes off."

His attempt to vilify winter came after a long list of seasonal details including torrential downpours that drowned small animals, tornadoes that whirled barns and cows through the sky, and droughts that dried up wells, fields, and men's spirits alike. Snowdrifts. Lightning strikes. Burr plants that ate you alive. Skunks and possums that roamed the night in gangs and barn rats that would upend a truck if they got a notion there was any food in it. "You afraid of bugs?" he asked and then shook his head as if it was too horrible to mention but then did anyway and ticked off beetles, mosquitoes, crickets, grasshoppers, dragonflies, and caterpillars that crawled up your pants legs. There were spiders as big as tarantulas in the basement and centipedes as long as your arm in the drains and mice in the walls and squirrels in the chimney, and they all had it in for you, and they all had rabies.

"Ever use well water?"

I shook my head.

"Well then." He raised his eyebrow and leaned his head back. "Let me tell you how orange it will turn your blonde hair then."

It didn't matter. The farm was exactly what I wanted—a refuge from everyone else—and when I left that afternoon, I clutched the hard-won lease to my chest like a briefcase full of money.

"Who *is* it?" Dustin called down again from the porch through the wind.

I shrugged, and as the truck plowed through a pile of wind-blown leaves and made the last upward bend in the drive, I clenched my jaws and waited.

• • •

By profession, I was a political press secretary. By intent, I was a professional liar. And after years of skirting the Golden Rule, after the speeches and the fundraisers and the late-night calls from frantic bosses, after missing the birthdays and graduations of my three children and then sending interns out to buy presents, after the backbends, breakups, breakdowns, and finally, *finally*, the sale of a well-received nonfiction book, which let me leave it all behind, at least for awhile, the farm's FOR RENT advertisement on the Internet and the solitude it promised looked like an attempt at communication from the Good & Great Upstairs.

I chose Northern Illinois, because my three children went to college here and settled in Chicago, and I wanted to make up for lost time. I chose McHenry County, because it was two squares away on the map from the city and had a nice shape. I chose the town of Woodstock, because I liked the name, and I chose this farm, because it was the only one for rent that I could find.

It was a good choice, too, because there was no cell phone service in most parts of the house, so I didn't have to return any calls, and there was no way to answer e-mails with only a dial-up connection. People who needed to get in touch with me resorted to sending letters in the mail, a *registered* letter in the case of one particularly needy friend whose husband was having an affair, and even then reception was iffy, because no one, including the post office, seemed to know exactly where McHenry

3

County, Illinois was. I could have listed my address as "Somewhere up by the Wisconsin border" and gotten more mail.

"I don't get it," Robert said in one of his late-night calls to me after I'd moved in. "Explain this to me again."

"I already did a thousand times."

"Yeah, but I still don't get it. You live on a . . . *farm.*"

Robert, a contract lobbyist I'd been seeing before I left, said the word *farm* as if it was a foreign place with a foreign name that had no slot in his vocabulary.

"It's only for a year. Just until I write the book. Then I'll be back."

"Yeah, but a . . . *farm?*"

It was a conversation that repeated itself over and over again. Whenever Robert called—and I happened to be in a part of the house that picked up service and I happened to decide to pick up the phone—the same words came out of our mouths like lines in a script. And it wasn't just Robert. Everyone I knew, even those who knew me best, including my parents, my kids, and my best friend from high school, asked, "Yeah, but a . . . *farm?*" as if I'd had some kind of nervous breakdown.

Which, I guess, I had. But it was well deserved. A person could lie to the public, ignore their families, and deceive their lovers for their entire lives, but they couldn't get away with perjuring themselves for very long without cracking up just a bit. And besides, I asked myself, who wouldn't escape their lives and all of their responsibilities for a year if given the chance? So after a while, when I grew tired of explaining, I just stopped answering the phone.

For Dustin, my son's childhood friend and now my twenty-three-year-old resident, things were different. When I invited him to join me on the farm—rent in exchange for chores—he assured me the isolation wouldn't bother him and suggested the peace and quiet would help him finish his résumé. For him, the farm was only a short-term layover between college and career, and the state of physical and mental solitude, otherwise known as being without broadband, only a temporary inconvenience. What he didn't realize, at least until after the first week, was that the only reliable way to communicate with the outside world was through smoke signals.

If he wanted to talk with his girlfriend, he had to take his cell to the only place that got absolute reception, which was, rain or shine, out the front door, down the hill of the yard, across the fence of the front paddock area, to the southeast corner of the northwest quadrant of the westernmost pasture on the property—where he had to stand between two large black walnut trees that dropped their loads like dive bombers. If there was strong wind or rain, he made the extra trip to the back end of the dairy barn. If there was lightning or a tornado, he drove into town.

So that morning, as the truck prowled around the last bend in the drive and I braced myself for an intruder, Dustin sensed a live human being besides me to talk to and bounded down the stairs from the porch to greet him.

• • •

"Name's Lenny," the man said as he bent down, picked up an empty cigarette box the wind brought in, crushed it in the palm of his hand, and thrust it into his coat pocket. It was made of canvas, the coat, like a winter sailboat cover, only streaked with dirt and paint and worn down in spots to sheen. A clump of burrs hung from the wrist, and he plucked them off without wincing. "Live just up the road."

He was robust, sunburned, and weathered for his fifty-or-so years. His John Deere cap sat at a serious angle, low and straight across his brow line rather than pushed back to the top of his head, and when his hand enveloped mine in a pumice-stone grip and I gave him a counterfeit smile, he didn't bother returning it.

"We just moved here," Dustin said with an enthusiasm usually reserved for those just released from a solitary, well-padded confinement.

Lenny nodded and glanced over at Dustin's old car plastered with bumper-sticker wisdom from John Lennon, Bob Marley, and Che Guevara: IMAGINE WORLD PEACE, a post-Katrina MAKE LEVEES NOT WAR, and SOMEWHERE IN TEXAS A VILLAGE IS MISSING ITS IDIOT.

"Figured that," he said and then grunted, which was a mistake on his part, because Dustin took it as an attempt at political discourse and lunged at the chance to make a new friend.

"Do you grow corn?"

Lenny's eyes swerved away from the car to Dustin's expectant face. "No."

"Because I saw this thing on the Discovery Channel about the thermodynamics of the corn-ethanol biofuel cycle and about how the fossil fuel energy used to produce it is actually more than the biofuel's calorific value. So I was thinking that if you raised corn for ethanol, you'd, you know, definitely be wasting your time."

"Well, I don't."

Dustin nodded. "But I guess you don't. So . . . I guess . . . that's good."

"I raise cattle," Lenny said, getting right to his point, "and I came round to see if you'd be interested in renting me your two back pastures for hay, and if you're not using that front paddock," he turned and nodded down toward the fenced-in area of weeds adjacent to the barn, "I'll rent that from you for two of my heifers."

I stared up at him for more explanation.

He stared back and waited for an answer.

"Heifers?" I finally said as I frantically searched my vocabulary for the word and came up blank.

"Yup."

I snuck a peek at Dustin, who shrugged, and when Lenny caught the exchange, he grinned half-cocked as if he suddenly found himself on familiar ground. He pushed the John Deere cap to the back of his head and leaned against the truck with hand on hip in a pose of nonchalance. It was a posture I recognized immediately, one that politicians and lobbyists assumed when they wanted to make a deal but didn't want to seem too eager, and I realized that Lenny mistook our confusion about the word *heifers* as collusion about what to charge for rent.

He swiveled his head toward the back of the truck and spit. When he turned his head back, his gaze was level and the grin was gone.

"I'll pay you what I paid the last tenant."

"Heifers," I said again, because I still didn't know what they were and didn't know what else to say.

He nodded slowly, "Yup," and looked out over the back pasture as if getting bored—another well-known tactic of deal makers. "Two of 'em."

"Two of 'em," I repeated as I stalled for time hoping a definition might make some kind of grand entrance. When it didn't, I felt a familiar tic start tapping in my left eye.

It occurred to me when the tic started that this wasn't a public negotiation about corporate tax breaks or a backroom deal about pension funds. There were no schedules to check, no party lines to adhere to, not one, single, soul-sucking agenda to consider. There weren't any lawyers or lobbyists twisting wrists to check watches: there probably wasn't even a suit, a gold watch, or a pair of wingtips within fifty miles. No one needed an answer from me except a sunburned farmer in muddy boots who only wanted to put two things called "heifers" in my yard.

But the thing about escaping stress is that it takes time to readjust, and your brain, which wants nothing to do with the word *heifers* bows with outstretched arms to the rest of your body and says, "Be my guest," out of sheer habit. And there you are, alone in a mindless body that can't handle this kind of responsibility, which as I'd learned from reading dozens of books about anxiety disorders and panic attacks, is the second thing about stress that damages your case most in the end: It convinces your brain—both left side and right—that you, its vessel, its whole reason for being, is incapable of handling the job. Instead, it sneaks out the backdoor, backpack stuffed with valuables, and leaves no forwarding address.

What *was* a heifer? An overweight woman was the best I could come up with, and just before the left side of my brain followed the right side out the door, it warned me not to let on.

I looked up so Lenny wouldn't see the tic hammering away in my eye and noticed the smoke again above the roofline of the barn, drifting now, indifferent, lazy in the way that it wandered with no place to go and all the time it needed to get there.

As an arrow of southbound geese flew just beyond the smoke's reach, it occurred to me that when I was this far away from the city, there were very few horizons. In the city, the landscape ended at the next building, the next corner, the next person walking toward me whom I had to avoid. It made me feel vulnerable. It made me feel trapped. There was no way to see where I was going. But here, when I looked up at the sky or out at the fields, I looked at distances that might take days to reach. Even at night I gazed out at millions of stars and beyond them a million more until I realized everything was reversed, that instead of looking out over land with a distant horizon, I looked at a place with no horizon at all.

And somehow that made me feel safe.

I looked back at Lenny. The answer to his question was simple. For the first time in a long time I didn't have to strategize anything, because for the first time in a long time there wasn't anything to strategize about. Everything I needed to see I could see. This man didn't care who I was, who I worked for, or whose ear I could bend. He kept direct eye contact and never once asked where I came from or how I made a living. He didn't want to know about my children, my educational background, or which side of the aisle I stood on politically. It was almost too straightforward—a simple question that needed a simple answer—but he'd never stop by to chitchat over tea, and in the end, that's all that really mattered to me.

Finally, with the relief of someone who finds what she was frantically hunting for right in front of her, I shrugged and said, "Sure, why not," and was surprised at how easy it was to do.

He nodded, and when Dustin broached the next subject—did he raise soybeans?—Lenny turned to me and touched the brim of his cap.

"I'll bring 'em round tomorrow," he said. "I'll be going."

"Wait," I said as he turned toward his truck, "was there a fire?" and pointed up to the smoke in the sky.

Lenny followed my hand and then rested his own hand on the door of his truck.

"Yeah. Barn fire. Last night."

"Was anyone hurt?"

Lenny nodded and stared hard at the smoke. "Lost some sheep."

"Sheep?" Dustin's eyes sparkled at the potential of another conversation, and he stepped into the shadow of the open truck door and rested his elbow proprietarily upon it. "I *just* saw a thing on the History Channel about how the sheep industry in the United States declined drastically after World War II because of wool-production subsidies and restrictions on grazing on public lands. Wow. Cool. I didn't even *know* you raised sheep around here . . ."

"We don't." Lenny dipped his head and looked at his boots. "They were more like . . .," he shrugged, ". . . pets."

I stared up at the smoke as I gave the difference between the death of pets and the death of livestock a respectable silence. Only now it was more than just smoke, now it was something a little too large, too raw, and too still alive to ingest: death and how it happened. My guess was that on farms like these it happened with a shrug.

"Did he have any other animals?" I finally asked.

"Yeah. Some of the sheep lived, and he's got chickens and, I don't know, some ducks or something. And horses. I think one of them is one of those wild mustangs that the government rounds up. I've seen the tattoo on his neck."

"I read something somewhere about those mustangs . . ." Dustin started.

"What's going to happen to them?" I interrupted.

Lenny shrugged again. "Dunno. The guy's Mexican or something, just moved here a couple of years ago and doesn't speak that much English. All I know is that winter's coming on, and he's got a whole lot of animals and no barn to put them in."

"That's too bad," I said.

"Yup, well. I don't have any room in *my* barn for them, and all the other big barns in these parts are pretty much gone."

Lenny touched the brim of his cap again, and as he climbed into his truck, I realized he'd never turned off the ignition.

After he rumbled down the drive and pulled out onto the road, I stood and watched the last of the smoke drift away. Half an hour before I would have thought about the smoke with satisfaction—my neighbor's barn burned down, but it was far enough away that I didn't have to worry and I hadn't even noticed—but now as I stared up at the sky, I thought about dead sheep, the emotional proximity of tragedy, and a wild mustang with no barn to protect him from bad weather.

• • •

Chapter Two

My sister and I looked out from the hayloft across squares of gold October corn and winter wheat that lay like a hand-stitched quilt between my farm and my neighbor's. From our vantage point we could see the black hull of the burned barn surrounded by sheep, horses, and a scattering of chickens and ducks all heads down grazing on brown lawn grass. In the front yard a woman pushed a small child in a tire swing. In the back a teenage boy filled buckets with water from a hose.

"Look at that," Susan said and pointed out to the neighbor's back field, where two men—one young, one old—walked cautiously toward a horse who moved quickly back and forth along a fence line.

The horse was brown with a black mane that seemed disproportionately thick and long to the rest of his body, and when he reached one invisible stopping point on the fence line and spun around to pace back toward another, it flew up and away from his neck like the tails of an opera coat snapped up by the wind. He seemed frantic, caught between threats on either side of him that only he could see, and several times he stopped midway along the fence and pranced in place as if trying to generate energy to jump. Only he couldn't. Even from our distance we could see that his weakened state—the outlines of his ribs and the peaks of his hipbones—rendered him unable. After he reared in a half-hearted attempt, he returned to pacing.

"Maybe," Susan said, "you could help them."

I raised my eyebrows. My sister was hearing impaired, so much of my communication with her was visual. Her hearing loss began as a result of nerve damage when she was a child and deteriorated slowly over time, so because she grew up hearing, she could talk and learned to read lips and body language. "I mean, there's plenty of room in here for *a lot* of animals," she said as she turned and surveyed the deep space around us.

The barn *was* big, as big as the city halls of most towns. On the first floor it held three ancient tractors, a pickup truck with twenty-year-old license plates, and at least ten decades' worth of broken tools, outdated furniture, rusted lawn mowers, tangled rolls of barbed wire, doorless green refrigerators, buckets of used motor oil, hand-painted signs—EGGS 4 SALE, BEEF 4 SALE, HAY 4 SALE—and other things gone useless.

On the second floor, though, the hayloft opened up like a cathedral, and each time I'd gone up there, the light played so differently it looked like another place. It was architectural op art of open space and angled beams and soaring heights, and as Susan waved her hand around its majestic emptiness, bars of dust-filled sunlight surged in through the windows and onto dozens of bales of stacked hay.

"Why not?" she asked.

My eyebrows snapped down, and I stared at her in disbelief. From the moment she and her two kids arrived to spend the weekend on the farm and meet the new heifers, she'd been on the run from wild animals.

"Why *not?*" I pointed to her small feet encased in my big boots and then out to the paddock where her own shoes, light-blue plastic garden clogs, stuck out of a pile of heifer manure.

"Have you forgotten what *happened* out there?"

• • •

Heifers, it turns out, are young female cows. I looked it up in the dictionary before Lenny brought them over, but when the "young female cows that haven't produced calves and are under three years of age" arrived, and lumbered out of their trailer and into the paddock, I understood why Lenny spent that entire morning stringing electrified wire from one fence post to the other. They looked more like mythological incarnations of beasts from the afterlife than the fuzzy, wide-eyed innocents I imagined from the written definition. Where I expected large versions of brown and white cocker spaniels with brass bells tied around their necks, there stood two black rhinoceroses with plastic orange tags in their ears.

"That's *them?*" I asked as I backed away and into Dustin, who himself took large steps backward.

"Yup," Lenny said. "Black Angus."

"As in Black Angus *burgers*?"

"Yup."

The enormous heads of the two creatures made slow passes back and forth to take in their surroundings. They were huge. They were whales on four pegs. The muscles in their necks must have weighed hundreds of pounds alone, and at one point, when they lifted their tails in unison, ten-pound meatloaves fell from their butts.

As we stared with open mouths, one of the behemoths slowly stretched her neck up like an armored tank positioning a gun mount skyward and let out a sound so explosive, so passionate, so beyond anything anywhere close to a moo, that a cannon firing off right next to our ears would have gone completely unnoticed.

AAAAHHHHHH-*OOOOOOOOOOOOOOOOO*.

Dustin reached the fence line two steps before me. He leaped off the ground like a professional hurdler with one leg stretched forward and the other cocked high behind him and would have cleared the thing had his front foot not grazed the top electric wire, which froze him in midair in that position for a considerable amount of time.

AAAAHHHHHH-*OOOOOOOOOOOOOOOOO*.

I dove underneath him and crawled under the bottommost electric wire. Later Dustin would claim that he saw a tunnel of light as the creatures bore down on us with fire streaming from their nostrils, but I actually saw a pair of large feet in sandals standing beside a burning bush.

Cows, apparently, are territorial. They will charge anyone or anything without a weapon who disturbs them, but Lenny didn't tell us about that until later, after we jitterbugged around on the front lawn for several minutes shaking off residual electric currents running through our bodies.

"Maybe," he informed us with a slight hint of a grin, "you shouldn't invade their personal space."

Susan and the kids—Nickolyn, nine, and Davis, seven—arrived two days later. They lived sixty miles south of the farm deep in the Chicago suburbs and spent the preceding forty-eight hours making cow scrapbooks, writing cow poems, and drawing pictures of themselves with complete life histories, "So they get to know us," Nickolyn said in anticipation of their trip. They made Play-Doh cows, baked buttercream cow crunch cookies, and guzzled a gallon of milk in one day so they could use it as a vase for a cow bouquet. When their purple minivan pulled in the drive, which bordered the heifers' paddock, the kids hung out the windows and screamed, "*Loooook!* There they *arrrrre!*" and waved hand-drawn, glitter-strewn WELCOME signs taped with long streamers.

I stood at the top of the hill by the house raking leaves. I smiled. Nicko-lyn had called at least seven times during the past two days to check on their status—Were they happy? Did they like the farm? Had I milked them yet?—but I never found the heart to tell her the truth. How could I explain that they were vicious future Big Macs without crushing her dreams and inflicting some kind of long-term psychological damage as a result?

I couldn't, and I didn't, but the realization that I should have came too late, because after the minivan pulled in, it didn't head up the hill to the house but stopped halfway up the drive by the paddock instead. Before I registered what was happening, the side door slid open, the kids and their yellow lab Cosmo jumped out, and the three ran like starry-eyed lunatics straight for the paddock gate.

Under normal circumstances it took approximately three long min-utes to walk from the top of the hill down to the paddock and barn. I assumed the original farmers wanted the barn close enough to the house to keep an eye on the animals but far enough away to avoid the smell of their manure, which I believed in the case of cows was poisonous, but the lives of my niece and nephew hung on whether they opened the gate or not, and I made it down the hill in thirty seconds flat. I was still too late.

Cosmo was the first one in. He was big for a yellow lab, about the size of a pony and awkward as a result, but he slipped under the bottom wire of the electric fence and ran in a flat-footed gallop straight for the cows. They saw him coming and cocked their heads. Meanwhile, Nickolyn and Davis gave up trying to open the gate and scrambled over the top.

"NOOOOO," I wailed as I raced toward them and flew past Susan just getting out of the van. "DON'T . . ." but by that time, Cosmo barked and bounced in circles around the heifers as Nickolyn and Davis ran toward them calling, "Come here cowwws, come heeeere," with arms stretched wide to embrace them.

I don't remember many details of what happened next. I would learn in the months to come that when faced with almost certain death, a person's mind just clicks off, leaving a blank, blue screen upon which instinct or guardian angels or extraterrestrial beings take over operations, but back then, back when the worst of my problems were only the two terrible cows, I was still fairly artless in the ways of survival. I think I ran into the paddock, and I think I grabbed Nickolyn around the waist and Davis by the scruff of his neck, and I'm pretty sure I dragged them out because they're still alive today, but really the only thing that sticks out as an actual memory is of Susan running past us in her light blue plastic garden clogs screaming, "COSMO, *NO!*"

Cows do not like dogs. They especially do not like suburban dogs who, having spent most of their lives in the company of hamsters, believe that cows are God's answer to their prayers. New, large friends playing prey. By the time the kids and I reached safety at the top of the hill, Cosmo's adrenalin reached religious levels. As he leapt in circles around the heifers with his tongue flying out of the side of his mouth in abject and sheer joy, he looked more like a revival attendee just cured of gallstones than the wolf he pretended to be.

Lightning bolts flashed out of the cows' ears. Jets of fire shot from their nostrils. They pawed the ground and flattened their ears, and when they saw Susan running toward them and the dog, they lowered their heads and . . .

AAAAHHHHHH-*OOOOOOOOOOOOOOOOOO*.

Somewhere between that spot and the electric fence, which she didn't know about, Susan lost her shoes. Somewhere between one side of the electric fence and the other, she also got a perm.

We spent the next two days trying to make friends with the cows so we could get into the paddock to retrieve the shoes. First, we gave them names—Miss 11 and Miss 12, based on the numbers printed on the plastic orange tags in their ears—and then we established the electric fence as the perimeter of their personal space and didn't cross it.

Next, we made a trip to Farm & Fleet, an agricultural big box at the edge of town, to buy them treats, but one of the employees, named Bob, haughtily informed us that Farm & Fleet didn't carry treats for cows.

"How come?" Davis asked him with slit-eyed accusation.

Bob looked down at him, then scanned the rest of us for help and upon seeing blank stares, looked back down to Davis.

"Because."

Bob then directed us to the salt blocks and told us to buy one of them instead.

Our next stop at the grocery store was equally as fruitless, because we argued about what Miss 11 and Miss 12 would like to eat. We discussed the pros and cons of giving them anything with milk or butter in it—"But that's like eating themselves," Nickolyn decided—and when Susan suggested whole wheat crackers, Davis informed us that cows preferred chocolate chips.

"They do *not*," Nickolyn said. "You don't know anything about cows."

"Yes I *do*."

"No you *don't*."

"YES I *DO*."

"*NO* YOU *DON'T*."

And so on until it got embarrassing and we dragged them out of the store.

Our final attempt to get the cows to like us was to write them notes. Nickolyn suggested that if we drew pictures of people petting cows and wrote things like, "We are nice," and then taped them on places like the water trough and the salt block, they might come around. The problem was that after we finished our notes, we had no safe way of getting in the paddock to tape them to anything. Davis came up with the idea of launching them from the hayloft in the form of folded airplanes, which was how we ended up on the second story of the barn on Sunday morning.

• • •

As Nickolyn and Davis propelled the last of their messages into the paddock, Susan stared with longing at her shoes down below. The idea of offering my barn to the neighbors for their animals was preposterous, and she knew it, but she had trouble letting it go.

She turned and waved her arms in a wide circle. "Why not offer them this stuff then?" she said.

"The hay?"

She shrugged. "They probably lost all of theirs in the fire."

I nodded, but I wasn't as excited about the solution as my sister hoped I'd be. It meant meeting more neighbors who might not be as willing to mind their own business as Lenny was.

"Maybe," I said.

Susan shrugged again and walked over to the kids, who'd become bored with the noncommunicative cows and jumped from hay bale to hay bale avoiding invisible alligators. "Come on guys," she said, "time to go home."

I looked back out the window at the neighbor's farm. In the field, the older of the two men had trapped the horse against the fence as the younger one swung a rope above his head in slow circles. Behind them, the sky purpled with an incoming storm and backlit the whiteness of the rope.

The horse trembled and danced in place as low bass thunder rumbled in the distance. When the man with the rope stepped toward him, the horse's legs tensed and he tried to bolt, but the old man waved his arms, and the horse backed up again.

I didn't understand. Even though he was larger than the men and possessed enough raw energy to flatten them like road kill, the horse seemed terrified. His hooves moved up and down in place like pistons, as if the ground below them was hot, and the muscles in his shoulders quivered with building pressure to each staccato beat. Rather than stare the men down, the horse's eyes searched frantically for a way around them. He could have run them over, but there was so much confusion from so much pressurized fear, the only release his brain registered was escape.

And that I understood. Fear swallowed confidence whole.

With a snap so fast I barely saw it leave the younger man's hand, the rope shot forward and encircled the horse's neck. The animal reared up, and the noose tightened. The man leaned back against the rope to pull him down as the horse threw his head left and right to escape it. The old man danced around them waving his arms. The younger man leaned farther back, but the horse reared higher and thrashed from the rope in crude panic.

I held my breath. I felt like a voyeur witnessing a great downfall, watching a horse disgraced. I didn't want to see it, but I couldn't pull my eyes away. I wanted to see the horse outwit the men, fly over their heads and run until he was only a smudge on the horizon heading for the safe distance of the incoming storm. Instead I watched his fear.

When he came down, I saw sweat soaking his heaving sides. The men weren't hurting him, but he was so afraid it was if they were. The old man lowered his arms. The younger man took one cautious step forward.

Suddenly, like a spring unloaded, the horse reared up again, higher this time, pummeling his front hooves in the air. He towered above them and screamed and whipped his head back and forth as white foam flew from his mouth. His front legs lashed out as the sweat-soaked muscles in his neck twisted from the grip of the rope.

Below him the old man danced. The younger man pulled against the rope and leaned farther back against the violent, thrashing, feral weight until finally, as if stripped of conviction and strength, the man sank in slow motion to his knees. He still hung on to the rope, but he knelt before the wild horse as if in prayer.

In the distance, the dark wall of rain moved toward them.

• • •

Chapter Three

It rained all night: cold and hard and accompanied by a northwest wind that drove heavy pellets of rain onto the roof that pelted the windows like a concert of thrown marbles. Gusts of cold air whistled through every crevice of the old house as tree branches scraped against its sides trying to claw their way in. I piled three blankets on the bed but still couldn't get warm and wondered if sound alone could make a person cold.

I was used to restless nights, but I'd thrown away the sleeping pills the day I moved in, and there wasn't a drop of wine, a tablespoon of cough medicine, or a Tylenol PM in the house. Meditation was out of the question given the incessant pounding of the rain, and shivering made muscle-by-muscle relaxation techniques impossible. When a particularly nasty gust of wind knocked out the electricity, it eliminated even using the microwave to warm a glass of milk, so I was on my own and stared up at the ceiling, waiting for the roof to cave in.

At some point when the rain softened a bit and I drifted into a thoughtlessness bordering on sleep, a different noise filtered in that seemed far away, like the early soft notes of a dream. But it abruptly turned so harsh and near and real that I shot up out of bed to listen. At first I didn't know what it was. It was so unfamiliar that I couldn't link the sound to a picture in my head, but as it continued and disentangled itself from the sound of the rain, I knew with a sudden stab of dread what it was: the sound of crying sheep.

Only they weren't just crying, they were wailing—BAAAAAAAAAAH, BAAAAAAAAAAH, BAAAAAAAAAAH—from all directions into the wind. They were cold and wet and out there in the dark and probably hungry. How could the neighbors stand it?

I stared out the window for half an hour before the rain picked up again and drowned out their laments. But even then, even once I burrowed back under the covers and vowed to get some sleep, I stared at the ceiling for a long time.

• • •

I walked down to the neighbor's farm the next morning. I'd decided to offer them the hay in my barn, and while I risked having them overestimate the offer as an attempt at social interaction, I didn't want to spend another sleepless night listening to wailing sheep.

It was sunny and cold and frost glazed the weeds on the side of the road that wound past a pasture of sun-spangled oak trees in tall, blowing prairie grass. I'd wrapped a cashmere scarf around my neck and put on my warmest coat, but it was only a leather trench and it along with my snot-strewn face were stiff from the cold by the time I reached the gate of the neighbor's driveway.

The scene was a page from a child's picture book: a red brick house; a long white fence; a yard full of sheep grazing in pairs like lawn ornaments. Somewhere a rooster crowed. A horse whinnied. An empty tire swing circled in the wind. It might have been the scene on a savings and loan calendar except for the piles of charred planks in a wheelbarrow, scattered buckets and shovels, and water hoses strewn like bandages across the dying grass. The smell of smoke still tinged the air.

The gate to the driveway was latched, and as I stood trying to decide whether to open it or just stand there and hope someone noticed me from the house, I saw the dark brown horse standing behind barbed-wire in the back field. His coat was matted from the rain, and his head was bent as if it was too heavy and he was tired of holding it up.

Suddenly a group of white geese emerged from under a pickup truck and surged toward the gate in a well-organized line of assault. The noises they made were more than honks, they were the trumpet blasts of elephants, and as they ran toward me with wild eyes and extended necks, they added hisses and shrieks and screams of attack that would have sent Navy SEALs running for the hills. The noise acted as a siren to every animal in the yard, and as sheep and chickens and ducks scattered in all directions, a huge white horse with black spots trotted out from behind the house. In his wake came two more horses and a pony, and as they converged at the gate and stared out at me—I was now rooted in the middle of the road—I saw the dark brown horse in the back field run back and forth along the barbed wire line that secluded him from all of the action.

I braced myself. At any minute the three horses and the pony would break through the fence followed by the geese, and even if I could somehow magically sprint, I'd never make it to the nearest tree.

Then the front door of the house flew open, and a small man stepped out and shuffled across the yard waving his arms and shouting commands in Spanish. The three horses and pony skittered away as he approached, and the geese dispersed with loud complaints.

The old man unlatched the gate and motioned me in, but I shook my head. I was safer in the middle of the road.

"Hi," I called and waved.

He stared at me, hands on hips, so I waved again. He cocked his head and waved back.

"I'm your neighbor," I pointed up the road.

The old man shook his head and cupped a hand around his ear.

"I'M YOUR NEIGHBOR."

He scowled and motioned me toward him with a sharp gesture that said he didn't care who the hell I was, he wasn't going to walk out to the middle of the road, so I stepped cautiously back toward the gate keeping a close eye on the geese who patrolled a distant perimeter of the fence and foamed at the mouth with the indignity of it all.

"Hi," I said again when I reached him and extended my hand. "I'm your new neighbor."

The old man just nodded, so I decided the best approach was a professional and immediate one.

"I understand your barn burned down, and I have some hay I thought you might be able to use for your animals."

He nodded again but didn't say anything.

"There's a lot of it in my barn, and I don't need it."

He shielded his eyes from the sun and stared at me.

"For the animals. In case they're hungry."

When he nodded again without saying anything, I realized he didn't understand me.

"Do you speak English?"

A grin of slight guilt pulled one corner of his mouth up and he shook his head. "No, no English."

I looked past the old man as I considered my options. Behind him, chickens darted between the legs of sheep and the three horses who yanked at late-autumn yard grass. The pony sniffed at a statue of Mary under a tree. A line of ducks waddled across mud indented with tire marks as a rooster on an old lawn tractor stretched his neck and crowed at the sky.

My eyes wandered back to the pasture where the brown horse paced along the barbed wire fence. His black mane was as long as it was thick, and as the wind swept it up, I saw a line of white symbols on one side of his neck. I remembered something Lenny said when he first stood in our driveway and told us about the barn fire, and my arm rose impulsively as I pointed toward the horse.

"Is that the Mustang?"

The old man turned. "*Si*," he nodded, "*mestengo.*"

"Mestengo," I repeated the word as we both gazed at the horse who, as if he understood our attention, stopped pacing and turned to face us.

The wind whipped his mane across his eyes, so I couldn't see them, but I felt his stare, and it was so direct that it either expressed a threat or a plea. Hatred maybe. Or longing. One extreme or another, but it didn't matter which, because it held all of my senses in custody. For that one moment there was no old man and no cold wind and no smell of burned wood: just the Mustang standing alone in a field that could have been anywhere in the world at any time in history staring at me through a tunnel of time and space and the windswept veil of his mane.

I had to yank my eyes away, and when I did, it felt like a gasp for air. "Why is he alone?" I asked.

The old man turned back to me and nodded. He didn't understand.

I'd already been here longer than I intended, so I motioned toward the sheep and then brought my hand to my mouth as if eating. I chewed with vigor and said, "Hay, I have," while my eyes widened and darted toward the sheep. When he didn't respond, I bent down, grabbed some grass, and shook it in the direction of my farm. "Food?" I said. "Animals? Food?"

He cocked his head. He looked at the grass in my hand and then at my mouth chewing away at imaginary food. I nodded my head toward the sheep, and when he turned, looked in their general direction, and shook his head, I stepped into his line of his sight, put two pointed fingers up at the sides of my head, and said, "Bah, bah, bah," as I chewed.

Ditches of incomprehension mixed with growing fear deepened on his brow.

I decided to try a different approach and mimicked a barn roof in the air with my hands. "Barn," I said and pointed up the road. Then I stabbed my fingers first toward the sheep, then toward the horses, then toward each chicken individually until finally one side of the old man's mouth crooked upward, and he looked at me sideways through squinting eyes.

"Barn?" he said.

"*Si, si,*" I nodded with excitement and chewed with renewed energy. "Barn. Food. Animals."

He smiled with suspicion. "*No es un problema para usted?*"

"*No, no problema,*" I said and shook my head for emphasis.

He nodded slowly and as his distrust gave way, a smile snapped to full salute across his face.

"*Gracias,*" he said as he grabbed my hand and shook it. Like Lenny's hand, the skin of his palm was as hard as a cowhide glove and nothing like the waxy, near-to-melting models I was used to. I wondered as I smiled back and tried not to wince if he could even sense my grip.

"*No problema,*" I said. "*No problema.*" And I felt my conscience shed guilt in pounds. I'd done the right thing despite my concerns about making new friends, and the benefit of it all was that my new friend spoke no English. How, I asked myself as I turned to leave, utterly perfect was that?

• • •

That night as I stared at a blank screen on my computer that was the first page of my novel, Robert called, and in the space of five rings as I watched his name blink on the phone, I predicted the tone and content of our conversation, questioned the point of dragging it out, and wondered how long it would take before he just stopped calling.

"Tired of being a hick yet?" were the first words out of his mouth followed by an exaggerated yawn, which meant he was out of the state capitol building after a fourteen-hour stint, probably at home, trying to unwind with a third cocktail before crawling into bed, getting five hours of sleep *if* he could get to sleep, and then starting all over again.

"Tired of being a lobbyist yet?" I asked.

"Not on your life, baby, not on your life." I heard him stretch and yawn again and pictured him loosening his tie. "I only need two more senators before it goes to committee, and I am hot right now, and I mean hot."

By "it" he meant tax-increment financing one of his clients wanted for a redevelopment project. By "hot" he meant he'd found money for the campaigns of any senators who sat on the fence, which meant he'd get their votes when he needed them.

Unlike in-house lobbyists who worked for one company or one issue or one cause, Robert was a contract lobbyist who worked for anybody who hired him. It took a certain amount of good-old-boy bravado and political brawn to succeed as a contractor at the state level, but when you did, as Robert did, you did so very well. One of his talents was his ability and timing to get to the point just when it mattered. No lawmaker had time to listen to the minute details of every issue that landed on the desk, and the fastest way for a lobbyist to fail was to actually try and explain anything. Robert knew this. He never wasted valuable face time feeling anyone out, because he predicted and anticipated what they'd think, what they'd say, and how they'd react before he ever set foot through their door. No small talk. No particulars. Straight to the point in a lunge.

Like anyone embedded in politics, a lobbyist's work bled into real life, and any relationships in that real life—those outside the capitol, which meant they were barely real at all—focused almost solely on the work, on the political existence, on the life that really mattered. The working life that could barely wait until the next morning's meetings. In our own relationship, Robert and I barely touched on anything as time-consuming as our feelings for one another. There was no talk of the future and no dwelling on the past. I knew everything about his client portfolio but nothing about his childhood or his previous marriage or his children. It was not an affair of heart but an affair of state, and when we talked, it was about capitol hall gossip and tax-increment financing schemes rather than about why I opted out.

But that evening as we talked, and Robert droned on about tax subsidies that would theoretically guarantee future tax gains, my fingers quietly typed "wild mustang" into a search engine box on my computer screen.

"They're going to argue that the redevelopment site isn't blighted," Robert said, "but I think we can get it anyway through eminent domain . . ."

The results that popped up on Google numbered 33,400,000, and after I scrolled down to take some of it in—mustang rescue groups, wild horse sanctuaries, the Bureau of Land Management's Wild Horse & Burro Internet Adoption Program page—I clicked on Wikipedia's entry for "Mustang Horse" and hoped for something concise. And with pictures.

". . . but I don't think it will come to that. I can get money into one of the PACS that can push it into the campaign funds . . ."

Wikipedia stated that the word mustang came from *mestengo,* a Mexican Spanish word itself derived from the Spanish *mesteno,* which meant "a stray livestock animal" or "any animal of uncertain ownership." While the word stray hit me as loaded with baggage, most of it tattered and smelling badly, the photos on the page showed well-nourished, well-muscled horses with coats that shone like shellac in the sun. Behind them, in every picture, were plains of scrub and mountains and places to go, and I thought with an unsettled catch in my throat about the barbed-wire fence surrounding the Mustang down the road.

". . . mucho dinero, baby, *mucho* dinero . . ."

Was Robert really saying "mucho dinero" as if anyone from the ethics commission who might be listening in wouldn't understand? Perhaps it was an attempt to be funny or just a bad euphemism for "bribery," but it sounded so crass as I looked at the pictures on the screen, that I pulled the phone away from my ear and stared at it. I even thought about just hanging up and blaming it later on bad reception, but eventually, when I heard him stop talking unknowingly to himself in the air, I put the phone back up to my ear

"Did I tell you about my neighbor's mustang?" I said.

"Huh?"

"My neighbor has a wild mustang, and his barn burned down, so I walked down there this morning and offered him some old hay I have."

"You have . . . old hay?" Robert asked as if I'd told him a joke he didn't understand.

"Yeah, in my barn."

"In your barn."

"Yeah," I said with a defiance that marked a bright line between his world and mine, "in my barn."

"Really."

"Really."

"Well . . ." he cleared his throat, and I heard him wrestle himself out of his chair in preparation of ending our conversation, "that's nice," which I didn't mind at all.

I slept well that night, at least for the first half, until the sheep started crying again, which yanked me awake for a little while. I drifted back off, though, as I imagined them eating my hay and being grateful and learning to speak human in order to thank me . . . "*Gracias, gracias* . . ." I dreamt of them all night . . . little, fluffy cotton balls with happy faces . . . "*Gracias,* bah, *gracias,*" . . . leaping over fences to help me sleep . . . on and on for the rest of the night . . . "Bah, bah, *gracias,* bah, bah Bah BAH, BAH, BAH, BAH . . .," until their bah-ing got louder and louder as if they were mad at me for something, and suddenly they called my name, "MELINDA, MELINDA," and I opened my eyes . . . and . . . saw Dustin standing in my door.

"Melinda, are you awake?"

I sat up and tried to focus on him, but sheep still called to me from my dream. "What's wrong?" BAH, BAH, BAH.

His eyes were wide, and he looked scared. "I think you should look out your window."

• • •

Chapter Four

Christopher Columbus basked in the warmth of fame and fortune as he watched the parade staged just for him at Seville one month after his return from the New World. His family had been ennobled, Queen Isabella appointed his son as page to Prince Juan, the heir apparent, and he'd been promised seventeen ships and at least one thousand men for his second attempt at finding and then conquering the rest of the world.

Before him in the parade, a line of flashy military horses pranced in full ceremonial dress. They were the famous Spanish Jennets just returned from the battle of Grenada where Spain expelled the last of the Muslim Moors after more than eight hundred years of occupation. The Jennets, bred almost exclusively for warfare, were the aristocrats of their own species and the choice of human nobility across Europe. They had chiseled features, highly refined silhouettes, and an elegant, natural gait that made the rider seem motionless in the saddle. They were considered the most desirable horses on Earth, and twenty of them were promised to Columbus for his trip back to the edge of the world.

There are some questions why it happened, but just before Columbus's second fleet set sail in September 1493, the twenty military horses promised him were replaced with what one eyewitness recorded as "small horses of inferior quality, very different from those that I had observed in the parade." The substitutes were at that time called Marismeno and considered short, ugly, and practically useless. They were primitive horses indigenous to the Iberian Peninsula whose direct ancestors were the stuff of cave paintings, and compared to the Jennets, looked like mules. Their coats were a dark dusty gray, and they had black-tipped ears, black muzzles, black manes, and black stripes on their legs and backs. Peasants used them for farm work because they were strong, cheap, and could survive for long periods without food or water.

These days, the Marismeno are called Sorraias, and the few who remain—less than two hundred in the entire world—are the very last of the indigenous wild horses of southern Iberia. They are now on the brink of extinction, but back when the world was still flat, Columbus called them "common nags" and complained bitterly of the unexpected exchange.

Despite their hardiness, most of the little horses who set sail for the New World that day didn't make it. The trip was difficult. The animals languished below deck in slings that rolled with the ship's movements and kept their legs from bearing any weight. For the five weeks it took to cross the Atlantic, the horses saw no sun, drank no fresh water, and received no exercise. In the following two decades, hundreds of Spanish horses of various breeds would make the perilous transatlantic trip to supply the conquistadors, but only half usually survived.

To make matters worse, the ships from Spain traveled through a belt of latitude about thirty degrees north of the equator that was known for hot, dry weather and almost nonexistent winds. Two of these bands girdle either side of the earth's midsection, and their domains over land include places like the Great Australian Desert, the Kalahari, and the Sahara. Where they control the seas, little, if any, sailing gets done.

When the Spanish sent supplies to the conquistadors along this route, their ships stalled in these doldrums near the West Indies, and horses were tossed overboard in an effort to save water. The sea was literally "strewn with the bodies of dead horses," according to historical accounts, and these ocean deserts were named—and are stilled called—the Horse Latitudes.

For those horses who did survive, the final passage from ship to shore was about as pleasant as a prisoner exchange. First they were blindfolded to prevent them from panicking. Then they were raised from below the decks with hoists attached to their slings and dropped unceremoniously into the water. Led by men in rowboats, they had to swim the rest of the way.

Columbus was reported to have been so angry about disembarking with the squat, ugly little ponies instead of the fine warhorses he'd imagined that he took it out on them by withholding food and water. He was, as history now suggests, afflicted with an overinflated ego and a smattering of mood disorders, but the horses who did survive his command were the first to step foot on the Western Hemisphere in more than eleven thousand years.

They were also some of the founding stock of what would become the American mustang.

Long before they alit on the shores of the New World, back in the second century, the Roman scholar Claudius Aelianus gave one of the earliest descriptions of what might have been the horses who accidentally sailed with Columbus: "They are small and not very beautiful," he stated but added that they were "extraordinarily fast and strong and withal so tame that they can be ridden without a bit or reins and can be guided simply by a cane."

The Roman's scientific knowledge of animals in the second century apparently didn't extend much beyond that. Aelianus wrote, for example, that if a horse stepped in the footprint of a wolf, it would go numb or that if a wolf's spine was thrown at a team of horses, they would immediately halt. He did, though, make one observation that anyone considering moving to the country to write his or her first novel would be smart to note:

"Nature has given animals many different voices and languages with which to speak, just as it has done with humans. Scythians have one language, and Hindus another; Ethiopians speak one tongue, and Sacae another; the languages of Greece and Rome are not the same. And so it is with animals. Each one has a different way of speaking. One roars, another moos, another whinnies, another brays, another bleats; some get by with howling, and others barking, and others roaring. Screaming, whooping, whistling, hooting, twittering, singing—these are just some of the ways in which animals speak."

• • •

Indeed, I thought some eight hundred years later as I turned in a confused circle among screaming, whooping, whistling, hooting, twittering, singing animals in my driveway and asked, "What's going *on*?"

Just a few minutes before, moments after a frightened Dustin woke me up, I'd flown down the hill toward the driveway with hair plastered to one side of my head, bra-less in my most god-awful pajamas, as a carnival parade of people and animals watched my graceless, flapping descent upon them from on high. I suppose there are times in every woman's life when she doesn't care what she looks like, but I for one hadn't been seen in public without makeup since I was about fourteen and never experienced such a moment until that morning.

Looking back, I should have at least put on a coat. But when Dustin first woke me up and suggested I look out the window, sleep still confused me, and what I saw—blurry horses, a pony, some sheep, and what must have been my neighbor's entire extended family and all of their friends yelling at each other in Spanish as they unloaded cages of chickens, roosters, ducks, and geese from an old wood-slated pickup truck—sent me sprinting down the stairs and out the front door in a sleep-dazed, panic-stricken departure from propriety. By the time I reached them, I was out of breath, and the fog of hyperventilation made the scene even more unreal.

"What's . . . ," I turned in a circle and looked for someone in charge, ". . . going on?"

No one heard me, because the animals, each in their own language, demanded their own explanations. Four sheep uttered guttural wails as a teenage boy and a tiny yapping Chihuahua corralled them in a tight circle. Up on the truck, ducks in wire cages complained in rapid-fire succession as chickens squawked, roosters crowed, and the geese screamed unrepeatable insults. When the pony, held to the back of the truck by a frayed rope around his neck, bayed up at the sky, the two heifers in the paddock adjacent to the driveway bellowed verbal abuses over the fence to the intruders who'd interrupted their breakfast. Between all of that and the sound of excited Spanish tossed between women in the back of the truck and men in cowboy hats trying to hold snorting horses on the ground, it was like standing in the middle of a high-school marching band tuning up. I wanted to cover my ears.

Behind me, Dustin yelled into my ear, "What's going on?" and I whirled around and yelled back, "You tell me. *You* saw them first." He shook his head and shrugged, and then his eyes widened as one of the sheep broke out of the circle, knocked over a cage, and sent emancipated barn fowl flooding across the lawn with small children, squealing with joy, running after them.

• • •

My neighbor turned out to be a man in his forties named Alex—short, I would later learn for Alejandro—and the old man I met at the gate the day before was his father visiting from Mexico. Alex spoke English, but as he pumped my hand and spoke above the cacophony, I couldn't comprehend what he said.

"Thank you. It is very kind of you. They probably would die."

I stared at him. "I don't understand."

"The weather. No food. My father, he just wanted to," Alex slashed his finger across his throat, "but then you came down and now everybody, they will be happy here."

"Happy here?"

Alex nodded and smiled. "My father, he said that when you came down yesterday and told him we can use your barn for our animals, he was very surprised. The people," Alex waved his hand up and down in the direction of the road, "they aren't so friendly here."

Then I understood, but I didn't want to. The old man had misinterpreted my offer of the hay as an offer of my barn, and now, as the frantic right side of my brain screamed *Do something!* to the left side that responded with, *Like what?* my body stiffened with paralysis under the lack of any command as an entire season's worth of *Wild Kingdom* played out on my driveway.

The sheep who had escaped the circle ran up the hill of the yard with the little dog in its wake barking in soprano and nipping at its heels. The duo scattered a group of chickens, then raced through two roosters who'd squared off and lunged at each other in midair, then headed in the general direction of two young boys. The boys bravely stood their ground with arms spread wide as if to stop the trajectory of the oncoming sheep, but quickly split and fled when they didn't comply.

Suddenly, though, the sheep stopped and turned and faced its tiny predator. It bent its head and lunged, but the little dog backed up just enough to stay out of the way and yapped from a safe distance with renewed energy. When a man holding the white horse yelled something in Spanish to the dog, the horse shied and backed up into a smaller yellow horse who in turn backed up into a wooden crate that cracked open and freed a dozen ducks who ran-waddled and quacked their way up the driveway like a herd of windup toys.

It was too much to take in. While I was used to chaos and dealing with problems under pressure, this was like a quicksand dream in which I couldn't react, couldn't speak, couldn't make my limbs move, and from which, it became increasingly clear, I couldn't wake up. It wasn't real. Deadlines were real. Yelling bosses were real. Scandals and press release typos and elections gone bad, they were all real, even out-of-control floor debate and four-day-old filibusters were things I understood and handled, but this . . .

I turned back to Alex. I had to say something to him, but Dustin, whose eyes suddenly widened to the size of dinner plates, said it for me . . . "HOLY CRAP!" . . . as the sheep and Chihuahua charged in a straight line our way.

• • •

Sheep, for the record, are not small and cute. They are big and fat, and sticks and leaves and clods of dirt get stuck in their wool and make them look like things in a small child's nightmare. Petting them is out of the question: They hate people. And they hate Chihuahuas even more, so when one chases them in your direction, you get out of their way.

• • •

Once Alex lured Dustin and me out from behind a big oak at the edge of the driveway, a woman in the bed of the pickup truck waved to get my attention. "Thank you," she called with a heavy accent as she smiled and pointed a chicken she held in her hands in my general direction, "Thank you very much." An old woman sitting next to her smiled too and nodded her head, and when I looked around, I realized everyone in the driveway was smiling at me and nodding their heads in thanks.

I shook my own head and held my palms up to indicate that their gratitude was misplaced and that they were going to have to get all of the animals out of here, but they apparently misunderstood it as a gesture of modesty, and they smiled and nodded even more.

I turned to Alex. I intended to be direct, to tell him that it was a mistake and that the animals couldn't stay. When I looked up into his eyes, though, I was a little stunned by what I now believe was my first glimpse ever at sincere appreciation in an adult. It was a soft look, warm, unstained by the politics of guile or manipulation. It was the look one might only recognize in a young child, because it said, *thank you*, and really meant it, and it took me completely off guard.

The old man shuffled over to us and said something to Alex, which included the words *loco* and *gringo* and made him laugh. Alex turned to me and looked apologetic. "My father, he says, yesterday he thought you were a little crazy when you come down. He says he didn't understand at first, because he didn't think people like you . . . ," he trailed off and looked for words but couldn't seem to find them, ". . . you know," he shrugged and gave up. "Thank you, you are very kind to us."

Before I could respond, a young girl came to us cooing to a small brown chicken she held cradled in her arms. Alex looked down at her and smiled.

"My name is Estella," she said as she stroked the head of the chicken who looked content and half-asleep, "and this is Brittany." She gently uncurled her arms and lifted the chicken up toward me. The chicken had hot pink painted toenails and squawked and flapped her wings in the air. I leaned away.

"She is usually *very* good," Estella said. "She's just upset about moving." She thrust the chicken closer to me, "Here, she likes to be held," and I had no choice but to take her.

The girl stared up at her pet in the hands of a stranger, and large, heavy tears welled up in her eyes. Her brow furrowed, and she took a deep breath. "She likes marshmallows," she said, and then as the tears breached her lids and spilled down her face, she turned and ran away.

Alex smiled after her. When the chicken complained about being held at arm's length in the air, he took her from me and nestled her into the crook of his own arm.

"I have insurance for the barn," he said as he stroked the bird's head, "and they will pay me. We will build a new one in the spring when the ground is soft enough to dig. We come down every morning and night to take care of the animals. No problem. You will not know they are here."

Then he pointed to the truck with his free hand where the women handed crates down to the men who carried them into the barn. "These chickens will give you eggs every day. Very good eggs. You take as many as you want. And the ducks, they will give you eggs too. Big eggs from the ducks."

By this point, the left side of my brain was rapidly calculating how many days there were until spring as the right side sang arias about omelet recipes. I knew I had to tell this man his animals couldn't stay, but I also knew there was no way to tell him that they couldn't.

"And the sheep, they will have babies soon, you will see. And the horses, you can ride the white one whenever you want. And the pony, the kids, they ride him all the time. And the yellow one is Mamacita. She is having a baby too . . ."

The horses. My eyes quickly scanned them—the big white one, the small yellow one, the pony, and a yet-unnamed brown horse—but I didn't see . . .

"Where's the Mustang?"

Alex turned away from me and looked down the road toward his farm. "There," he said, and I followed his eyes to where two men walked toward us with a horse between them. I recognized the Mustang immediately: the small body, the thick black mane, the dance of fear as he tried pulling away from the ropes attached to a halter on opposite sides of his face. One of the men yanked down on his rope to still the horse, but this seemed to scare him more, and his front end veered one way and his back end another.

"He does not go by the other horses," Alex said.

The other man yanked on his side of the rope, harder this time, from his own fear I guessed, and the Mustang danced in a frantic, confused circle around him. Alex yelled something to the men in Spanish, which woke up the chicken who'd fallen asleep in his arms. The men were so focused on calming the horse, though, they didn't look up at us. When Alex yelled again and one of the men spared a glance, the Mustang reared back and pulled the men with him. The chicken squawked, and when Alex turned back to me, he handed her over.

"I go down and help them," he said but hesitated and then pointed his thumb back over his shoulder. "He does not go by the other horses," he said again but this time more seriously, as if giving me instructions, "And you no go by him either."

I shook my head as much as in confirmation as to clear it. I still couldn't seem to wake up. I stood in my front yard shivering in my worst pajamas holding a chicken named Brittany with hot-pink toenails surrounded by rioting farm animals who were, I slowly conceded, moving in with me. I had to make some sense of this, I had to understand something, so I said to Alex as he backed away, "Why I no go around the Mustang?"

He smiled, but it was sad. "*Es loco,*" he said as he raised his hand and then twirled his finger in small, serious circles at the side of his head. "He is crazy."

• • •

Chapter Five

I walked down to the back pasture the next morning and panicked when I didn't see the Mustang. The pasture, a field about the size of two square city blocks, was covered with waist-high prairie grass that blew like waves in the wind, and spotting any one thing in it was as hard as spotting a small boat from the beach on the wide horizon of the Pacific. Lenny told me once that in the heyday of the farm—back when dairy ruled this part of the country, several dozen milk cows provided a decent living, and manure was the fertilizer of choice—clover and alfalfa blanketed every tillable field from McHenry County, Illinois, to the Canadian border. When the last dairyman left this farm back in the 1950s, though, the tall native prairie grasses—Indian Grass, Switch Grass, Bluestem—made a victorious return.

My chest tightened as my eyes scanned the field for the horse but saw nothing. Alex warned me repeatedly the day before that the Mustang was hard to contain and to call immediately if he ever got loose, but when I dug in my pocket for the cell phone, I remembered it was on the porch where earlier that morning I'd left yet one more incoherent message on Robert's voice mail.

Over the past twenty-four hours I'd left a whole series of incoherent messages on my kids' phones, my sister's phone, my parents' phone, and just about any other phone with voice mail that would listen to me, including Robert's:

"There are chickens and crowing roosters all over my lawn. There are chickens everywhere. Call me when you get a chance."

"There are two pregnant sheep in the barn and their husbands, the rams, actually ram you when you go near them. Call me."

"One of the horses is a wild mustang. He's beautiful, but I think there's something wrong with him. Mentally I mean. *Why* haven't you called me *back*?"

But as of yet, I hadn't heard from a soul.

My near hysteria was a combination of excitement about living on a farm that now had real, live farm animals and of fear of those same farm animals who were . . . real and live. In total, I thought there were about forty-three in all, not counting Miss 11 and Miss 12, but I wasn't sure because it was hard counting chickens when they all ran around looking alike.

The day before, after Alex and his father surveyed the buildings and fields on the property, they ushered eight ducks, six geese, and maybe twenty chickens into the fenced-in yard of a large, old chicken shed up on the hill near the house.

"*Perfecto*," Alex said to his father when they were done.

Then they put the four sheep and the normal horses—the big, white horse; Mamacita, the yellow pregnant mare; the pony; and the brown horse they referred to only as "the two-year-old"—into a pasture adjacent to the heifers' paddock near the barn.

"*Bueno*," Alex said and dusted off his hands as if a hard day's work was done. But his father immediately said something in a sharp, accusing tone and pointed to the end of the driveway where the Mustang danced between the ropes still held by Alex's two friends on either side. Alex nodded slowly. The father said something else, more severe this time, and Alex looked at the ground and nodded again.

"My father, he says you do not have a good place for the Mustang."

I looked down toward the horse and then motioned to the heifers' paddock. "Can he go in with the cows?"

The father seemed to understand what I suggested and said, "No, no, no," as he shook his head with near violence. Alex looked back at me and smiled as if to a child who'd just suggested a pony should live in the house.

"No," he said. "The Mustang, he is wild from the mountains, and he is how do you say . . ." he trailed off and stared down at the horse and muttered a word in Spanish several times before looking back at me. "He is, you know . . ." he made two cups with his hands and shook them before his chest, "full."

"Full?"

Alex looked at his father and then back at me. "Yes, you know, he is . . . ," he shook his cupped hands again but this time moved them down toward his crotch, ". . . full."

I stared at his crotch. Then I shot a look at his father, who grinned and nodded his head. When I looked at *his* crotch, he stopped grinning and pointed to the Mustang and said something to Alex as if to change the subject.

Alex nodded. "The horse, he is not cut. He . . ." he bounced his cupped hands again, "can have babies."

"He's a stallion?"

Relief flooded Alex's eyes. "*Si, si,*" he nodded and looked at his father, who smiled with relief himself and nodded back, "He is a stallion. He is wild and he is a stallion and he does not like the cows."

They eventually decided the Mustang would go in the far back pasture where a rotted wood fence patched with barbed wire surrounded the large field of prairie grass. As they led him back toward it, the horse's nostrils flared, his eyes darted in all directions, and his ears pitched sideways and forward and sideways again to take everything in. He trotted in place between the two men like a wound-up spring, and when they finally reached the gate of the pasture, stress and exhaustion creased the two men's young faces like age.

Alex's father unlocked the gate. When the Mustang saw the field open up before him, he immediately stopped prancing and pulling from the rope. In less than two seconds his eyes took in the shape of the field, the perimeter of the fence, and the distance between where he stood and where he wanted to be. Then, like something shot from a barrel of a gun, he charged forward dragging the two young men behind him. Bursts of panicky Spanish broke out as Alex and his father ran after the horse, who pulled the two younger men through the tall grass as if they were on skis.

As the Mustang raced toward the back end of the field, one of the men let go of his side of the rope, fell, and disappeared in the grass, while the other, who'd wrapped the rope around his hands and couldn't get free, was dragged on his butt across the ground. When the horse reached the back fence, he finally stopped. He turned and looked down at the man at his feet and then at Alex and his father running toward him. I thought he'd bolt again, but he stood quite still even as Alex walked cautiously up to him and unfastened the ropes. As Alex's father helped the man on the ground stand up, the Mustang, now free, shook his head, rounded his back, and ran off kicking his back legs up in the air behind him. It was, I guessed, his way of giving them the finger.

After the men lumbered and limped their way back to the gate where I stood, my jaw still unhinged from what I'd just seen, Alex's father looked back out over the field now serrated with paths of trampled grass. He shook his head and mumbled something. Alex answered him, and then turned to me.

"My father, he say this fence no good. He thinks the horse get loose. But I tell him," Alex shrugged and swept the field with his eyes, "there is no other place for him."

• • •

The first *mestengo* was a young male horse named El La Drone who escaped an army of six hundred men and fourteen other horses who marched with Hernán Cortés toward Mexico City in 1519. Until then, the only horses in the Western Hemisphere were those brought by the Spanish to the newly conquered islands of the Caribbean where farms were set up to breed horses for war on the New World continents. El La Drone was born to a mare on a ship traveling from Spain bound for one of the stud farms.

While El La Drone was bred and trained to be a warhorse, he was still an animal who needed a herd. For years after his escape, he was seen running with a band of deer who were the closest thing he could find to other horses in the entire New World. After he stole a mare from another traveling Spanish troop later in his life, wild horse herds grabbed a foothold in the Americas.

For the next one hundred years the descendents of El La Drone and any other Spanish horses who escaped captivity eked out a living in the deserts and plains of Mexico. They were warhorses, and they were tough and they adapted. If one of today's domesticated horses found themselves alone in desert scrub, they'd probably last a month at most. The hardy Spanish horses, though, were bred to go without food or water for long periods of time, and they worked out ways to survive. They learned, for instance, to chew prickly pears for moisture when water was scarce, and to this day wild mustangs break through ice with their hooves to get to water, which is probably something no domesticated horse could figure out before he died of thirst.

But in addition to their brains and brawn, the first fugitive horses in North America escaped with the characteristics shared by all equines, characteristics that helped them thrive under harsh conditions. Namely, everything about them was big. They had big necks that allowed them to both eat grass without lying down and raise their heads high one second later to search for predators. Their huge eyes were set on either side of their heads, so they saw much wider spheres of the world around them than animals such as humans, whose eyes only saw what was right in front of them. Their nostrils were big enough to smell even another animal's fear, and their ears, like satellite dishes, turned simultaneously in all directions, taking in high-frequency signals of danger. They also had big stomachs to digest the bulky, un-nutritious desert scrubs and grasses, and their legs were long enough and their hooves strong enough to take them the fifteen to twenty miles a day they needed to go to find those scrubs and grasses.

For the Spanish horses, though, one of their biggest advantages was their fear. It made a home in every cell in their bodies. While in prey animals like humans, fear is considered a weakness, in prey animals like horses it is a trait honed to perfection. A horse who knows when to run is a horse who will survive, and the Spanish *mestengo* was a horse who knew when to run. For next several hundred years, they ran. And they ran north. And as they ran north, they increased their numbers so that by the time they reached the valleys, lakes, and mountains of the Great Basin encompassing much of what is now Nevada, they figured in the hundreds of thousands.

• • •

As my eyes skimmed the field repeatedly and found no horse, Alex's parting words from the day before sent adrenaline sprinting through my bloodstream.

"If he gets out, you call me right away."

"I will," I said, still in shock over the Mustang's stampede into the field and nodding my head up and down like a bobble-headed dog on the dashboard.

"If he get out, you no go near him."

My head changed direction from up and down to left and right. "I won't."

"You call me right away."

Up and down. "I will."

"You understand, yes?"

Up and down with more momentum. "I understand."

Had he actually thought I'd try to catch a loose horse who five minutes before dragged experienced men twice my size through a pasture the length of a football field in about two seconds flat? Maybe he knew independent, strong-willed women who would be so inclined, but I was even afraid of the chickens.

Now, with my cell phone up on the porch, I realized I was alone and surrounded. To get back up to the house, I'd have to not only traverse a yard land-mined with barn fowl, I'd have to avoid a renegade horse hiding somewhere just waiting for the right moment to attack me. I knew it was absurd. Somewhere in my head I knew the chickens wouldn't hurt me and the horse was probably in another state by now, but the whole situation was so absurd that my reasoning, fried from years of politics, still hadn't taken it all in and sorted things out.

So my hands tightened on the rail of the gate as I reasoned that the safest place for me would be *in* the pasture where the Mustang obviously *didn't* want to be. I slid my hand to the chain on the gate and unlatched it. Slowly, I slithered through the opening, and when I reached the safety of the other side, I spun around quickly and relocked the gate.

I turned back to the field and surveyed my new position. Swaying grass. A few scattered oak trees. A small black bird balanced on the stem of a weed. The only sound was the wind as it blew through the grass, and the quiet seemed so foreign that I had to try hard to hear it. An old apple tree. Clumps of milkweed. A hawk flying slow, silent circles in the sky. It was all so . . . introverted . . . and beautiful. And because of it I closed my eyes for just a second to listen to the still.

When I opened them again I saw him. By the fence. The Mustang was *in* the pasture, and as our eyes locked over the top of the blowing grass, I realized he'd been there watching me all along.

As I flattened against the gate and then climbed up over it backward, the Mustang never moved, just stared. And he stared as I backed away from the gate. And he stared as I turned and fled for the house, and I felt his stare on me the entire way.

I felt it throughout the whole night and into the next morning. I woke up, made my coffee, and felt it. I brushed my teeth and felt it. I felt it when I got dressed, when I ate a piece of toast, when I searched my purse for some last vestige of the cigarettes I gave up when I moved here. He was out there, staring up at me.

It was a ridiculous, overly dramatic assumption on my emotions' part. I told myself this as I climbed the stairs to the bathroom and put a new nicotine patch on my arm. I had a novel to write, and this was wasting my creative energy. He was just a horse, uncastrated and crazy maybe, but still just a horse.

When I went back downstairs with my common sense back on track, I poured another cup of coffee and turned on the computer. I sat down and stared at the screen that was empty except for the words "Chapter 1." Then, as I got my artistic juices flowing by deleting "Chapter 1" and rephrasing it "Chapter One," a hideous scream not unlike an old woman being boiled in oil suddenly erupted. It was so loud, it reached me through the walls of the house from all the way down by the barn.

From that point on, and for the rest of that winter, common sense wouldn't even get its foot through the door.

• • •

Chapter Six

What I saw when I looked out the window flashed like rapid-firing frames in a silent film: Mamacita and the pony running frantically along the fence line of their paddock; the sheep tearing as a unit in wild circles; the white horse cowering in the corner with red splashes across his chest; and in the center of it all two rearing, frenetic brown horses—the Mustang and the two-year-old—blood and foam flying as they ripped at each other's throats.

One of them screamed again.

But it wasn't just a scream, it was a high-pitched shriek of fury that ricocheted against the walls of the barn and echoed through the rest of the valley. It was a horrible sound, a head-on crash of rage and madness so threatening, so convincing, so lucid in its purpose that I could *see* it.

"Dus-*tin*."

As I yelled up the stairs to my still-sleeping boarder, my fingers frantically clicked down the list of numbers on my cell looking for Alex's name.

"Dus-*tiiin*."

Another scream outside. I ran back to the window. Mamacita and the pony now ran in circles with the sheep, as the white horse backed up into the fence. It bowed from the white horse's weight, and I thought it might snap, but he suddenly bolted forward as one of the brown horses— I couldn't tell which was which—chased the other one his way.

I ran back to the stairs as I clicked through the numbers again. When I finally found Alex's name, I hit "talk" and then yelled up the stairs with the most bloodcurdling yell I could manage.

"Dus-*tiiiiiin* wake *up*."

Alex answered, and I flew back to the window and blurted. "The horses, they're not in separate pastures. They're fighting. The Mustang and the two-year-old. They're killing each other. Can you come?"

"I am not home," Alex said. "I work in McHenry today. I will call my father. He will come down. I will be there soon."

I heard Dustin tromp down the stairs, and I ran to him and jabbed my finger toward the window.

"Hurry," I said to Alex. "You hurry."

Dustin gave me a questioning look, then scratched his head and yawned as he shuffled to the window.

"I call my father right now," Alex said. "I be there soon."

Just as Dustin looked out, the horses screamed, and he jumped back from the glass. Then he stretched his neck forward to take another look without getting too close, and the horses screamed again.

"Holy crap."

• • •

It's thought by some that the Comanche adopted their most threatening war screams from their horses. A woman who witnessed a peace treaty gone bad between the Republic of Texas and the Comanche in 1840 described it as ". . . so loud, so shrill and so inexpressibly horrible and suddenly raised, that we women . . . for a moment could not comprehend its purport."

By that time—the mid-1800s—the Comanche were well-known not only for their ferocity in battle but for the bond they had with their horses, which in large part made their ferocity possible. Less than two hundred years before, the Spanish to the south and the Americans to the east barely recorded their existence in what are now the states of Colorado and Kansas. But after a revolt by Pueblo Indians against the Spanish in 1680 resulted in the release of thousands of Spanish horses into the southern plains, the Comanche moved south to capture them and made a name for themselves. They were, as noted by George Catlin in the early 1800s, ". . . the most extraordinary horsemen I have seen yet in all my travels."

A Comanche rider could, for instance, ride a horse at full speed and pick up a coin from the ground. It astonished the first Americans who saw it, but it was one of the first tricks taught to Comanche children who later in life used it for the imperative task of picking up fallen comrades in battle. They could also hang from their horses' sides from a thin strip of leather to avoid an enemy's bullets or arrows. This little trick didn't go unnoticed either, and Homer Thrall wrote in 1879 that the Comanche was ". . . half horse, half man, so closely joined and so dexterously managed, that it appears as one animal, fleet and furious."

What really rendered onlookers speechless, though, was the way the Comanche caught their horses in the first place. After the Pueblo Revolt in New Mexico, freed Spanish Colonial horses wandered the plains in the thousands. As they spread north in ever-increasing wild herds, the Comanche moved south to meet them. They were sturdy little horses that Catlin later described as varied in color, like hounds in an English kennel, with thick, heavy manes, ". . . very profuse, and hanging in the wildest confusion over their necks and faces—and their long tails swept the ground." They were also extremely hard to catch. "There is no other animal on the prairies so wild and so sagacious as the horse; and none other so difficult to come up with," Catlin wrote. "So remarkably keen is their eye, that they will generally run 'at the sight,' when they are a mile distant . . . and when in motion, will seldom stop short of three or four miles. I made many attempts to approach them by stealth . . . without ever having been more than once able to succeed." The Comanche learned how to do it, though, and they did it with pomp and flair.

One of the most dramatic ways to catch a wild horse was with the lasso—a thin rope of braided rawhide about fifteen yards long with a sliding noose at the end. When a Comanche set his sights on a particular stallion in a wild herd, he mounted his own horse, coiled the lasso around his arm, and took off full throttle until he ran in the middle of the stampeding band and alongside his member of choice. Unlike the Spanish horsemen in Mexico or the American ranchers who came later, the Comanche didn't swing their ropes over their heads and fling them in hopes of hitting the targets. They didn't have to. They rode so fast and so well and so close to the horse of their intentions, they simply tossed the noose of the lasso over the animal's head. Once it tightened, the Comanche slid off his horse and pulled on the rope hand over hand until it choked the stallion to the ground.

After that, it was easy. As the horse lay there gasping, his front legs were tied together, and once he was secured, the noose was loosened so he could breathe again. Immediately the Comanche bent over the mustang's head and blew air into his nostrils, and from that point on the horse was his.

Balduin Mollhausen, a German writer traveling through the western plains in the mid-1800s witnessed the Comanche at the top of their wrangling game: ". . . at present the catching of the wild mustang is an occupation or a sport, to which they give themselves up with all the wild passion of which these untamed children of nature are capable."

As dramatic and exciting as capturing wild horses was, the Comanche usually found it easier to just steal them. And they were proficient at that too. They stole so many horses from the Spanish ranchers in Mexico, New Mexico, and Texas, that by the late 1800s, an American government official reported that one Comanche camp had fifteen thousand horses alone. They were the largest brokers of horses between the Spanish to the south and the Native American tribes to the north, and once the Americans headed West with their skinny, blue-blooded strains that couldn't take the heat, there was no ceiling to the Comanche's rise to power.

Over and over, the Spanish government tried to negotiate some kind of peace with them, but the Comanche with their horses held the cards. They were so sure of themselves that at one point they agreed to leave the Spanish colonists alone but only if the Spanish government promised to turn over every single horse in Mexico. Even years after the Comanche's fall from rule, they clung to their confidence and claimed that they had only let the Spanish stay to raise their horses in the first place.

The end of the 1800s marked the end of the Comanche reign and the end of the Plains Indian horse culture altogether. After almost three hundred years, it was over. But the Spanish mustangs who made it possible for the Spanish to control South America and Mexico and then later made rulers of the Comanche, still ran free from the southern plains north all the way into Canada. Once they started breeding with the American's European light breeds, they became the American mustang and numbered in the millions.

• • •

I was the first to reach the paddock. Dustin ran behind me as he pulled on his coat, "I don't think we should be doing this," he said as he followed me the whole way down the hill. But I couldn't stand the sound of the screaming that sheered every nerve in my body. It was an inexpressible sound. No words could describe it. No signs could represent it. It was a shock wave more than a sound and knocked out a city's grid worth of reasons not to make it stop.

I climbed over the fence as the two horses, about ten yards away, faced each other and then rose from their back legs until their heads were silhouettes against the sharp morning light in the sky. They faced each other and beat their front hooves in the air as if in warning that this might get bad. They seemed suspended in the stance, balanced on their hind legs with hooves beating *back down, back down, back down* until some silent bell finally went off between them, and they launched for each other's throats.

That's when stallions scream: when the moment of posturing is over and they have to follow through. They pin their ears back, show their teeth, and then scream right before they lunge. Horse people call it "the stallion squeal."

"STOP IT," I yelled and bent down, picked up a small rock and threw it in the horses' direction.

They never looked my way. Their front hooves were locked on each other's shoulders and their faces were lost in the manes of each other's necks. They were so entangled in each other's rage, I couldn't tell them apart.

I turned back to Dustin, who still stood on the other side of the fence. "*Do* something."

The horses came down, and in one movement the smaller of the two twirled and ran away. As the other pursued with head stretched low and forward, ears flat, teeth barred, I saw the string of strange white symbols tattooed across his neck.

They tore through the sheep and then along the perimeter of the fence past the cowering white horse, then past Mamacita and Albert, and then past Dustin who, still on the other side, picked up a stick and waved it their way. The smaller horse stopped. He turned back to the Mustang, and they squared off, reared up, and dove screaming for each other again.

This time blood flew. "STOOOP IT," I yelled and picked up handfuls of dirt and flung them uselessly at the horses' sides. But they didn't stop, and I didn't know what else to do, so I whirled around and yelled for Dustin to "*Do* something" again.

That's when I saw the old man walking up the driveway and almost wept with relief at the sight of him.

"Hurry," I yelled as the horses unlocked and flew to another corner of the paddock where they reared up at each other again.

But the old man seemed nonchalant. With a calm I couldn't understand, he unlocked the gate and ambled over to me as if this was just any old day in the country.

"*Cuerda,*" he said, and when I shrugged, he looked over to where Dustin stood on the outside of the fence staring at the horses. The old man let out a whistle that was loud and sharp enough to claim decades worth of practice, like the cracking of a whip, and when Dustin looked over, the old man raised his voice and said, "*Cuerda,*" again. He twirled his index finger in the air, "*Cuer-da,*" and Dustin offered up the stick he still held in his hand. The old man scowled and mumbled something that included the words *gringo* and *estupido,* which I interpreted to mean that he didn't want a stick, and then he turned, looked over at the horses, and shook his head with disgust.

By now sweat drenched the horses' bodies. They reared up at each other and squealed, but this time when their chests met midair, the smaller horse only clung to the Mustang for balance. He was tired. He made half-hearted attempts to avoid the Mustang's teeth on his neck, but his eyes were dull and his movements were slow and his back legs finally gave way, and he fell.

The Mustang stood over him. Then, as foam and sweat and blood dripped down, he raised one of his hooves and pounded into the smaller horse's body. I screamed and lurched forward to try and scare the Mustang off, but the old man caught my arm.

"No," he said. He raised his palm and patted the air telling me to wait.

"But . . ." I turned back and motioned to the Mustang who now stood back from the small horse still on the ground. The Mustang snorted, ears forward, and stared hard now at the smaller horse trembling by the fence.

Just as he started a tail-raised trot toward the white horse, Alex pulled up the driveway and jumped out of his truck with two coiled ropes in either hand. He climbed over the fence and threw one of the coils to his father. Without a word between them, as if they'd done this a million times before, they fanned out on either side of the Mustang.

The Mustang didn't seem to see them. He arched his neck and focused his eyes on the white horse instead, who backed against the fence until it cracked. The old man gave a loud whistle to grab the Mustang's attention and waved the rope in circles above his head. The Mustang stopped his advance and looked at the old man with his rope. Then Alex whistled from the opposite direction, and when the Mustang turned and saw him, his ears dropped, his tail lowered, and his sides heaved in panic when he realized how cornered he was. He looked like a different horse.

As Alex's rope flew toward his head, the horse rounded his back and then bolted between them. Before the empty lasso dropped to the ground, the Mustang flew across the gate he'd flattened earlier to get in and ran for the back of his pasture.

The old man watched him and shook his head. Alex rewound his rope and watched him too. Dustin climbed over the fence and bounded toward the dented gate on the ground, glancing out at the Mustang, then back down at the gate again.

At the other side of the paddock, the small horse stood up and shook his body of dust. The white horse, still trembling, paced along the fence line looking for a way out. Mamacita and the pony and the sheep huddled by the barn.

My hands shook. My head hurt. I realized I was out of breath. Alex walked over to me and gave me an embarrassed kind of smile, and I stared at him as if I'd just woken up from a dream.

"Does this . . ." I managed to make my mouth say, "happen very often?"

• • •

Chapter Seven

Alex and his father replaced the gate, and Dustin, finally able to use some of his third-year engineering skills, fortified it with some old wood he found in the barn. He added a layer of barbed wire for good measure. Then Alex's father tended the wounds on the small horse and the white horse, none of which went more than skin deep, as Alex and I leaned against the fence and stared out at the Mustang. We stood there a long time without talking.

Finally, I asked Alex what *cuerda* meant. He looked at me sideways and raised his eyebrows. "*Cuerda?*"

"Your father," I said, "before you got here, he kept saying '*cuerda.*'"

Alex smiled. "He meant he wanted a rope. *Cuerda* is a rope."

I nodded, and we stared at the Mustang some more. People who lived in the country seemed able to stand right next to another person for a long time without talking. It made me uneasy. In politics, people spoke quickly, very quickly, covering as much ground as they could in as little time as possible. There was no chatting about the weather, no small talk unless it had some point. People who spoke slowly or who broached prohibited subjects like family or medical problems or ethical misgivings were considered inept, because no one cared, because no one had time to listen. Speaking quickly was an art form, and many new interns fresh from the halls of academia learned their most important lessons in the halls of the Capitol as they raced alongside a frenzied lawmaker on his way to a meeting and were yelled at to "Get to the damn point already."

So for me, standing next to Alex in a silence that extended beyond three seconds was as uncomfortable as standing in a new pair of shoes. There were so many points to get to.

"So . . . your father doesn't seem very happy about all this," I said and rolled my eyes around to take in the field, the paddock, and the barn.

Alex smiled and shook his head. "No, he is very happy right now. He is feeling smart."

"Smart?" I turned and looked across the paddock at the old man who muttered to himself as he dabbed some kind of salve on the small horse's neck. "He seems mad."

Alex shook his head again. "No. He is feeling, how you say, *justificado?*"

"Justified?"

"Yes. He warned me I should not keep the animals here."

"Here?" I said and spun my eyes around the farm again. "You mean he doesn't want the animals to be here?"

Alex frowned and waved his hand back and forth as if he'd issued an insult and wanted to wipe it away. "No, no, not what I mean, He thinks you are very kind. He is just very . . . what is the word . . . *practico?*"

"Practical?"

"*Sí.* He have a farm in Mexico. I grew up there, and the animals, they are not like here where we treat them so nice. Like children, yes? He thinks I am crazy because I have them."

"But you said he has animals too."

"Yes," Alex said and turned to look at his father, "but he likes to eat them."

Alex grew up outside a small town in Durango, Mexico, where his mother cooked on a wood stove, his eleven brothers and sisters rarely wore shoes, and his father, who built their adobe house with his own two hands, made his living plowing the corn and bean fields with two horses. When boys who weren't going to stay on the farm turned seventeen, it was almost expected they would cross the border.

"It's just the way of things," he said and shrugged.

Alex's family had relatives in Chicago, so he left the village one afternoon with four friends and his cousin, and they headed in that general direction. They set out not knowing where they were going and carrying nothing that would help them get there—no money, no change of clothes, no food—but it was an adventure they'd prepared for most of their lives, and they left in big strides. "We wanted to *run* out of town," Alex said.

About three days out, though, the adventure turned bad when they got lost in the desert. Their shoes, old and ill fitting to begin with, gave out, and they trudged for three weeks on bare feet. When I asked him what they had for food and water, he said "snakes" and "animal troughs" when they could find them, but then he told me the worst part was crossing the Rio Grande River, whose current nearly ate them alive. "My cousin, he did not want to cross. He turned back then. He went home."

Once they negotiated the border, Alex spent more than ten years getting to Chicago. He made his way north on a string of family friends and odd jobs and learned English, got married, and had four children along the way. When he arrived, he started his own fencing business and bought the small farm down the road.

"The American Dream, yes?" he said and laughed and swept his hand across the paddock of bleeding, trembling, braying animals around us.

Much to his father's disappointment, Alex didn't buy the seven-acre farm to raise animals to eat but to have as pets for his family. He wanted his sons to ride horses and his daughters to make friends in 4H. Even though they collected eggs laid by the chickens, it was an afterthought rather than a purpose, and his oldest daughter, now a sophomore in high school, never admitted to her friends that she ate homegrown eggs.

"My father, he does not understand this," Alex said. "He complains when he visits."

I looked over at the old man who still grumbled to himself as he checked the brown horse's front hooves. When he seemed satisfied, he stood up and stared at the animal as if it was an old truck someone painted to hide rust. He threw his hands in the air, and the horse spun away.

"He was especially mad about the Mustang," Alex said as he sighed, turned back to the field, and rested his forearms on the gate. "He says we have no business with a horse like that. And maybe," he shook his head and sighed again, "maybe he is right."

I looked out over the top of the grass at the Mustang who, apparently unfazed by the havoc he caused in the paddock earlier, grazed in his usual distant spot.

"Where did he come from?" I asked.

The answer crossed Alex's face in a shadow of guilt or shame or sorrow, I couldn't tell which, maybe all three, but he went dark for a second before he came back to himself and turned to me and laughed. "You have some cerveza?" he said.

• • •

The spread of the Spanish horses north happened so quickly—from the Comanche in 1680 to the Shoshone by 1700 to the Blackfeet in Canada by 1740—that historians now refer to it as The Great Horse Dispersal. In that time, horses changed the lives of Native Americans so dramatically that T. R. Fehrenbach wrote that it was "one of the most rapid and widespread technological diffusions in human history." But it was more than the trade among people that broadened the horses' range, because it was the wild herds that did most of the traveling.

Whether they escaped, were dumped, or were born in the wild didn't matter in terms of time or space. They found each other, and the mountains and plains of the American West were such perfect places for the horses bred for war that by 1850 it was estimated there were two million of them running free. No Mexican rancher, no Native American tribe, no American settler could have bred them as quickly as they did in the wild when left to their own devices.

Part of their success was based on social instincts that somehow survived hundreds of thousands of years of domestication by man. These instincts, like little survival handbooks or perhaps more accurately like step-by-step instructions on political theory, kept them together in organized groups, which in turn kept them alive.

A wild horse herd is made up of smaller bands, each with a strict social order. These bands are called "harems," which by Turkish definition are "sacred, forbidden places" where one male guards his females from the advances of other males but, which by wild horse definition, are simply "family."

The band is controlled by a lead stallion who protects a group of up to twenty mares and their offspring from mountain lions, bears, and other stallions. Other than breeding, his main job is defense, and the stallion spends most of his time on the physical fringes of the family watching for potential enemies. The day-to-day activities of the band, however, are managed by the lead mare, who is usually the oldest female in the group. She controls where the band travels, when they eat, and who gets to drink first when they reach a watering hole. When a band of wild horses runs from danger, the lead mare directs their escape while the stallion stays protectively in the rear.

A stallion with a healthy, functioning herd rarely acts aggressively toward any member of his family. In fact, wild stallions often help mares raise their young and can be very affectionate and nurturing. The bond between father and sons can be particularly strong, and it's not uncommon for lead stallions to take their colts out on patrol with them when they're old enough.

Noted documentary producer Ginger Kathrens—whose studies of the Pryor Mountain horse herds brought worldwide attention to the stallion, Cloud, and his band—once witnessed a stallion named Bigfoot trying in vain to care for his orphaned son. The foal's mother died a few months after he was born, and Bigfoot, despite his responsibilities as the herd leader, tried his best to guide and protect him.

"The old stallion would sniff the colt lovingly," Kathrens stated in *Natural Horse* magazine, "but he could not give his son what he needed to survive. I did see one pathetic attempt by the foal to try to nurse his father. Bigfoot responded by turning quietly to the colt, then walking with him to the water hole. But a three-month-old colt can't survive on water."

Likewise, Mary Ann Simonds, a wildlife ecologist who studied wild horses for thirty years, saw many demonstrations of tenderness on the parts of stallions for their sons. "At a BLM roundup I witnessed, one of the young stallions that had been captured was injured and seemed to be doing badly," Simonds told *Horse Connection* magazine. "Another stallion stayed with him to protect him, licking him, obviously trying to help him feel better. Theirs was clearly a very close relationship, undoubtedly a parental one."

Things change, though, when the youngsters in a band reach about two years of age and the stallion indicates it's time for them to leave the family. In order to avoid inbreeding and the dilution of genetic strength, the fillies and colts reaching sexual maturity have to emigrate. There's no negotiation, and while young females at the encouragement of their mothers quickly join other bands, the young males have a harder time letting go. They often follow the band at a distance for some time before the lead stallion finally uses his full force to drive them away.

Research by Joel Berger on horse herds in the Nevada Great Basin found that one colt sent away from his band spent the first six months trailing the family. Ten months later, he had moved farther away and within a year was seen sixteen kilometers away from the group. He returned, however, in the next year, and it took him several more months to finally realize he couldn't ever rejoin the family. While the young females who initially left the band joined other bands, the colts had to make their own, and, as Berger pointed out, "Young emigrating males possessed neither the skills nor the body weights needed to acquire harems."

So it's not an easy departure for the colts. For any social animal like horses or humans, leaving a family wouldn't be, but it's how they disperse, it's how they re-create themselves to carry on, and for humans as much as for the wild horses of the American West, it's just the way of things.

• • •

Alex first saw the Mustang two years before while on a job in the next town. He was hired by a man to build a fence strong enough to contain the wild six-year-old stallion he'd recently purchased for $125 from the Bureau of Land Management, but when Alex saw the horse, he realized right away that no fence on Earth would contain the anger built up inside him.

Alex had been around horses all of his life. He'd seen them born, he'd seen them die, he'd seen them at their best and at their worst, but until he met the Mustang in a small town in Northern Illinois, he'd never seen their fury.

"The horse, he was in a small pen," Alex told me as we stood at the fence and watched the Mustang graze. "He had no room to move around. The man, he no understand horses, and he put barbed wire up to here," he raised his hand above his head, "because he said the Mustang kept getting out. The Mustang, he was full of cuts from the barbed wire."

The horse was also full of welts, Alex said, which told him the man tried beating him into submission. There were marks of abuse all over his body.

"The man, he was afraid of this horse, so he got mad and hit him."

The Mustang was also too thin, Alex said, near starvation with a dull coat, shaky legs, and jutting bones to show for it. Despite this, though, the horse snorted and pawed the ground and turned constant circles in his small pen, and when Alex first approached him, he summoned enough energy to flatten his ears and lunge at Alex in aggression.

"I heard many stories about wild mustangs, but I never saw one before," Alex said. "I grew up hearing about how strong they are, how you say, pride, proud? But this one, he was very weak and I felt bad for him."

Alex looked out at the Mustang again. Then he shook his head and pushed a stream of air through his lips tinged with apologetic regret. "So I told the man I would give him five hundred dollars if he let me have the horse."

Alex shook his head again and after a few beats of heavy silence, turned to me and laughed. "I never saw a man so happy."

At the time, Alex's parents were visiting, and when his father heard about his son's purchase of yet another useless animal who was, on top of everything else, a wild mustang, he nearly packed his bags right then and there to head back for the comfort of Mexico. He wanted to be in a place, he said, where people had common sense.

"He does not understand why I go to a job to make money and come back with *less* money and a crazy horse instead. He was very mad at me."

I nodded. Then I furrowed my forehead in parental commiseration. "I'd be very mad too," I said.

Alex smiled. Then he looked over his shoulder at his father who stood, hands on hips, staring with palpable disapproval at the horses and sheep around him. "Yes," Alex said and turned back to the pasture. "I understand." Then he gave a loud, sharp whistle across the field to get the Mustang's attention.

The horse looked up. The grass hid everything but his shoulders, neck, and head, and he stared back at us across the field as if daring us to come out and get him. He seemed so aloof, so unapproachable, so much farther away than the physical distance could describe.

"Why does he fight?" I asked.

"My father? He does not fight. He is just mad."

"No," I said. "The Mustang. Why does he fight with the other horses?"

"Ah," Alex said. "He is, how you say again, stallion? The white horse, he a stallion too, but he is weak and runs away, so they do not fight most of the time."

"But what about the brown horse?" I said.

"The brown horse," Alex pointed out to the Mustang, then turned and pointed back to the two-year-old to build a connection between them. "He is the Mustang's son."

• • •

Chapter Eight

During the next week, we settled into a kind of routine. The old man, Alex, and Alex's oldest son, also named Alex, came in the mornings and at night to feed and water the animals. In between, Dustin and I—afraid of the free-roaming geese—stayed pretty much in the house and checked on the new residents periodically by looking out the windows. After a few days of this, Dustin announced he needed to "get away" for the weekend and fled for the safety of his girlfriend's apartment in the burbs. I wondered if I'd ever see him again.

Left alone in the old house up on the hill, my imagination went slightly feral. The wind, which was almost constant and turned more vociferous at night, made the house feel like a battered old boat in rough seas, and each door, window, and clapboard creaked so loudly under the strain that a burglar or a ghost or whomever or whatever got in first would have to shout in my ear before I heard them. It was dark too. Even after I turned on every light in the place, I felt watched by 125 years' worth of phantoms.

Before I went to bed, I lodged a kitchen chair underneath the knob of the front door. Then I warmed some milk, grabbed *How to Write a Novel in 30 Days* from the couch, and headed up the stairs for my room. I hummed the whole way up, because I'm a firm believer in faking things, and once I nestled in under the blankets, I started to feel more at home. This *was* my new home, I reminded myself, and I had to get used to things.

Looking back, it was inevitable that I would call 911 that night, given how creepy an isolated, old farmhouse can be when one is alone and suffering from writer's block, nicotine withdrawal, and a right-sided brain that was bored and looking for something to do. I was also undergoing chemical changes from my abrupt departure from the Prozac, Xanax, and Ambien that until recently got me through my days and nights, so three pages into the book, when some awful flying thing suddenly intruded, dialing 911 seemed like the natural thing to do.

My instinctual analysis indicated the thing was a space alien. It was suddenly just there, this thing, this half-animal, half-extraterrestrial prop that swooped in from the darkness of the hallway and circled my room like a battery-operated UFO. It was hideous whatever it was. It had the face of an old man and the wings of a pterodactyl, and it cruised in silent, ever-tightening circles in the air space right above my bed.

I didn't know what I was looking at. I stared at it for a full minute before the left side of my brain cleared its throat and said, "Consider being afraid," and the right side started screaming expletives. But by then it was too late. All I could do was gasp for air and clutch *How to Write a Novel in 30 Days* to my chest for protection.

It occurred to me as I rolled off the bed and grabbed my cell phone along the way to call my children and my parents to tell them how much I loved them, but my fingers under the influence of incomprehensible fear punched in 911 instead.

"I'm sorry, ma'am, I didn't understand you," the dispatcher said after I whispered that something was flying in my bedroom trying to attack me.

"It's circling," I said, "above my bed."

"What is your location, ma'am?"

"*Under* the bed."

"No," the dispatcher said, "I meant, what is your address?"

I couldn't remember.

"Ma'am?"

I was so scared, I couldn't remember. I stared at the bed slats above me and tried to concentrate. Where *did* I live? In an old farmhouse in the middle of nowhere was the best I could come up with, and just before the left side of my brain followed the right side toward the EXIT sign, it warned me not to say the words *space alien* and added as a parting shot not to tell the dispatcher that I couldn't remember my address.

"Ma'am?"

"Hold on. I'm thinking."

I turned my head sideways, stared across the bare wood floor of the bedroom, looked for a landmark, a clue, anything that might remind me where I was—specifically numbers attached to a street name attached to a town—but all I saw were dust mites careening against the bottoms of unpacked cardboard boxes when the shadow of the alien swooped above them. The light dimmed for a second as it flew over the lamp shade. Dust balls rolled again.

"Ma'am, I see you're calling from a St. Louis phone number, is that correct?"

"St. Louis. I live . . . I used to live . . . but now I live . . ."

She interrupted me and said, "Ma'am, are you alone in the house?"

"Yes."

"Can you describe the thing that's flying in your room?"

"It's a . . . thing . . . something like a . . ." Since I couldn't say "space alien" I said, ". . . hairy toy airplane," instead, and that's when a slight note of cynicism entered the dispatcher's voice.

"And it's flying above your bed, ma'am?"

"Yes. In circles. Above my bed."

"Ma'am, it's probably just a bat."

I stared again at the slats on the underside of the bed and tried to take this in.

"Ma'am, did you hear what I said? It's probably just a bat that's in your room."

A bat. "Just" a bat she'd said. I wondered what would happen if I just hung up.

"Ma'am?"

"Yes?"

"Are you still under your bed?"

"Yes."

"OK," she said, "here's what I suggest you do . . ." The dispatcher then informed me that bats in the house were common at this time of the year, and it wouldn't attack unless it had rabies, which it probably didn't since it was flying around. All I had to do, she said, was open all the windows and wait for it to fly out on its own. She said she could send the animal control officer out if I thought this was an emergency, but he'd be a while, because he was off duty, and she'd have to wake him up.

I wanted to ask her to send a SWAT team instead, but I thanked her for her time and hung up.

I turned my head sideways and looked across the bare wood floor again. Then I slid my head out from under the bed just far enough to see the ceiling. Nothing. No dimming light. No sign of the bat whatsoever. After a few minutes, I wondered whether he'd given up looking for me and pushed my shoulders out very slowly to get a better look. Still nothing.

I decided to take my chances and pulled myself out from under the bed. I lunged for the closest window, and as I yanked it open, the bat suddenly alit from the curtain where he'd been hanging all along. I screamed. Then dropped to all fours and crabbed from the room as fast as my hands and knees could carry me.

Later, as I stood on the driveway in my pajamas, white furry slippers, and black trench coat and stared up at the silhouette of the lighted house and waited for the bat to fly out the window, two things occurred to me. One was that the bats, the animals in the barn, and the wild Mustang in the back pasture were all part of living in this place, and since there couldn't possibly be anything worse than what I'd already encountered, it should be easier from now on. As soon as the bat flew out the window, I told myself, I'd get a good night's sleep and wake up refreshed, ready to write, ready to start the rest of my new life.

Then, as I looked back up at the house for some sign of the bat, a second and more profound thing occurred to me, one which would haunt me for the rest of that night and for some nights to come: There were screens on all of the windows.

• • •

The next morning, after zero hours of sleep in my car, I went straight to Farm & Fleet to find something to "deal" with bats. Under normal circumstances I wouldn't kill anything, and somewhere in the back of my head I thought bats might be mammals, which made killing them seem that much worse, but I was tired, undergoing all kinds of withdrawals, and too afraid to go back in my house to take the screens off the windows. I figured the Wal-Mart of agriculture had to have something to kill kindly, though at that point, still dressed in my pajamas, white furry slippers, and black trench coat, I really didn't care if it was kind or not.

I walked several miles' worth of aisles in Farm & Fleet before I paused to get my bearings. Nothing on the shelves made sense—row upon row of chains, tractor parts, metal and plastic gadgets of every size and shape—but nothing that had anything to do with bats. Around me, men with work gloves and heavy, mud-caked boots lumbered around with tractor tires and bags of feed on their shoulders. Like some secret society, they all seemed to know what they wanted and where to find it as I stood there in my pajamas and slippers feeling lost and inappropriately dressed.

As I would learn in the months to come, the type of shoes people wore to Farm & Fleet said everything about them. Back in the Capitol, everyone from the most influential lobbyists to the newest unpaid interns wore the same shoes—men in wingtips and women in low pumps. In Woodstock the shoes were as varied and definitive as social security numbers. If you wore old cowboy boots, it meant you had horses. If you wore *new* cowboy boots, it meant you had hired hands to take care of them. If you wore galoshes, you had dairy cows. If you wore work boots, you farmed. If you wore gym shoes or sandals or at the very worst, white fluffy slippers, it meant you were a suburban transplant probably there to buy bird-feeder food and didn't, by any interpretation of the name of the store, belong.

I definitely didn't, not then, and as I stood there in an aisle of huge rolls of bailing twine trying not to look so blonde, a voice behind me said, "Do you need help?"

I spun around and saw Bob, the man who several weeks before informed my sister, the kids, and me that cows didn't eat treats. "Thank god," I said and really meant it and all but hugged him on the spot. He backed away, but my desperation got the better of appropriate behavior. "I need something to kill a bat," I said as I clutched his sleeve. "Anything. Right away."

He looked at my hand. Then he looked at my slippers. Then he took another step back to clear a safe distance between us. "A bat, you say?"

"Yes," I nodded gravely. "I haven't slept. I'm afraid to go back in the house. I need something to kill it."

"You need . . ." he said slowly as if trying to make sense of a foreign phrase, "something to kill a bat?"

"*Yes,*" I said with more hiss than was probably polite, but I was so tired and wired, and he didn't seem to understand the urgency.

He crossed his arms, rocked back on his shoes, and looked up. "You know," he finally said after he must have examined every square inch of the ceiling, "bats *are* good for insects."

I stared at him. I couldn't tell if he was serious or not. He just stood there with his arms crossed rocking back and forth almost as if daring me to challenge his statement. I took another step toward him, dug my fingernails into the palms of my hands, and slowly repeated the words to make sure he understood them.

"I . . . need . . . some . . . thing. . . to . . . kill . . . a . . . *bat.*"

I said it with enough venom to kill an elephant, but Bob just looked up at the ceiling and rocked on his shoes again. Then he frowned, shook his head, and looked back at me with a steady gaze. "We don't have anything like that."

He said it so definitively, with such a stinging moral finality, that I suddenly felt ashamed of both my intent to kill the bat and him. I took a step backward and unclenched my fists.

"Nothing?" I said as hopelessness overwhelmed me. "Not even something to scare it away?"

He shook his head again and shrugged.

I looked down, and when I saw the marks left by my fingernails in the palms of my hands, I realized how close I'd come to losing control. I never lost control, my career had depended on it, and if by negligence control ever did give me the slip, I just popped a Xanax or took a smoke break or gulped some wine to find it again. There, standing in the middle of Farm & Fleet, though, I didn't have any of those things, and my throat suddenly tightened at the thought of it. Before it even fully registered, pressure built behind my eyes and tears, the kind that sting, the kind that have a life of their own, the kind that make one embarrassed to be one's self, rolled down my face, pooled at my chin, and dropped to the floor by the cupful. It was ridiculous, and I knew it, but I couldn't stop.

"Whoa there," Bob said, and when I looked up, he held his palms out toward me and waved them as if trying to stop traffic.

"It's just . . ." I gulped for air, "I'm afraid of the bat and I haven't slept all night, I haven't slept since I moved here because there are all of these animals in my barn and this wild horse who's crazy, and I don't know what's going on with my life and . . ."

Bob, obviously afraid, interrupted me and told me there might be something he had that could help me.

"Follow me," he said, and he turned, and I followed, and I continued following down the aisles of the store as I wiped my eyes and told him the rest of my woes, ". . . and I'm writing this novel but I can't seem to get started, and I only have enough savings to see me through two to three years at most . . ."

First we walked through a section of rattraps, gopher traps, mole traps, yellow jacket and flying insect traps, live animal traps, and Overnight Flea Traps. I thought we'd arrived at our destination, and I was so relieved that I laughed out loud at the silliness of my earlier fear and told Bob as we passed snake repelling granules, squirrel baffles, fly bombs, deer repellents, and propane foggers that I'd dedicate my second novel to him. "I'm dedicating this first one to my kids of course," I said. But Bob didn't seem very grateful, didn't answer at all in fact, just kept on walking deeper into the bowels of the store.

Next we entered a section called Outdoor Living full of things that would have been more at home in an armed forces storage unit: camouflage coats, knives, air rifles, bullets, human-scent masking sprays, slingshot ammo, binoculars, crossbows. As we walked, my mini mental breakdown finally gave way to something sane—a sudden and overwhelming nervousness about killing a bat with a crossbow—but when I tapped Bob's shoulder to tell him this wasn't such a good idea, he just picked up his pace and kept walking.

Next came the Protective Gear section. Then the Boats & Motors section. Then the Fishing section with river, lake, and ice fishing subsections each with subsections of their own. When we finally got to the Camping section and Bob stopped to look around, I was sweating under the trench coat and out of breath.

I couldn't imagine why we were there. Nothing among the shelves of waterproof matches, compasses, and portable toilets could possibly kill a bat. There were tent repair kits, tick removers, solar-powered can openers, and packages of freeze-dried Hearty Beef Stew, Potatoes & Pork in White Sauce, and Fettuccini Alfredo with Chicken but no bat poisons or traps whatsoever. Then I saw the axes. And then I saw Bob head toward them.

"Are you crazy?" I said, control once again taking a dive in the deep end. "People kill bats with *axes* around here?"

Bob turned and stared at me. It was a look of irritation mixed with pity, a scathing combination when it's directed toward you, so I slunk back into myself and shut up.

Bob then zeroed in on a shelf just beyond the axes and pushed his glasses up on his nose as he scanned it. Finally he pulled down a small package wrapped in cellophane and handed it to me.

I looked down at it: Stay Away Polyester Mosquito Net.

"Put it over your bed at night," Bob said, "and you should be just fine."

I stared at the package in my hands trying to decide if this was a joke. Then a woman's voice on the loud speaker called, "Bob to hydraulics. Bob to hydraulics," and by the time I looked up, he was moving so fast back toward the sanity of the motherland and mud-caked boots, I didn't think anything on Heaven or on Earth could have stopped him.

• • •

Chapter Nine

It took us several weeks to get the bat to leave, and sleep was hard to come by. For one thing, I insisted we keep every light in the house turned on twenty-four hours a day. For another, we had to keep the windows open, so as I tried to sleep under the mosquito net I'd nailed to the ceiling of my room, and Dustin tried to sleep with a tennis racket cradled in one arm and a croquet racket he found in the garage in the other, we were embedded in every sweater, coat, glove, sock, hat, and scarf we owned.

For yet a third thing, there was the Mustang. Barely a day or night went by when we didn't at some point hear squeals explode from the bottom of the hill, which meant he'd broken through the fence again and another fight had started.

Occasionally when I ran down to the paddock, I found father and son only posturing over the fence. At those times, I discovered that if I shouted and waved a shovel in their direction, they usually turned and ran their separate ways. Most of the time, though, I found them together in the paddock locked in violent hugs, thrashing and gnashing and screaming their rage while the other animals ran in terrified circles around them. At those times, I called Alex, and it got to the point whenever he saw my name on caller ID that he no longer said, "Hello" when he answered but, "I'll be right there."

There seemed no way to keep the Mustang on his side of the fence. Every time Alex and his father came down to break up a fight, they ended the episode with patching up whatever new holes he'd created, knowing it was futile. He crushed wooden slats, pushed down wire-mesh panels, and ripped through barbed wire as if it were fine thread. Even the gate— a strong metal structure meant to hold in cattle—was so battered down after a few days it looked like a piece of plastic run over by heavy machines.

But what seemed like uncontrollable rage on the Mustang's part was something more intricate than raw emotion alone. As I would learn throughout the rest of that winter, it wasn't even really an emotion but a physical impulse fueled by whatever flowed in the Mustang's blood that in the wild had kept him—and the rest of his family—alive.

Alex told me that *the* day he brought the Mustang home, the stallion jumped his fence and bred Mamacita. Less than a year later, the foal was born and for the following year and a half the three, along with the pony, lived as their own little herd. But then Alex bought the white horse—also a stallion—and even though he bowed to the Mustang's leadership from the start, tensions grew within the family because Mamacita was pregnant again, and Alex didn't know if the Mustang or the white horse was the culprit. In addition, the foal, now deemed a colt, was hedging on sexual maturity, and the Mustang began to feel threatened.

The Mustang wasn't susceptible, though, to unrefined passions. His response to the new threats didn't stem from jealousy, resentment, or covetousness on his part but rather from the knowledge that the white horse wasn't fit to lead a herd and his son, now two years old, needed to get out there, learn the ways of the world, and then start a family of his own.

In the wild horse herds, it's all about experience. Very few bands are governed by young stallions, and the lead mares are almost always the oldest in the group. It's a hierarchy that works well, because the young ones don't have the skills necessary to keep the family together.

In healthy wild bands led by a mature stallion and mares, for instance, the stallion is strong enough and wise enough to fend off other stallions from breeding his mares. He then selectively chooses which mares he himself will breed, and they never include females he's related to or any under the age of four years. When foals are eventually born to the younger mares, the older mares in the group help the younger ones raise them.

Research by the International Society for the Protection of Mustangs and Burros (ISPMB) shows, however, that in herds continually broken up and rearranged by government roundups, only the most immature stallions and mares are left to lead them. The results can be devastating. The young stallions, for instance, aren't physically or mentally strong enough to fend off other stallions who themselves are young and immature and break into the band to breed indiscriminately. Fillies as young as one become pregnant and either die during the foal's birth or don't know how to take care of their offspring once it's born.

As Karen Sussman, president of the ISPMB told a reporter for *South Dakota* magazine, ". . . you can imagine what happens in a community if younger and younger stallions are allowed to take over who don't have the education that is usually taught to them over a period of years by the harem stallions. It's like having a school run not by professors but by sixth and seventh graders."

When left alone by humans, wild horse bands follow old social orders, which dictate that band stallions push their two-year-old sons out of the nest so they can *learn*. While at first it's difficult for the young stallion to leave his family, he eventually finds other young stallions in the same predicament, and together they form bachelor herds. It is within these bachelor herds that they grow to true adulthood. They play fight, play protect, and even play mount each other at times, and when they're ready, and *only* when they're ready, they venture out to find fillies and mares who will join them to start a new family.

For the father and the son in my backyard, the old social order played out as required. Alex told me the fights started several months before the fire, and while at first they were just aggressive snorts and nudges on the father's part, they eventually turned into full-blown attacks powered by atomically powered commandments of instinct. For the Mustang, his son's presence wasn't a threat to him as an individual but a threat to the survival of his species. He wasn't on the defense over his right to rule the herd; he was on the offense to protect it and could no more control his aggression than he could his own breath.

The problem was that they were fenced in. For the wild mustang stallion, seven acres was a tiny space, and for the two-year-old son who'd never known anything else, there was no distant horizon to run to, no bachelor herd to join, no other place for him to go.

• • •

At the beginning of December, Lenny took the heifers away. Even though an electrified fence protected Miss 11 and Miss 12 in their own field from Alex's animals, Lenny said horses and cattle didn't mix. An animal, he told me, would eventually get hurt, and he couldn't afford for it to be his two heifers.

I felt badly about it, as if I'd broken our agreement, but I never liked the heifers very much and it freed up the electrified front paddock for Mamacita, the white horse, Albert, and the two-year-old. With an empty field now between them and the Mustang and with their own field forti-fied with five thousand volts of hot wire, they could lead an easier life. The rest of us could too. For almost a week, the Mustang stayed in his pasture, and the only squeals we heard were when one of the other horses accidently touched the fence.

One morning, however, I woke up and heard it again. At first I thought that maybe one of the horses had just gotten tangled up in the wire, but when I threw on my coat, opened the front door, and looked down the hill, I saw the Mustang charging through the front paddock behind the two-year-old and the white horse.

Before I even got down the porch steps, the white horse in the lead ran straight into the fence and then plowed through as if it wasn't even there. The two-year-old, who'd been right behind him, skidded to a stop when he saw the opening the white horse created. But before he could react, before he understood that it offered him escape, the Mustang rushed up behind him. The father spent no time deciding what to do. He flattened his ears, curled back his lips, and sank his teeth into the two-year-old's rump.

The son kicked out his back legs and caught the Mustang square in the chest with enough force to throw the older horse to the ground. Then the son turned on him. I thought he'd attack while his father scrambled to get off the ground, but the two-year-old seemed confused, and before the Mustang pulled himself up, he fled to the far corner of the paddock.

Had he run through the hole in the fence, had he taken a few seconds to calculate the differences between outrunning his father in the freedom of the yard and fleeing to another place in the enclosure, he would have avoided the beating he got. But he didn't take the time to figure it out. He ran on impulse, and as soon as he reached what felt like safety, he turned and found himself cornered.

This time when they squared off, there was no posturing between father and son. The Mustang immediately reared up and lunged before the two-year-old got his front hooves off the ground. As he went down, the young horse twisted his body and pummeled his front legs as if trying to escape on sheer air.

Meanwhile, a mass exodus ensued on the opposite side of the paddock: the sheep, Mamacita, and the pony all followed the white horse through the opening he created, and they fanned out across the lawn, each in a different direction. The sheep ran full throttle up toward the henhouse, the pony sprinted behind the garage, Mamacita trotted in confused circles, and the white horse galloped so fast up the hill he left a track of torn-up grass and dirt that all but smoked behind him.

At first I didn't know which way to turn, who to try and catch and in what order, but when I saw the two-year-old disappear under the writhing muscle of the Mustang's mass, I ran back to the house and called Alex.

"I'll be right there," he said.

• • •

Dustin had once assured me he could catch the sheep if there were ever a problem. After I phoned Alex, I screamed a wake-up call to Dustin, which included not only the usual "W*aaake up*," but a blazing-fast summary that practically came out in one syllable, "The Mustang broke through the fence and the white horse broke through the fence and everyone is loose in the yard and you have to catch them . . ."

Dustin stumbled down the stairs bleary eyed and mumbling "Okay. Okay," armed with the tennis racket in his hands.

"I'm going down to the paddock," I said as I headed back out the front door. "You get the sheep."

He nodded and rubbed his eyes with one hand and held up the tennis racket with other. "I'll get the sheep," he said.

I ran down the hill and through the hole in the fence straight for the fighting horses. The two-year-old was still on the ground, and the Mustang drummed up and down on him with such force, I heard air escape the two-year-old's young lungs with each beat. There was no time. I couldn't just stand there and wait for Alex, so I surged toward the Mustang waving my arms and reached him before I realized what I was doing.

When he saw me coming, the stallion backed away from the two-year-old and turned toward me instead. I was about ten feet away from him, but the look he gave me stopped me dead in my tracks. He stared with a cool disdain, surveyed me like a lion would a rabbit, and then he picked up one hoof and pawed the ground as he snorted cold, white air from his nostrils.

I'd never been this close to him before. Every bone in my body wanted to turn and run, but I felt paralyzed by his very nearness. I saw his eyelashes, a tiny patch of swirled white hair on his nose, the soft, thin skin around his nostrils that billowed like sails when he snorted. And his eyes—the color, the diameter, the depth—were so close, they bored easily through my audacity and went straight for my guts and warned me how insignificant I was.

I was nothing. I was a speck on the pavement. I was barely worth the time it took for him to look my way. He stopped my "attack" with that one single glance that said, *Back off before I have to hurt you.*

But I couldn't move. I was nothing, and I couldn't move because of it. His stare reduced me to such an irrelevancy that I had little physical sense of myself. Mentally, I wasn't even there.

Suddenly a loud whistle whipped through the air and the stallion turned his head. He looked across the paddock as Alex and his father ran our way, and immediately his gaze turned dull. Like he did every time when he heard the whistles and saw the men coming with their swinging lassos, he turned into a different horse. The challenge was over. Now he was the threatened one. And there was no dishonor, embarrassment, or shame in it at all, because a smart horse knows when to run.

• • •

Alex decided the only way to keep the two-year-old safe was to put the Mustang in a stall. There were four of them side by side in the barn, and while they were old, built in the 1800s, they were strong enough to hold draft horses who at one time pulled the wagons.

"I don't like to keep him in there," Alex said as we stared into the twelve-by-twelve box meant only to house a workhorse at night when he slept, "but I see no other way."

Inside the box the Mustang paced tight circles. He tried kicking his back legs at the walls, but there was barely enough room for him to turn around let alone provide him enough space for a solid strike. I winced when he tried and then tried again to break down the wall, but he was trapped, and he understood this, and eventually went back to circling again.

"It's only until spring," Alex said almost to himself. "Then we'll build him his own big barn."

Outside, the old man went to work fixing the hole in the fence. He'd already mended the gash in the two-year-old's rump and then easily chased Mamacita, the pony, and the white horse back into the paddock from the yard, where they seemed uneasy about running free.

The four sheep, on the other hand, still sprinted across the lawn with wild abandon, and as Alex and I moved from the Mustang's stall to the open barn door, we saw Dustin waving the tennis racket behind them.

A light snow started to fall. It was feathery and dry, the first one of the year, but Alex looked up at the clouds and gave a soft whistle as if a deep-winter blizzard might be on its way.

"My father will go home now," he said. "He leaves when it snows."

I nodded with sympathy, even though I was glad the old man would be gone. "You'll miss him," I said with as much empathy as I could manage.

Alex laughed. Then he shook his head and laughed some more. "No. We talk on the phone, and he'll be back next year. But he is a big help to me. In winter, there is much more work to do. My sons, they help but only on the weekends, and Maracella, my wife," he turned to me and grinned, "she is pregnant now."

I smiled and gave him my congratulations, but I didn't really care as much about the new baby as about what "much more work" meant for me. People asked for favors in different ways, but they almost always came after compliments, gossip, or warnings that dripped with valuable detail, so I always knew when they were coming, and always with reimbursement in mind. Alex, though, seemed so unaffected by pretense and my brain was so unfamiliar with deciphering *nice* people, that I wasn't sure if he'd just asked for my help or not.

I decided it didn't matter. I had no time, there was a novel to write, and I couldn't help with the animals anyway, because I was afraid of all of them. But I had to offer him something.

"Dustin can help you," I said.

In the time it took for Alex to raise one eyebrow and look at me sideways as if I'd just offered a quarter for a one hundred dollar bill, the two rams up on the hill stopped running from the waving tennis racket and turned to face it instead. They were tired of playing this game, and as their wives fled to safety, the two rams rounded their necks, bent their horns to the ground, and charged for Dustin with murder flaming in their eyes.

For as much time as he spent in science books, Dustin was in good physical shape. He threw the tennis racket with perfect precision, and it landed and caught on one of the ram's horns. Then he turned and flew across the lawn in precise arcing patterns worthy of an NFL receiver. But the tennis racket closed in behind him. By the time he disappeared around the back of the house, it had made contact at least four times with Dustin's posterior end.

Alex laughed and said he'd better go help. But he stood there in the doorway of the barn for a minute and looked back up at the sky. The clouds hung low, like heavy wet blankets on a clothesline, and he sighed as slivers of snow floated down and landed on his face.

"It's very hard when the winter comes," he said.

• • •

Chapter Ten

Winter comes quickly to the northern prairies. It swoops down from northwest Canada in late November and circles overhead for almost half a year. Under its shadow, everything scatters: birds flee south; fish dive low; land animals run for whatever cover they can find. Long before the first snowfall, every insect is dead and every piece of vegetation stiff with rigor mortis. Long after, snow dunes bury them in a desert terrain scavenged by hawks, coyotes, and red foxes.

That year, the cold came early. By the first week of December, the streams froze, and almost overnight, the ponds, lakes, and well pipes to the barn all followed. By mid-month, when the northwesterly winds clashed regularly with easterlies off distant Lake Michigan to the east, I was hauling buckets of water out to the animals morning, noon, and night.

It was my new job.

After Alex's parents left for Mexico, I watched from the house as he made the twice-daily rounds by himself. At first I didn't feel too guilty, because it only took him half an hour to take care of all his animals, but once the pipes to the barn pump froze, he had to bring water in large plastic drums in the back of his truck, which he then siphoned off into smaller containers that he lugged to various destinations. It took him more than an hour each time, and when I saw his wife Maracella helping him one day, pregnant and carrying buckets of heavy, sloshing water, guilt in full armor chased me down to the barn.

Maracella, who was shy, spoke very little English. When I first approached her that morning, grabbed the bucket from her hands, and told her she should go home, she didn't understand, only heard accusation in my voice, and looked fearfully to Alex for rescue. After he assured her I wasn't a threat, she smiled timidly, looked down at her belly, and then said something softly in Spanish.

"She says to tell you she grew up on a farm and is used to this kind of work," Alex said. "She says she is fine. This is no trouble for her."

"She shouldn't be here," I said with a little too much indictment. "*I'll* help you instead."

Maracella seemed to understand, because she shook her head and spoke to Alex with more force in her words this time.

"She says you have already been too kind. This is no trouble. You have other things to do."

I quickly realized there would only be one way around this, so I forced my mouth to smile and put a hand on Maracella's shoulder. "Tell her," I said as I looked at Alex, "that there's nothing I'd rather do."

Alex eyed me with suspicion as he repeated what I said. Then Maracella looked at me directly for the first time with her brow wrinkled in disbelief.

"No, really," I said with the kind of enthusiasm that accompanies a failing lie. "I'd *love* to help."

After I spent the next ten minutes shoring up the propaganda with how much I loved animals, how much I'd always wanted to live on a farm with animals, and with how much I'd always wanted to take care of them, Alex and Maracella finally pretended to believe me. At first I thought I'd really convinced them that my life's ambition was to spend time in a barn, but after I learned what was actually involved, I knew they were just being polite.

There is nothing worse than barn work in cold weather. Especially when you don't have the right gear. I didn't own a pair of waterproof gloves, so when I hauled buckets of water down from the kitchen sink, it spilled out and froze my thin, leather Amatos into planks of solid ice. I also didn't have a warm coat, so I layered until I could barely move, but the barn—with its cement floors and stone foundation—held in the cold air like a thermos bottle that a trench coat and three angora sweaters couldn't fight. I didn't own a hat, so I wrapped cashmere scarves around my head and knotted them in place under my chin, and since the only flat shoes I had were leather loafers and running shoes, I wrapped plastic bags around them in an attempt to keep my feet dry.

The chickens, geese, and ducks came first. When Alex opened the door to the henhouse in the mornings, they charged toward us in an orchestral stampede complaining about the weather and demanding their breakfast with an audacity usually reserved for wealthy old women. As Alex scooped grain out of a fifty-pound bag and I poured water into black rubber bowls, the chickens dive-bombed us from their perches, the ducks exploded with arias of starvation, and the geese honked and hissed and ridiculed my outfit as they stabbed at the plastic over my shoes. After about a week of this, I brought the tennis racket with me.

Next came the animals in the barn. Every morning, Alex climbed the stairs to the upper story where the hay and straw were kept. The hay— heavy, green bales of timothy and alfalfa grass—was used for food, and the straw—lighter bales of thin, gold wheat stalks—was used for bedding. Alex tossed three bales of hay and four bales of straw down a shoot each morning, and my job was to divvy it up among the sheep and horses.

The four sheep slept in their own stall at the far end of the barn. When I opened their door, they hurtled out as one, but as three of them dashed for the hay, one of the rams—they took turns—made a point of making a point. What that point was, I never figured out, but making it involved smashing their heads against the stall door behind which I always cowered. Once the smashing was done, the ram of the day joined the others, and I waited for the window of opportunity when he had a mouthful of hay to run on tiptoe past them.

By this time, Alex climbed down from the hayloft, and all I had to do was water the horses. On the first day, Alex insisted that I feed the hay while he heaved the buckets of water into the galvanized trough, but when the white horse, the pony, the two-year-old, and the pregnant Mamacita saw me coming with their meal, they surrounded me and ripped it from my arms. I was trapped, encircled by a street gang of teeth, and the more I twisted in circles to avoid them, the tighter the circle became. I panicked and yelled for Alex to come help me, but by the time he pushed his way through the horde, I was close to passing out, and the hay, stripped like a field under locust attack, was completely gone.

From that point on, I did the watering. I learned that if I carried two buckets at a time instead of one, the weight on each side counterbalanced the other and my shoulder sockets were less likely to unhinge. I also learned the importance of pouring slowly even though it took more concentration and strength, because if water splashes onto a trench coat and freezes it to angora, which in turn freezes to the naked body, later they all have to be ripped off like bandages from hairy skin.

The worst of the barn work, however, was the mucking. In farm circles, the word *muck* is used both as a noun and a verb. It is used to name not only the objects ejected from an animal's back end but also to name the pile upon which those objects are put and to describe the physical activity of a human putting them there. Thus, a farmer mucks muck into a muck pile.

Most of the animals had no concern about sanitation issues. As the ducks and geese paraded across the front yard gossiping and complaining, they left long trails of steaming cylindrical turds behind them without missing a beat of conversation. Likewise the chickens didn't care who saw them raise their tail feathers and squeeze out the phlegm-filled globs of former food, dropping and plopping and spraying it on nests, food, water, and each other whenever and wherever the mood struck them. Even the sheep, who were mammals and theoretically answered to higher evolutionary codes of conduct, crapped all over the place.

The horses managed their excrement to a certain extent. Mamacita and the pony never pooped on their food, and the boys created a single mountain of manure called a "stud pile" within a specific area of their paddock.

For stallions, building stud piles isn't just a tidy way of eliminating fecal matter, it's a way of life. Even when they've shown the door to every conceivable piece of waste, they always find more to reinforce their stud piles. Entire bodies of research have been conducted on these feats of civil engineering, and they all conclude that stud piles are a brilliant compensation for a stallion's genetically limited resources.

In the wild, horse territories are mobile. A stallion's province isn't measured by physical boundaries such as tree lines, mountain ridges, or streambeds, but by the individual members of the family itself. Since the family is always on the move, the probability of bumping into another band is high, so stallions need a way to warn others when they're entering scared ground. Since a horse's sense of smell is so acute, stallions exploit what smells the most.

Like all prey animals, horses depend on odor much more than sight to warn them of bad things on the horizon. They have huge nostrils that take in more scent per molecule than those who stalk them, and the part of their brains that deciphers odors—the olfactory lobe—is so convoluted and compressed within a tiny space that when flattened out, it's much larger than the olfactory bulbs of predator species such as humans. It's like a balled-up piece of paper, and the density of odor receptor cells in a horse's brain is so immense, he uses scent instead of space to measure physical distance.

Because stallions usually live most of their lives on the periphery of the bands they protect, dropping a load is an easy, surefire way for them to mark the boundaries of their family. It's a pile of notification, a no-trespassing heap, a mound of threatening graffiti that not only tells other stallions who he is but how strong he is, how close he is, and how determined he is to protect his mares and foals.

When he's not on the fringes of his family, the stallion spends a lot of his time covering the manure and urine of his mares with the smell of his own. When a mare defecates, the stallion trots over and conducts a formal investigation, which includes pawing, sniffing, curling his lips, flaring his nostrils, and then depositing his own feces or urine on top.

"When a stallion enters a new area, he may prance from one fecal pile to another, performing this ritual sequence at each," explains Sue McDonnell, founding head of the Equine Behavior Program at the University of Pennsylvania, whose research found that "repeated defecation in a particular area results in accumulation of fecal matter into large mounds, which are known as 'stud piles' . . . which often accumulate along fence lines of pastured horses. Stud piles may be used by several stallions, resulting in large stud piles along common paths."

The stud pile created by the white horse and the two-year-old along the fence line of their pasture wasn't just "large," it grew to the size of an earthwork that archeologists would one day probably want to excavate. When Alex put the younger stallions in stalls and let the Mustang out for exercise, the wild horse, who spent most of his adult life maintaining the sanctity of his stud piles, added to this domesticated version with ecclesiastical fanaticism. The stud pile grew almost half a foot each day, and after I put Dustin in charge of the mucking, he spent hours on the computer researching animal waste disposal techniques and finally and authoritatively designated the "mass of excrement" as "un-muckable" due to bulk weight per unit volume.

And so it grew until it rose to the height of the electric wire at the top of the fence and shorted it out. It didn't matter, though, because the heifers were gone and the horses were separated by stalls, and since it didn't smell too bad—frozen horse turds don't smell like anything—we eventually learned to ignore it.

• • •

What I couldn't ignore was the Mustang's confinement in the box. Alex let him out each morning but only for the time it took for us to feed, water, and clean out his stall, which meant this animal, who grew up never knowing constraint of any kind, now faced an entire winter with a half an hour's worth of freedom a day.

There wasn't enough room in the stall for him to pace back and forth as I'd seen him do along fence lines, so he circled and circled, first one direction then the next, until he wore a hard-packed track in the straw. The only time he stopped circling was when he stuck his head out the top half of the door when someone, usually a sheep, walked within striking distance of his outstretched neck. Once I saw him grab one of the rams by the thick wool on the back of the neck, lift him off the ground, and fling him like an old washrag to the other side of the aisle.

The other stallions, the two-year-old in particular, quickly learned that if they stood just beyond his reach, they could taunt him with arched necks and flattened ears and receive no penalty other than the Mustang's furious squeals as he banged against the stall door with his front hooves. The Mustang's anger was bigger than himself, heavier, tougher, more focused on its purpose, and it bullied and harassed him and poked him with sticks until every part of his body, from the horn of his hooves to the hair in his mane, quivered with what he couldn't express. Several times I saw the two-year-old get too close, and when the Mustang made contact with his outstretched teeth, his legs and chest rammed against the stall door until the wood panels splintered and bowed, and the solid frame loosened from steel hinges.

And then, when the two-year-old pulled back and ran away, the Mustang started circling again.

Alex reinforced the panels on the stall door and tightened the hinges, but the two-year-old turned increasingly bold with his taunting, creeping closer each time, so Alex finally nailed a wire fence panel over the opening with hopes this would create enough buffer.

Physically it worked for a while. Without the opening that provided momentum, the Mustang could only rear up at the door instead of forcing his full weight against it. But now the two-year-old was free to stand at the wire panel and ridicule him, and when he wasn't there, the Mustang no longer had the freedom to stick his head out into the aisle. He was completely isolated, yet forced to watch his son, his mare, the white stallion, and the pony bond as a family without him. Despite him. As if he wasn't there.

I spent time down in the barn after Alex went home in the evenings. I stood by the Mustang's stall and looked in at him through the mesh, but if I cooed or hummed or signaled him in any way, he rushed at the door with his ears flat and threatened me with his teeth.

I brought some carrots down with me one night thinking that might help our relationship, but they were too big to squeeze through the wire squares, and when I snapped one in half, the horses outside heard it and ran into the barn like ravenous, flesh-eating lunatics. I threw the entire bag to fend them off, but they overlooked the obvious in their frenzy and chased me all the way down the aisle. Even after I slid through the barn door and slammed it shut behind me, they pawed and called for their carrots. As someone later told me somewhere along the line, "If you think horses can't count, take three carrots into the barn, but give them only two." It was a statement I learned to live by.

After the first big snowfall in mid-December, I stopped going down to the barn at night. For one thing, it was too much work getting dressed in my layers and plastic bags, but for another, I sensed my presence in the barn upset the Mustang more than it relieved him. He seemed so angry, but I didn't know why, and there was nothing I could do but stand and watch him circle.

In the meantime Alex, Dustin, and I fell into a quiet routine. There were some mornings when the only thing we said to one another was "Good morning," then spent the rest of our time working to a silent rhythm we kept while doing all of the chores. It was like meditating. It was a time when nothing but the smell of hay and the sound of animals chewing entered my head at all, and when I was done, I almost didn't remember doing it.

And everything ran smoothly for a while.

• • •

Chapter Eleven

I felt like the tour guide of a Christmas Nativity scene gone terribly wrong.

Before me, what was a charming country barn decked with holiday decorations only a week ago, now looked like a Halloween house of horrors. Behind me, my family—my parents; my ninety-five-year-old grandmother; my sister and her family; my youngest daughter Sarah and my middle son Jacob; my oldest daughter Alicia, her husband Adam, their two kids; and Adam's mother—followed me wide-eyed and whispering in a tight huddle down the main aisle of the barn.

Around us, shredded red-fabric bows littered the floor and pine garlands, ripped from their moorings, hung loose from the rafters like cobwebs. A herd of life-size plastic reindeer lay trampled and dismembered among broken bales of straw matted with newly dried blood that also splattered in diagonal patterns across the whitewashed dairy barn walls. Confined in their stalls for the day, the sheep turned into possessed spirits wailing to be free, as the white horse, wrapped in blood-soaked white bandages that kept coming loose, roamed the aisle like a listless, unraveling mummy.

It was Christmas Day, and the week before, after Dustin left to visit his family in Maryland, I had shoved my novel and my ongoing search for health insurance into the back of a drawer reserved at this time of year for adult responsibilities and spent hundreds of dollars at Farm & Fleet on garland, bows, inflatable candy canes, acrylic snowflakes, and red-scarved plastic penguins and brought them home and hung them from anything with a surface across the entire seven acres of the farm.

It was the first time in several years my family would all be together in one place at one time, and I wanted it to be worthy of a Norman Rockwell painting. I wanted the adults to believe in Santa, the small kids to remember it always, and my own kids to understand how sorry I was for so many years of half-hearted attempts. We would be an old-fashioned Currier & Ives family, and in our own little world, at least for one day, we'd be free of professional duties, term papers, and pressures to succeed. Most of all, and with enough well-placed stage props to help us suspend the disbelief, we wouldn't let regrets control our lives. Not for that one day.

I wrapped swags of green fur around the top rail of the fence that bordered the driveway, nailed plastic red bows on the windowsills of the henhouse, and strung blinking white lights from extension cord to extension cord wherever there was an outlet. I hung a five-foot wreath over the barn door, and inside, where the "animals of the manger" lived, I decked out every stall door, milk stanchion post, and ceiling beam I could reach.

When Alex first saw the barn in its new holiday glory, he turned in circles and stole sideways glances my way, afraid to look me in the eye. Finally, after he took in the swags of synthetic pine boughs, the clusters of plastic holly, and the family of life-size deer that had to be propped up on bales of straw because the rams kept attacking them, he turned to me and asked if everyone in America did it this way.

They would, I thought, if they just had the time.

Later that afternoon, as an incoming front full of snow loomed dark at the edge of the western fields, Alex brought Maracella and his youngest son and daughter to the barn to see what Americans did with their spare change and time. The kids were impressed, but Maracella, as kind and shy as she was, couldn't hide a look of bewildered surprise that advanced quickly toward alarm when she saw the deer family up on their tower of straw. She whispered frantically to Alex and then called her children to the safety of her arms. It wasn't until I brought cups of hot chocolate down from the house, and we sat on warm bales of hay and I assured her through Alex that decorating animal barns was an ancient western European tradition—which I assumed somewhere in history it must have been or should have been if it wasn't—that she seemed to settle down.

That night, the furious winds of the storm roared in and ripped all of the outside decorations from their windowsills and fence posts. When I trudged down the hill the next morning to meet Alex for chores, I found decapitated penguins and upended sleighs jutting like tombstones from the new snow. When I finally got to the barn, I thought we must have left the sliding doors open the night before, because the inside ornaments lay as windswept and scattered as those in the yard.

I saw Alex's silhouette at the far end of the aisle next to a horse.

"What *happened?*" I called as I took in the chaos, the utter disaster all around me.

Alex waved me toward him, and as I stepped over shattered bales of straw and flattened piles of synthetic greenery, I saw the blood sprays broadcast across the walls.

"What happened?" I said again, but when I got closer to Alex and the horse, I didn't have to ask a third time.

The white horse, shaking, wide-eyed, and worried, had gashes and bite marks all over his chest and face. I immediately looked to the Mustang's stall, but as he circled, I didn't see a mark on him. Then I noticed the two-year-old in the next stall over, and he did.

"They fought last night?" I asked as the new order of things unfolded in my head: the two-year-old, no longer harassed by his father, was taking over the herd, and the white horse, a big oaf with no ambitions, was the only one standing in his way.

Alex nodded.

"And now the two-year-old has to stay in a stall too?"

Alex, with a look of strain I'd never before seen on his face, slowly nodded again.

• • •

On Christmas night, after the dinner was over and the adults played Scrabble in the kitchen while the kids played upstairs with their new toys, I sat with my grandmother in the living room by the fire where we sipped steaming strong Bailey's and coffee.

"Did you have horses growing up?" I asked as we stared over our mugs at the fire.

She smiled, lowered her mug, and nodded slowly as her childhood from almost one century before played out in the dancing flames. She was born in 1910 and grew up on a farm in Southern Illinois where the German immigrant family wasted nothing—not a scrap of food, not a page of newspaper, not a drop of water—to keep the place going year after year.

Her grandfather, whom she called *Vada*, butchered his cows when they stopped giving milk, boiled his hens when they stopped laying eggs, and could pet one of his pigs with affection in the morning then slit its throat and have it hanging in hams and ropes of sausage in the smokehouse that night.

"The horses and the other animals weren't pets," my grandmother said. "They couldn't be, or we'd starve."

I sipped my coffee and watched her stare at the fire.

"There weren't any grocery stores like we have now," she went on as if I'd accused her of being cold-blooded. "So imagine what it would be like if you had to take a pet dog and slit her throat, drain her blood into a big iron pot, and cook it over an open fire while you cut the rest of her body into edible pieces, salted them, and hung them on hooks in the smoke-house. Then you'd throw all the rest—her organs and fat and gristle—into the boiling pot of blood, where they cooked all day while you stirred them down into a mush that you later stuffed into the linings of her own intes-tines. And then imagine, my dear," she paused and pointed an arthritic finger at the fire where the past and the present comingled, "that you had to eat it."

"I'd starve," I said, and she nodded.

"I believe you would."

But despite the gruesome necessities, Vada did have one weakness. This is what my grandmother called it and what his family and neighbors apparently thought of it as, a weakness, like a wanderlust spirit or innate bad judgment regarding the weather or anything else that disqualified a farmer from being a good one: He loved his plow horse, Blue.

"No one understood it," my grandmother said, "but for many years after that horse stopped working, Vada took care of him as if he was the hardest-pulling draft horse in the country. He never made over him, never petted him or cooed over him, or anything like that, and when folks asked when Blue was going to the renderer, Vada just grunted and said, 'When the time comes.'

"But the time came and went, and Vada still kept the old horse in good hay, still kept his hooves trimmed, and still let him out to pasture every morning and brought him in again every night.

"And each Christmas, year after year after year, even when Vada's back was hunched over and he could barely walk because of the arthritis," she paused, stared at the fire, and chuckled at the next thought, "Vada trudged out to that barn with a piece of my grandmother Mutti's best china and gave Blue a piece of our Christmas cake."

A long moment passed during which I couldn't read her face. Then she chuckled again and pulled a piece of lint off her sweater. "It took Mutti hours to make that cake."

I let her think of her grandmother for a while. Then I asked, "So, what ever happened to the horse?"

"Oh," she paused as if she had trouble remembering and then finally gave up and shrugged. "I think after Vada died, that would have been sometime during the Depression, he probably went straight to the renderer."

• • •

Renderers of horseflesh made a pretty good living during the first forty years of the 1900s. They were dark years for horses, but particularly hard on the wild mustangs who now, after several hundred years of fresh water, wide stretches of grazing land, and reproductive freedom, ran across the deserts and mountains of the American West by the millions.

The bad times started in earnest for them after the San Francisco earthquake in 1906. When the cleanup of the city began, every available draught horse on every ranch and farm from Southern California to Oregon was shipped in to haul away twenty-five thousand buildings worth of rubble, but within weeks they were all dead from exhaustion.

In a 1907 *Harper's Weekly* article, Rufus M. Steele wrote:

> *There are more horses than the city ever held for before, and these are barely more than half enough. The loads must be drawn, and the horses to be had are the horses which much tug and heave and plunge until the loads are moved. A half hour's walk from Market and Kearny streets at any hour of the day will lead you to a dead horse—dead in the harness—worked to death. The vans that carry off the carcasses are busier than the vans which carry drunk men to jail. And the men whose business it is to bring in new horses to replace those who go out in the struggle are growing more and more desperate.*

The men whose business it was to find new horses were private contractors, and with quick wits they turned their eyes to the endless supply of fresh animals who ranged from Missouri south to Texas, west to California, and all the way north to Canada. In Nevada in 1910 there were more wild horses than humans. Not only were they plentiful, but they were strong, healthy horses who had no owners and therefore came free of charge. Thousands of them were rounded up and shipped on trains to San Francisco where the horse market, according to Steele, looked "like a bull day in Wall Street."

From that point on, wild mustangs were on the house.

Tens of thousands of them were captured, broken, and sent overseas to Europe during World War I. "The little western pony may not be up to cavalry standards," stated the *Idaho Daily Statesmen* in 1916, "but he is a good little Ford, and will get you there and be up and about the next morning, and if cactus is the only food, he will take it and smile, leaving the regulation Packard waiting for the oats to catch up." None of them, however, came back. Those who survived were sold to Paris butchers or British families on the brink of starvation.

After the war, the scarcity of horses in Europe turned their flesh into a rare delicacy used in Norwegian sausages, German sauerbraten, Swedish stews, and Belgian steak tartare. The meat was rich, sweet, and tender with age, and the Italians sliced it into carpaccio and ground it up into savory salami, while the Dutch just salted it and put it straight onto bread.

The demand for horsemeat in Europe was too strong to ignore, and a second generation of private contractors started rounding up wild mustangs in the American West again. They shipped them by the thousands in railroad cars to processing plants in the Pacific Northwest, and by the 1930s, when the Depression ramped up the American demand for cheap, high-protein dog food, hundreds of horse-packing plants dotted the West Coast.

"The wild horse packing industry, born since the war, goes on day by day," stated the *Oshkosh Daily Northwestern* in 1930, "and as far as can be seen the numbers will continue and the supply remain unexhausted for years to come."

The horsemeat sent to Europe was shipped in fifty-gallon barrels that held fifteen-pound chunks of salted flesh. One of the biggest packers of eastern-bound horsemeat was Schlesser Brothers in Portland, Oregon, which slaughtered three hundred thousand wild horses between 1925 and 1930 alone. In an interview with the Center for Columbia River History, Edward Schlesser, who worked for his father in the heyday of the plant, said, "They boned all the meat, pickled it and put it into barrels. The barrels were rolled onto railroad cars and were shipped to New York. From there they went to Holland where they used the meat in their smorgasbords.

"At that time," Schlesser continued, "we were killing about one hundred horses each day. Train loads of horses would come in once a week."

In the meantime, the Ross Dog and Cat Food Company in Los Alamitos, California, entered the wild horse butchering business and used 180,000 pounds of wild horse flesh in Dr. Ross' Dog and Cat Food between 1924 and 1939. The company thrived on selling the red and yellow tin cans, which didn't state that they contained almost pure horse meat but advertised instead that they were packed with "scientifically prepared food" that contained "exactly the right proportions of pure, lean meat and other ingredients for a perfectly balanced ration."

About ten years into Dr. Ross's business, complaints about how the company treated the wild horses it processed started flooding in. The *Los Angeles Times* reported in 1933 that twelve horses in a load of seventeen coming in from Arizona died of either starvation or thirst or were trampled to death in a small truck bound for Dr. Ross's killing floors. One year later, the company was charged with animal cruelty when a shipment of 950 wild horses from Arizona and New Mexico arrived at the factory in trucks with many dead inside. One writer stated that the wild horses who regularly arrived at the dog food plant were, "decrepit, bony, a half-starved creature, barely equal to the long trek from the sales corral to railroad shipping points."

And eventually, under public pressure and with a dwindling number of wild horses left, Dr. Ross gave up on slaughtering them and instead turned to whales and sea lions for his pet food.

Meanwhile in the Midwest, an aggressive businessman named Phillip Chappel created Ken-L-Ration dog food made from horsemeat that became so popular he couldn't keep up with demand. He slaughtered 32,900 wild horses in 1933 alone, and the railroads were so busy shipping them from the southwest north to Ken-L-Ration processing plants near Chicago, they designated their cargo as "chicken feed" to avoid legal requirements to treat them humanely. Many of them arrived dead, and those who didn't were halfway there when they arrived only to be jammed into small corrals where Ken-L-Ration workers finished the job.

In 1923, according to the annual report of the Bureau of Animal Industry, 149,906 pounds of horsemeat were canned into pet food. By 1933 that number increased to over twenty-nine million. After that, the use of horsemeat declined, because there weren't enough horses left to use, but horsemeat was still used occasionally for American pet food until it was banned in 1970.

It is still legal, however, for "kill buyers" to purchase horses in the United States and sell them to contractors in Canada and Mexico, where horsemeat is still in fashion.

Renderers back in the 1920s and 1930s killed the horses by slitting their throats or putting bullets in their heads. Today in Mexico and Canada, renderers use bolt guns on horses—quick, nonpenetrating shots to the head—which on cattle usually kill instantly. But many point out that these bolt guns don't work as intended on a horse's brain.

The reality is that a horse's brain is farther back than a cow's. Horses often regain consciousness and feel the pain of being shackled and hoisted to the rendering area. As one advocacy group noted, "They are very much aware of being butchered alive."

• • •

The day after Christmas, when everyone was gone, I hid a candy cane in my coat pocket and took it down to the barn. I passed by the two-year-old, who stood in his stall staring out as if confused about why he was there, then ducked under the necks of Mamacita and the white horse in the aisle, pushed past the pony, and went straight to the Mustang's stall.

The candy cane was thin enough to push through the wire, but it took the Mustang several minutes to stop his circling and investigate.

At first he just stared at the red and white striped stick poking in at him. Then he stretched his neck forward to get a magnified sniff. His tongue came out, hesitatingly, touched the very tip of the candy, then darted back in where it rolled the flavor of peppermint around in his mouth.

His eyes widened and started to glisten. His ears shot forward. He licked his lips. Then he stretched his neck closer and gently, slowly clenched the stick between his front teeth. When it was secure, he yanked his neck back with a sudden and violent jerk and pulled the candy cane with him.

He circled quickly with the new thing in his mouth and turned his head into the far corner of the stall for some privacy, where he chewed on the brittle sugar with a sound like crunching broken bones.

Meanwhile next door the two-year-old figured out something was going on and kicked at the wall between the two boxes. I jumped back at the impact, but the Mustang, lost in the raptures of peppermint, didn't flinch and kept crunching the candy.

When he was done, he turned back to the door with a look I thought might be ecstasy, as though he'd never known anything could taste so good. Then he pushed his muzzle close to the wire, looking for a little more. I flattened my hand against the mesh so he could smell it, but when he realized there was nothing there but my hand, he flattened his ears, curled back his lips, and threatened me with his teeth. Then he started circling again.

I gathered up all of the leftover candy canes, about twelve in all, and for two days, before the supply ran out, the Mustang refused to eat anything else. But whenever his treat was done, he went back to his circles and glared at me each time around as if chased by a hate that he couldn't outrun.

• • •

Chapter Twelve

A blizzard is not defined by the amount of snow that falls but by how hard the wind blows and how low the temperatures drop. People in the upper-Midwestern plains know this from childbirth, grow up watching as many weather reports as they do Saturday morning cartoons and can follow jet streams and pressure gradients and colliding fronts as easily as sports scores by the time they reach sixth grade. Weather is what defines people in the Snow Belt; it's what makes them tough.

In Chicago on New Year's Day, when the average temperature is about fourteen degrees, hundreds of people gather at North Beach, where at noon they disrobe, run into Lake Michigan hollering like Vikings, and stay there for as long as they can. While some claim it's the best way to cure a New Year's Eve hangover, most people—including my own children, who made me watch them participate that year after Christmas—feel it's a way to define themselves as Chicagoans. It doesn't matter how cold it is or how much snow they have to traverse on bare feet before they get to the water: For the members of this elite club it's a way of showing the rest of the world how tough and resilient and farther up the food chain they are than anyone else on Earth. It's their stallion pile.

I preferred experiencing the weather from inside the window of my house.

And while native Chicagoans defined a blizzard as clashing fronts that pumped out torrents of snow, winds of at least thirty-five miles an hour, temperatures plunging below twenty degrees, and visibilities of less than four hundred yards, I defined it by whether I could see the barn or not. After the first of the year, I couldn't most of the time.

The first blizzard brought wind chills of twenty-five below zero, seven inches of snow, and gales that swept it across the roads and fields at fifty miles an hour. Wherever these sheets of snow hit a corner on a barn or house or silo, it amassed into drifts that made getting down the hill almost impossible without skis, which didn't matter anyway once the wind blew so much snow onto the porch that I couldn't open the front door.

The second blizzard, just a few days later, took the temperature down to forty-five below zero, and by the time I made it to the barn, the water in the buckets that I carried already started to freeze. Anything with moisture—from the three-foot-deep trough in the paddock to the snot-swathed whiskers on the horses—froze solid. The water in the snow itself crystallized cold, and when the wind drove it onto exposed skin, it felt like a wildcat's claws digging in.

During these storms, Alex, like most of the people in the area who worked seasonal jobs, hooked a plow to the front of his pickup and cleared driveways and parking lots for twenty-four-hour stretches at a time. It was steady work, because once the plows scraped the asphalt clean, another storm rolled in, and then another and another, until there were twelve-foot towers of hard-packed snow surrounding every paved place, and people started to feel claustrophobic.

One morning after a particularly hormonal blizzard struck and Alex came to do chores, dark half-moons hung below eyes that hadn't seen sleep in two days. He moved slowly and carelessly and lost his temper with the sheep. I asked him if he was all right, and he said, "Oh, sure," but at one point when he bent down to pick up a bucket of water and lost his balance, I told him to go home. I'd take care of the animals myself.

"No, I'm fine," he said.

"No you're not," I said and then started talking fast, like I did back in the Capitol when I had to convince someone of something important. "I know exactly what to do, the sheep get three flakes of hay, the horses get a flake and a half each, the chickens get two scoops of scratch, and the ducks and geese get two scoops of cracked corn, so it's no problem, and the only thing I can't do is let the horses out of their stalls, but you can do that later after you get some sleep, and Dustin will muck out the sheep's stall in the meantime, and everyone will be just fine, so go home."

"Yes, but . . ."

"You just go home, get something warm to eat, and then go to bed and sleep as long as you can, because it's supposed to snow again tonight and you'll have to be rested and not worrying about the animals," I pinched the sleeve of his coat and started leading him to his truck. "And besides," I added, "I'm going to Farm & Fleet this afternoon to get some warm clothes and good gloves and a hat and some thick boots, so the work will be easy for me, and you won't have to think about the animals at all." He followed me like a sleepwalking child being led back to bed, and all I had to do was give him a nudge from behind when he climbed into the driver's seat, slam the truck door closed, and point authoritatively down toward his house, and he was gone.

I stood there in my bulked-up trench coat and plastic bag–covered loafers wondering what I'd just done. Then a gust of incoming northerly wind ripped the scarf, tied under my chin like a babushka, from my head.

• • •

"You'll never believe where I'm shopping for clothes right now," I said into the cell phone balanced between my ear and shoulder as I held a pair of Carhartt overhauls up to my body to check for fit. "Never in a million years."

On the other end, about one hundred thousand miles away in Southern California, my best and only lasting friend from high school, Claudine, gasped with the cynicism allowed women like her, who owned their own marketing companies in balmy climates and wore blingy gold sandals and off-white linen twelve months out of the year.

"Not one of those outlet malls in the middle of a cornfield?"

The overalls, made of stiff cotton sandstone duck and lined with what felt like bulletproof Kevlar, were too heavy to hold up with one hand, so I just tossed them onto the pile in the shopping cart and headed for the matching coats.

"Nope."

My cart was heaped with anything I found that looked capable of challenging the weather: bags of salt to melt ice; an ergonomically correct snow shovel; a pair of light blue waterproof, insulated rubber gloves; a pink and black plaid wool trapper's hat with earflaps and adjustable chinstrap; six pairs of advanced-fiber socks with a Thermal Overall Grade of 2.34; and a pair of snow boots with waterproof nylon uppers, foam insulation rated to minus forty degrees, a bulky fleece collar and gusset tongue, a thick rubber shell, and humorless rubber treads that looked serious enough for moon travel.

"Target?"

"Nope."

"Not . . . ," Claudine gasped dramatically, "Wal . . ."

"No. I'm in Farm & Fleet."

"Farm and what?"

I perched the phone between my ear and shoulder again as I pulled a Carhartt coat off the rack. It was as heavy as the overalls, and the blanket-lined canvas had triple-stitched seams, a significant zipper, heavy-duty snaps and Velcro closures, and two deep front pockets presumably for tools.

"Farm & Fleet," I said again. "But listen, I was actually calling to find out what health insurance company you use."

A year before, a spider bit me on the face while I was sleeping, and it swelled so badly, I ended up in the emergency room the next day. After conducting an MRI to see if the swelling was affecting any part of my brain, the doctors found three brain aneurysms. While the two surgeries required to clip the aneurysms were relatively simple procedures for the neurosurgeon, and even though once an aneurysm is gone, it's gone forever, when I left government work and applied for private health insurance, company after company denied me coverage because they deemed an aneurysm a "preexisting condition" whether you actually still had one or not.

"Wait," Claudine said, "I'm still stuck on the fact that you're buying clothes at a place called Farm and Feet."

"Fleet," I said. "F-L-E-E-T."

"What's a fleet?"

"I don't know."

By now the cart was too heavy to steer in a straight direction, and it dawned on me as I zigzagged out of the women's section and headed toward the animal food aisles at the opposite end of the store, that I'd have to actually wear the suit of armor piled up in the cart that I could barely push. I almost turned around to put it all back, but I spotted Bob out in the open stacking shelves at the end of an aisle, and he was the man I needed to talk to.

"I've got to go," I said. "Can you e-mail me your insurance company's information?"

"I don't think they'll cover you," Claudine said. "Not with a preexisting condition."

"It's *not* a preexisting condition."

Bob saw me coming, and when I waved, he stood up and then took off down the nearest aisle. He moved quickly, as if he'd been paged, but I was pretty sure I hadn't heard his name on the loudspeaker.

"Wait," I yelled and pushed the cart into high gear, which immediately sent it careening to the right, where it thudded up against a solid stack of bagged barn lime.

"You're going to have to get a job," I heard Claudine say as I tried to convince the cart to get back on track with one hand and to switch the phone to the opposite ear with the other.

"What?" I stopped maneuvering the cart, so I could concentrate on the thing I thought I heard her say.

"You're going to have to get a job to get health insurance," she confirmed.

"There are no *jobs* here," I said and almost laughed as I thought of trying to find a political position in a place where I only knew a cattle farmer, a fence contractor, and a Farm & Fleet sales associate.

"Any job. Something low stress. Work in a boutique or a jewelry store or something. Anything. You *have* to have health insurance."

I stared at the cart. I'd moved to the farm to get away from a job, but as I gazed down, the coat, the overalls, the boots suddenly all implied potential injuries—hypothermia, falls on the ice, dislocated shoulders from carrying buckets of ice. And then I looked up, noticed a display of live-trap cages with pictures of raccoons and thought of wild animal bites and rabies as well. Horse kicks, rusty nails, bruised ribs from rams, dysentery from well water, gangrene from goose bites, they all lay in waiting for me like stalkers.

I shook my head. I'd think about it later. I had more important things on my mind. "Have to run," I said as I snapped the cell phone shut and headed off with my cart to find Bob.

• • •

I found him in the plumbing aisle. He stood there staring at a shelf of white plastic pipe things with no other customer in sight, and I wondered why he'd fled so quickly.

"*There* you are," I said as I aimed the cart in his general direction and barged forward as best I could. The problem was that once I got going, it was hard to stop, and Bob had to jump out of the way.

"I need something to keep a water trough from freezing," I said as I leaned my weight in the opposite direction of the trajectory of the cart and stopped it just before it crashed into the shelves. "Whew, that was a close one."

I turned to Bob and smiled, but he still stared at the edge of the cart that nearly knocked down hundreds of the white plastic pipe things. Finally he looked up at me and adjusted his glasses. "A water trough you say?"

I nodded.

He looked down at the Carhartt coat at the top of the pile in the cart. Then he looked at my loafers, then my thin trench coat, then back up at my face and readjusted his glasses again. "You don't have a heater for your water trough yet?"

Impatience got a foothold, and I stared at him hard. "No. I do not have a heater for my water trough yet."

He shrugged, looked down at the floor, and shook his head as if he felt sorry for me and for any animal unfortunate enough to be associated with me. Who at this time of year, his shaking head said, wouldn't have a heater in their water trough yet?

"Can you just show me where they are," I demanded rather than asked.

He shrugged again, sighed, and said, "Follow me," with a weary tone that bordered on rudeness.

He started to turn away, but my cell rang, and when I saw Dustin's name, I grabbed Bob's sleeve, flipped open the phone, and held up one finger to stop him.

"Melinda?" Dustin's voice sounded panicky. "Where are you?"

"Farm & Fleet. What's wrong?"

Bob crossed his arms and rolled his eyes.

"I'm down in the barn. It's the horses," he said, and in the near background I heard a high-pitched scream, followed by loud banging, followed by the clatter of the phone dropping.

"Dustin? Dustin? What's going on?"

The horse screamed again, then another bang, then another scream.

"Dustin? What's going *on?*"

I put a palm over my free ear so I could hear what was happening from wherever Dustin's phone landed.

Banging. Another scream. Dustin's muffled plea to stop.

"Dustin?" I yelled as loud as I could, and then Bob uncrossed his arms.

Another clatter of the phone being picked up and Dustin's breathing coming fast and hard.

"The two-year-old broke down the wall, and . . . ," he stopped, gulped for air, "the Mustang fell, and his leg is trapped under the door, and he can't get up and . . . ," he gasped again, "the other one is pounding on his chest."

"Oh my God," I said and looked in terror at Bob. "Get him away. Get him *away.*"

"I can't. I tried. There's blood everywhere. What do I do?"

I shook my head frantically as I stared at Bob, whose eyes widened behind his glasses. I didn't know. I didn't know what to do.

"A shovel," I said. "Get a shovel and bang him in the head. Or a pitchfork, stab him with a pitchfork. Do whatever you have to do. Use a board, whack him in the testicles with a board. I'll call Alex. Just get him away from the Mustang. *Hurry.*"

I hung up and dialed Alex's number. Bob opened his mouth to say something, but Alex answered, and I screamed at him to get to the barn.

"I'll be right there," he said and hung up.

I dialed Dustin's number. When I heard, "Hi, this is Dustin, please leave a message at the tone," I slapped the phone shut.

"*Shit,*" I said and stared at the phone.

Bob took a step toward me. "What's . . . going on?"

"Shit."

I opened the phone and redialed with shaking fingers. Dustin picked up this time.

"Melinda?" His voice was soft in a disoriented way, and then he choked as if he was crying.

I heard another squeal in the background, but it was milder this time, more sedate and sure of itself, heavy with conquest and finality. Every hair on my arms went stiff. I tried to keep my voice steady.

"What is it, Dustin? Tell me what happened."

"Jeezus," he said, and then his voice cracked open into a full-blown sob. "I think the Mustang is dead."

• • •

Chapter Thirteen

I ran out of the store on the physics of a bad dream. I couldn't get traction, couldn't move fast enough, couldn't span the distance toward a goal that got farther and farther away. I slid and fell on the slush that accumulated on the tiles between the sliding doors of the entryway, and I fell again on the ice in the parking lot. When I finally reached the car, I found a new layer of snow-turned-to-ice covering the windshield, and since I still hadn't gotten a scraper, and it would take ten minutes to thaw with the defroster, I clawed a credit card out of my wallet and scratched wildly at the glass.

When I cleared a circle large enough to see through, I got in the car and dumped the contents of my purse on the passenger seat to save time finding the key. I jammed it into the ignition and twisted it forward, but the engine groaned under the strain of the cold and no amount of pressure on the gas pedal could get it to catch. I twisted the key, pumped on the pedal, leaned into the steering wheel, and yelled, "Come *on*," but the engine refused to wake up.

I banged on the steering wheel with my palms then fell back against the seat. I remembered my dad telling me something about "flooding" an engine that didn't want to start. So I waited, and as I sat there and watched new snow cover the clearing on in the windshield, I grabbed the cell and called Dustin.

"Hi, this is Dustin, please leave a message at the tone."

Then I dialed Alex's number. "You've reached Durand Fencing . . ."

I didn't want to think about why they couldn't answer their phones. Or wouldn't answer their phones. But as I stared at the snow-covered windshield, I saw it anyway. All of it.

I saw the Mustang on the floor of his stall, saw him try to pull his leg out from under the door, saw him look up at his son towering above him with a look that questioned whether the time had finally come. I saw the two-year-old raise his hoof over the Mustang's chest exactly as the Mustang had done to him so many times before. He hesitated, held his hoof in the air for just a second too long, unsure of his intent, undecided, which gave the Mustang enough time to try to free himself. But there wasn't enough time. He couldn't pull free. And the failed attempt only solidified the two-year-old's hunch that the hoof. Should. Come. Down.

And it did. And then it did again. And as it did, something changed in the young horse's brain that made the doing of the thing impossible to stop. It wasn't rage, and it wasn't revenge. It was something he knew. Something he learned. Something that whispered directions in his ear in a voice that was calm and cool and composed. Nothing personal. Just business. The way of doing things.

The air in the car was so cold, I could barely feel my fingers or toes. If it didn't start, I'd have to go back in the store and ask for help, so I gripped the steering wheel, leaned forward, and begged out loud with frozen, white air streaming from my lips for the engine to turn over. I twisted the key. The engine grunted. I pushed on the gas pedal, and the engine rolled over, groaned, rolled over again, then finally snarled and woke up.

I pumped the gas as I turned the defroster on full blast and the windshield wipers on high speed. I couldn't see through the snow on the back window, but I shoved the gear into reverse anyway and then tore out of the parking lot on wheels sliding left and right on the ice.

Seven miles of slow going stretched before me. No number of plows or amount of salt could keep the snow from falling and then packing down to hard ice on the road. I leaned forward over the steering wheel to see through the windshield wipers that slapped back and forth across the small hole, but it was like looking through the lens of a telescope that wanted to take in the whole sky when I had to focus on one tiny spot three feet in front of my car.

The cell phone rang. Without taking my eyes from the hole, I reached over and patted the contents on the passenger seat until I felt its familiar shape. When I snapped it open, I heard Dustin's voice rambling something before I got it to my ear.

"...it's an emergency," he said.

"What? What's an emergency? I didn't hear you. What's happening?"

"The Mustang ... his leg ... Alex is here ... there's blood everywhere ..."

The windshield wipers whipped across the hole and tore away at its edges. I could see a little more now but not enough to concentrate on both steering and Dustin's voice. I slowed and pulled over to what I thought was the shoulder of the road as Dustin babbled on.

His panic was enough to yank me out of my own. "*Dustin*," I said sharply to get his attention, to reach across the airwaves and slap him out of it. "Slow down. Back up. Just tell me what's going on."

Dustin inhaled. Then he rewound and spoke slowly, connecting the nouns with the adjectives and the subjects with the predicates, pronouncing each syllable like its own word to make sure I heard him this time. "Alex needs bandages and antiseptic. He wants to know if you'll get them at Farm & Fleet."

"The Mustang?"

"He's not dead, but he's hurt badly, really badly, and we need bandages and antiseptic and stuff like that."

The relief I felt that the Mustang wasn't dead couldn't fight the implication in Dustin's voice that he might be soon.

"We need to call a vet," I said.

"No. Alex said he'll take care of it."

"But ..."

"Alex said he'll take of it, but you have to hurry."

There was density in Dustin's voice, a firmness that I didn't understand but that told me not to argue, so I hung up, turned the car around, and headed back to Farm & Fleet.

• • •

Very few wild horses die as a result of wounds inflicted by another horse. As battle scarred as they are, most wild stallions know when to back off, and with hundreds of thousands of acres of mountains and deserts and plains all around them, there's plenty of room to run. Besides, there are other threats to worry about: mountain lions, lightning strikes, starvation, getting mired in mud, getting left behind—there are so many ways a wild horse can die, that some proponents of rounding them up and placing them in captivity claim it would be cruel not to.

Yet, if a wild horse makes it through his first six months of life, he has a good chance of dying thirty to forty years later of old age. Adult mustangs in the American West have almost no predators and relatively few of the health issues like colic, lameness, dental wear, or parasites that usually claim the lives of domesticated horses by the time they're twenty. Instinct, the natural selection of survivors, and the protection of the herd make them one of the most successful species on the planet.

The highest percentage of natural deaths among wild horses is with the foals. When a foal is born, his legs are almost as long as an adult's, which makes balance unpredictable, like walking on stilts. And while it is his legs that will protect him later in life, they're not such an asset when he's three days old. A mountain lion, bobcat, or coyote won't attack an adult horse unless it's sick, lame, or stuck in snow or mud, but they will go after a wobbly little foal. One research project that followed a female mountain lion and her two kittens over ten months in Nevada found that over three-quarters of their diet consisted of wild foals. Another study found that of thirty-three foals born into a Nevada herd one year, half were missing within several months, and of the twenty-eight carcasses later found by the researchers, the vast majority were killed by mountain lions.

A foal's family will protect it as best it can. Mares, stallions, and older siblings will try to chase off a predator that gets too close, but there's only so much they can do. In one Nevada herd, researchers watched coyotes approach young foals again and again only to be chased off by the older horses. In one case, though, the researchers watched a coyote kill an unhealthy foal who could neither stand nor suckle from its mother. The study found that the foal was alive and lying near its mother and other band members, who had stayed close to the birth site. But later that day, the band's stallion aggressively herded his harem, including the new mother, out of view. The foal continued to lie in the sagebrush and its ears were occasionally seen twitching. Forty minutes later a coyote approached and pounced.

What the science couldn't measure was whether the stallion's decision to drive the family away from the foal was emotionally difficult, or if it was as quick and easy as drinking water on a hot day. Quantitative science avoids such questions, because instinct and emotion among mammals, including humans, are so closely intertwined it's hard to pick them apart. Either way, the stallion still had to make the decision: The foal was sick and would probably die of starvation because it couldn't stand up to nurse, and because the healthier foals were endangered by circling predators, he chose to protect whom he could.

Under normal circumstances a stallion will do anything he physically can to keep his family intact, but it's usually a private affair rarely seen by human eyes. In June 2011, however, photographer Sandy Standridge witnessed just such an episode, and her pictures and the story behind them went viral overnight.

Standridge was photographing a wild mustang family—a stallion she named Champ, several of his mares, and their colts and fillies—grazing along the banks of the Salt River in the Tonto National Forest in Arizona. As Standridge clicked away, another horse band arrived at the opposite side of the river, and among the newcomers were two colts playing at the water's edge who caught the stallion's attention. After watching the colts play for a few minutes, the stallion and his own colts started to cross the river to join in, but when they did, one of the younger fillies followed her father and brothers in.

"I thought, 'No, don't do that, the water's too swollen,'" Standridge said in one interview. "And at first it's OK, she's upstream, and she's going across, but suddenly the water catches her."

The filly was small and lightweight compared to her father and older siblings, and while she was safe at first on the upstream side of the bigger horses, the current soon pushed her into the middle of the group. She panicked and went under. When she popped back up and her head and gaping mouth reached for the sky, the stallion tried to grab the back of her neck to keep her from going under again. He couldn't hold on to her though, and the current swept her from the group.

As she headed downstream, with her eyes wide with terror and her mouth open to gasp for air, the stallion broke from the group and followed. When he reached the filly, he gently put his mouth on the back of her neck and then, as she struggled underneath him, he guided her back to the bank.

"He holds on to her, and he brings her back around to my side of the shore," Standridge said, "and doesn't let go until she's safe."

It was an emotional moment for Standridge, but she managed to keep her cool and continued taking photos. The last one shows the stallion, the shaken filly, and the filly's mare standing together on the shore as three birds land on their backs.

"Some people think that horses don't have a soul," Standridge said, "but the soul of a horse is much bigger than man knows."

Mark Bekoff, a professor emeritus of ecology and evolutionary biology at the University of Colorado, Boulder, saw the photos. Bekoff, who studies the ways compassion, empathy, and emotional bonds contribute to a species' survival, wrote in *Psychology Today* that Champ's rescue of the filly shows that "Anyone who has systematically studied or casually watched animals knows they form close and enduring bonds. Common sense along with good old Darwinian theory also shows that if humans have something, animals do as well. If we form friendships so do they. We all need others we can count on."

While the strong bonds among wild horses help protect them from mountain lions and swollen rivers, they aren't bulletproof. Shortly after Standridge documented the filly's rescue, she found the body of one of Champ's colts who also crossed the river that day under a tree with two high-powered bullet holes in his head. No one found out who did it or why, but as I would learn in the weeks and months to come, that was nothing new: Bullets and poisons and airplane stampedes killed so many mustangs deemed "pests" during the first half of the twentieth century throughout the western states that data about coyote kills turned irrelevant, and one dead horse lying under a tree barely made the statistics at all.

• • •

I pushed an oatmeal cookie through the mesh of the Mustang's stall, but he wouldn't look at it. I'd been to the grocery store three times in the two days following the attack, but nothing I brought him, not peppermint candy or sliced carrots coated with honey and rolled in sugar, lured his head up from where it hung. Two days' worth of hay sat at his feet.

"Come on big guy," I said as if urging a battered boxer from his corner of the ring. "Eat something. You can do it. Come on."

He stared at the floor. His ears stood at the halfway mark between attention and sleep. His neck muscles slacked, his tail hung low, and his back sagged to a sway. Even when the two-year-old kicked at the newly reinforced wall between them, the Mustang didn't register the event.

"He'll be OK," Alex told me on the afternoon of the fight after I returned from Farm & Fleet and pestered him to call a veterinarian. "He's just a little banged up."

I'd returned home with bags of horse aspirin, medicated pads, surgical tapes, bandage wraps, and antibiotics in powders, liquids, and creams. I'd grabbed everything that looked medically related off the first aid shelves—vitamin B-12 gels, apple-flavored electrolyte salt supplements, hydrogen peroxide teat dip for cows—anything that looked official or important or was certified, sanctioned, or endorsed by any group or person with "Dr." in front of his or her name, and when I got home and dumped it all out, it rolled and unspooled and tumbled to the far corners of the bloodied barn floor.

As Alex picked through the goods, the Mustang stood head down in the aisle. The two-year-old was temporarily in the back pasture, where he whinnied in protest about being alone, but the Mustang stood quiet and motionless in the barn. There was no emotion in his pose, nothing to indicate anger or fear or resentment, not even pain, and as I took in the bite marks on his neck and chest and the swelling wound on his front left leg, I asked Alex again why he didn't call a veterinarian.

"No need," he said without looking up at me.

Dustin, who'd been inspecting the shattered wood of the wall between the two stalls, looked over at me, shook his head, and scowled. I didn't understand, even when he put his index finger to his lips, so I turned on Alex again.

"When Dustin called me, he thought the Mustang was dead. That's how badly he was hurt."

Dustin stepped out of the stall. "I *thought* he was dead, but he was just trapped under the door and couldn't get up. He seems okay now."

I stared at Dustin. "Okay? Look at him." I jabbed my finger at the stallion, who seemed oblivious to our presence. "He's in pain. He's just . . . *standing* there."

Alex, who rested on his haunches, picked out a roll of white bandage wraps, a tube of antibiotic cream, and a plastic jar of powdered aspirin. Then he stood.

"I will give him aspirin for the pain," he said. "And the antibiotics and the bandages, they will be enough." Then his eyes darted to the rest of the things still on the floor. "You can return everything else."

"But ..."

Alex looked up from the things in his hand at me, and anger and frustration and apologies for both fought for control of his eyes.

"I cannot build fences when the ground is frozen, and the money from plowing isn't enough. I cannot afford health insurance for my family right now, and I cannot pay for an animal doctor."

His words came out like a confession, as if he'd done something wrong and was now ashamed and hoped declaring his guilt out loud for the whole world to hear would somehow end it all.

"That's OK," I said and placed my hand on the sleeve of his coat. "I can pay ..."

"No." Alex jerked his arm away from my hand, and in that instant changed from a repentant man to an angry one, lost and unwilling to ask for directions.

I immediately saw my mistake and tried to fix it. "I meant, I'll *lend* you ..."

"No."

Alex turned away from me, walked over to the Mustang, and ran his palm down the horse's injured leg. When the Mustang didn't flinch or try to pull away, Alex went to work covering the wounds with the cream and then wrapping the bandages around them. I watched him for a few minutes, stole some pleading glances at Dustin who wouldn't look back at me, and then, before I said something I knew I'd later regret, I walked out of the barn.

• • •

Chapter Fourteen

I spent a week in the house brooding about testosterone, angry at Alex's pride, Dustin's complicity, and the entire male gender's inflated sense of self-importance—including the Mustang and the two-year-old, who were as guilty as anyone. For seven days I sat inside blaming male CEOs for my lack of health insurance, the mailman for delivering bad news about my stock portfolio, the weatherman for his interminable blizzard predictions, my college journalism professor for teaching me nothing about plotting novels, Bob for being haughty, Robert for not calling, the rams for ramming, the roosters for crowing, and my father for not giving me enough warning about life in general.

My mood wasn't helped by the conclusion that I had to find a job. I'd never actually had to look for work before: I was offered a newspaper job covering education while I was still in college, which led to another newspaper job covering politics, which led to the congressional press secretary position, which led to the state senate post. And they always came by word-of-mouth. I'd never looked through the want ads, never broadcast my résumé, and never sat through a formal interview where there was anyone besides me in the running. I was always lucky that way, and now, when I had to find a job in the real world, I didn't know how.

I wasn't qualified for anything in McHenry County anyway. I couldn't keep books or run a cash register or manage a kennel. I knew nothing about human resources or automotive repair. I couldn't even type very fast. My experience included writing and schmoozing, and that was about it, and none of the ads I saw online mentioned the need for those particular skills.

Not that I didn't send my résumé out. I did. It was just that no one responded. I concluded they were probably all men.

When Dustin announced one morning that he *had* found a job and that it involved working in a halfway house in town for men with emotional challenges, I responded with, "How appropriate," and then reminded him with a poisoned little stab that he still had to muck out the stalls.

"Uh, that might be a problem," he said and told me that he'd be spending his nights working at the halfway house and that at home during the day, he had to sleep.

"So who's going to muck out stalls when Alex is plowing?" I said.

Dustin said nothing, just looked at the floor as the answer blinked on and off in the air between us like a pawnshop's neon sign: *The female will—The female will—The female will.* I didn't speak to him for the rest of the day, and when I hauled water down to the barn that night, I didn't speak to Alex or the Mustang or the two-year-old either. As far as I was concerned, they all belonged in a halfway house. Instead I spent time bonding with the mare and the ewes. Heavy with pregnancy, they were in the same frame of mind as I was, I figured.

The final assault on my disposition that week came when I took breaks from the job hunt and went back to my research on wild horses. I'd become somewhat obsessed about why the Mustang acted the way he did, and while herd behavior explained his attitude toward his son, it didn't account for why he hated people so much.

Probably, I thought as I Googled "mustangs" and let the bad mood run loose in my brain, it was because most of the people he'd come into contact with were men.

• • •

One morning in 1950, Velma Bronn Johnston was driving to her secretarial job in Reno, Nevada, when a truck hauling what she thought was cattle cut in front of her. She and her husband lived on a horse ranch just outside town, so she was used to seeing livestock trucks on the road, but this one dripped blood in its wake, and when Johnston got closer, she realized it was full of horses. "They were injured and bleeding," she told *Sports Illustrated* in an interview twenty-five years later. "And the only thing keeping some of them from falling down was that they were packed in so tightly. One horse's eyes had been shot out."

Johnston followed the truck to a rendering plant that processed horse-meat for pet food. She got out of her car, hid behind a bush, and watched as the back doors of the truck swung open and the horses tumbled out. What she saw horrified her: Most of the horses had large chunks of skin scraped off their sides; many had buckshot wounds; a small foal lay inside the truck trampled to death.

Five days later she went to the local office of the Bureau of Land Management (BLM) to complain. She was nervous about being there, but as a book about what would become her crusade related, "As Velma entered the dreary county building and made her way to the BLM's office, she remembered one of her father's sayings: 'Act like lady, think like a man. That way you'll get respect *and* you'll get what you want.'"

When she introduced herself to the agency's local range manager as Mrs. Charles Johnston of the Double Lazy Heart Ranch, he immediately assumed she was there to complain about wild horses on her property and assured her the BLM was doing everything it could to get rid of them. He assumed he was commiserating with a rancher's worried wife and told her private contractors using airplanes were rounding up "the vermin" as they spoke.

After that meeting Johnston researched wild mustangs, and what she learned about the "range clearance" programs of the BLM spurred her and her husband Charlie into a lifelong campaign to stop them.

The "clearance" started after the Civil War, when Congress passed a series of laws to encourage citizens to settle in the West. These legislative acts turned over 270 million acres of federal land to private owners, mostly in Kansas, Oklahoma, Texas, Colorado, and New Mexico. Many of these new settlers manipulated the homesteading laws to amass huge tracts of land for grazing cattle and sheep. With free rangeland at their disposal and no federal regulations to burden them, the ranching industry exploded in the American West, and overgrazing that damaged soil and depleted water resources eventually contributed to the Dust Bowl, a nearly ten-year-long brownish haze that saw crops blown away and made the simple act of breathing difficult.

In response, Congress in 1934 passed the Taylor Grazing Act, which created grazing districts on public lands that ranchers leased from the government. But it also put the ranchers in charge of administering these leases—and created loopholes they could drive a herd of cattle through. One section of the law, for example, stated that a certain percentage of forage on public lands should be allocated for wildlife. The mustangs who competed for depleted resources with commercial cattle and sheep, however, were deemed as "feral" instead of "wild" and weren't protected.

When the new agency's acting director, Archie D. Ryan, stated in 1939 that "A wild horse consumes forage needed by domestic livestock, brings in no return, and serves no useful purpose," he launched "range clearance" programs that encouraged ranchers or the men they hired called "mustangers" to kill or round up as many wild horses as they could.

The horses, though, weren't easy to catch, not in the beginning anyway. Mustangers tried everything from hoof nooses to lariats to out-and-out stampedes to corral the wild horses into captivity. The men were cowboys and used to compliant cattle who moved en masse whenever and wherever they were told. The mustangs, however, thought things through and had escape plans and rank-and-file roles to carry them out, and the cowboys spent entire winters plotting tactics for the following summer's roundups.

One of the earlier ideas they came up with was to simply wear the wild horses out. If they ran them long enough and hard enough, they'd eventually drop from exhaustion, and then they hoped that roping them would be as easy as roping wooden rocking horses. What they found, however, was that the wild horses were in much better shape than their own mounts, and the only way they could outrun them was with relays. Several mounted cowboys ran the band in circles until their own horses gave out, and then a second group of men and their fresh horses took over. What the mustangers didn't anticipate was that the wild horses figured out that they were being chased as a group rather than as individuals and veered away from the encircled band one by one. As mustanger Charles Barnum told *McClure's* magazine, "At length the pursuers find that they are trailing only one or two horses, and give up in disgust."

Once the mustangers realized they couldn't outrun the horses, they tried to outwit them instead. They knew, for instance, that the band's stallion would lead the family away if he saw a corral trap. When this happened, the mustangers forced their own horses to catch up with the stallion and then veer him back toward the trap, hoping at least some of his family would follow.

"But experience or instinct has taught the wild leader not to turn," Barnum stated, adding that seven out of ten bunches of wild horses will simply not turn. "I have ridden neck and neck with these game old stallions; I have beaten them across the nose with my quirt until their faces were drenched with blood, only to have them slacken sufficiently to dodge behind my horse and thence to continue on their contrary way."

The mustangers also tried to trick the wild horses into corrals by placing quiet domesticated horses in an area adjacent to the trap. They called it a *parada,* and when the running wild horses saw the gentler horses ahead of them, they headed toward the new group in the *parada* instead of veering away. When the cowboys urged the tame horses into the corral, the wild ones usually followed. But over time, the wild horses figured it out, dashing into the *parada,* through it, and away before the hands could stop them, sometimes bringing the gentler horses with them.

And once a wild horse escaped being trapped, he never fell for the ploy again. "It has always been the weaker and poorer horses that have been caught in largest numbers: the cream of the herds—the strong, the fleet, the capable, and crafty—escapes," Barnum concluded. "The elimination of the poorer stock has improved the breed, and the standard is higher among these wild horses today than among domestic animals."

As the wild horses got smarter, the mustangers had to find ways to keep up. They eventually resorted to poisoning their watering holes and shooting them with long-range guns. Once airplanes came onto the scene, wild horses were run over cliffs or chased into corrals where they waited for transport to the slaughterhouses. The airplanes were an enemy the wild mustangs couldn't outrun. In a detailed account in *Popular Science Monthly* titled "How a Cowboy-Aviator Hunts: The world's most thrilling sport . . . ," reporter Arthur Chapman described it as a "thrilling race" that pitted the cunning and speed of wild horses against the "marvel of modern science—the airplane."

Chapman wrote in the purple prose the magazine's readers enjoyed:

Out of the mighty depths of the Grand Canyon rose a humming roar that thundered through the spacious silence of the plateau as a great winged creature shot from the chasm of the North Rim and swooped downward, like a giant bird of prey. With a scream of warning, the large stallion lunged forward, a flashing streak of white, while the pack of wild mustangs pounded the desert at his heels. Madly they tore across the waste of sagebrush and cactus in a terrified race to shake off the strange menace from the skies.

The plane swooped down so close to the terrified horses, the reporter said it cast a shadow over their running bodies, and he couldn't hear their pounding hooves anymore. "Mile after mile the relentless pursuit continued. Now a raw-boned mare at the rear of the band faltered, stumbled, and fell. Now a spotted colt wavered and lagged behind, all atremble. The terrific pace was beginning to tell."

When they could run no more, the airplane finally banked away and left behind "a sweating band of exhausted trembling broncos—easy prey for the unerring lariats of cowboys," whom the reporter praised lavishly for saving the rangeland from the "menace" of wild horses.

But these weren't typical lariats. The cowboys dropped large truck tires attached to lines that not only slowed the horses down but often broke their necks when the rope snapped taut. The horses who survived the initial onslaught and were dragged to the ground by the lariats were immediately trussed up by the legs and pulled up a ramp into a truck waiting to transport them to the renderer.

It was just such a truck that Velma Johnston saw that morning in 1950, and by that time the two million wild horses who roamed the West at the turn of the century dwindled to fewer than twenty thousand.

Johnston's ensuing grassroots campaign for protection of wild horses, termed by one opponent "busybody women's clubs and elementary schoolchildren," was pretty much ignored by the livestock lobby at first, but as the general public learned what was going on, they started paying more attention. Once, when Johnston entered a state committee meeting to testify against airplane roundups of wild horses, a local rancher yelled out, "Well, if it isn't Wild Horse Annie," in an attempt to ridicule her, but the attempt backfired, the name stuck, and it became synonymous with the growing sentiment among the American public that wild horses on public lands should be left alone.

It was Johnston's quiet demeanor and modest approach that attracted much attention. She was never openly emotional. "Because I am a woman, I cannot afford to indulge in anything bordering on the sentimental. There isn't a thing wrong with emotion. It is a very important part of our lives; but when a woman begins on it, fighting a man's battle in a man's world, she has three strikes against her to begin with and I had to learn to talk on that level. What personal feelings I have are something different."

To the American public who followed her campaign, Wild Horse Annie was a simple and unpretentious woman who squared off against a ranching lobby of commercially minded businessmen and hard-core good old boys, many of whom threatened her life when her campaign started threatening them. About midway through her career as the country's leading advocate for wild horses, she began carrying a gun to her door whenever anyone knocked.

Before she died of cancer in 1977, Wild Horse Annie's work resulted in two federal laws: one in 1958 that banned air and land vehicles from hunting down wild horses on public lands; and the other in 1971, the Wild Free-Roaming Horses and Burros Act, declared wild free-roaming horses and burros "living symbols of the historic and pioneer spirit of the West" that enrich the lives of the American people. And because these horses and burros are "fast disappearing" from the American scene, the act declared that wild free-roaming horses and burros "shall be protected from capture, branding, harassment, or death" and considered an "integral part of the natural system of the public lands."

While the 1971 law was intended to protect wild mustangs from their human predators, one year after Johnston died, it was amended to allow the BLM to "remove excess animals" on public lands by rounding them up with helicopters and motorized vehicles. Once the "excess animals" were contained, the amendment stated, the BLM would try to adopt out what horses it could. But there was much room for interpretation. Horses deemed old, sick, or lame, the amendment stated, would be destroyed "in the most humane manner possible." And those healthy horses and burros for whom adoptive owners could not be found would also be eligible for destruction "in the most humane and cost-efficient manner possible."

• • •

I stopped sulking around the house once the Mustang started eating again. When Alex took off the bandages and revealed wounds that were healing well, my temper eased some more, and I further convalesced by convincing myself that mucking out the stalls was good exercise.

My mood really improved, however, when I stumbled across an ad for a saddle shop that needed a marketing manager. After listing job responsibilities including graphic design, press release writing, newsletter creation, and website administration, all of which I could handle, the ad closed with "Knowledge of horses required."

It didn't matter that the store was thirty miles east toward Chicago or that I'd be using skills I hoped I'd never have to use again. It was a full-time job with health care benefits, and when I delivered a buffed-up résumé to the store in person, I assured a woman named Karen that I was more than qualified for the job as I handed her my manila envelope.

I stuck to that story until the end. From the time the owner of the store, Frances, called me, through the ensuing interview at the store, and during the call later when she told me I had the job, I assured her I knew *all* about horses.

And at that time, after bonding with Wild Horse Annie's spirit and still sore from mucking stalls, I really thought I did.

• • •

Chapter Fifteen

The first question asked by the women who surrounded me on my first day at the store had nothing to do with whether I was married or had children or lived in the area. No one even asked who made my purse or who styled my hair. While the initial inquiry by my new coworkers was simple enough on the surface, it was one I wasn't prepared for, because as five women encircled me all with the same big question mark in their eyes, I felt the weight of it right away.

"What kind of horse do you have?"

I sensed the question was equivalent to asking someone in politics whom they worked for, because the answer either drew a circle that encompassed you both or slashed a line between that neither would cross. The answer, once spoken, would define the boundaries of small talk, the allocation of secrets, and how far they'd go if you ever needed their help. In other words, everything you needed to know.

I rummaged around in my brain for a response, but instinct told me not to try and summarize Alex's fire, the hooligans in my barn, or the episodes of natural selection that played out among them every day. It was too much information, too many causes and effects to condense into fast talk, so I stood there and said nothing at all.

One of the women, Judi, laughed, leaned toward me, and put her hand on my sleeve. "Don't worry," she said. "We're like a group of mares in a pasture, and you're a newcomer, so we're just sniffing you out."

Judi was the store's saddle fitter, tall and elegant and trained in England by the Society of Master Saddlers, which made her one of the lead mares. While under normal social circumstances her words would have eased the tension built up by my lack of response, to this group my answer seemed as important as telling them my name, and they just stood there, and they stared at me, and they waited.

As the tic that preceded a panic attack started drumming behind my left eye, I reminded myself that my answer to these women wouldn't change the course of democracy. I further reminded myself that panic attacks were simply neurochemical dysfunctions that overdramatized mildly intimidating situations, and that the minute the health insurance kicked in, I'd refill every one of my antianxiety prescriptions, and then some, so everything would be ok. But the thing about panic attacks is that the more you try to ignore them, the worse they get.

"A Thoroughbred?" one of the women asked.

"No," another one said. "I bet it's an imported Warmblood."

The first woman laughed. "She wouldn't be *working* if she had an imported Warmblood." And then they all laughed the way people do when they share a necessary burden. I smiled knowingly without knowing a thing, but the act of physically moving my mouth upward in commiseration and thereby establishing my inclusion in their herd was enough to distract the panic.

"I have stallions," I blurted out, liking the weight of the word, and liking even more the silence it brought to the group, until the silence lasted for more than a minute and started to feel uncomfortable.

"Stallions?" someone finally asked. "You're a breeder?"

The last time I'd heard that term used was by a lobbyist for the Lesbian-Gay-Bisexual-Transgender coalition who came to my office late one night with a bottle of wine, two plastic cups, and a folder full of talking points for senators who opposed the same-sex marriage ban scheduled for debate in the morning. He was an old friend—which meant an ally I'd known for more than six months—and as we drank and loosened up from the day, he called the sponsors of the bill "breeders," whom he defined as people who thought they were the only ones allowed to reproduce, when they should probably be doing anything but.

I looked at the women around me who looked back and waited for an answer. "Well, I'm not exactly a breeder ... you see ... there's this mustang and his son and this other big horse who ..."

"A mustang?" someone said, "You have a *mustang?*" and as it was said, the group seemed to take a collective step away from me as if the word was something too hot or too contagious or too awful to get near.

• • •

The reason "What kind of horse do you have?" is such an important question among equestrians is that a horse's breed or type usually indicates what side of the fence one rides on—either Western or English—much like a person's chosen political party, Democrat or Republican, indicates what kind of bumper sticker one uses.

Both styles of riding have three things in common: They require a specific kind of horse and saddle; they're considered sports that symbolize times long gone; and they compel their riders to turn up their noses at the other for not understanding the true purpose of the horse. Western riders dress like cowboys, ride in big heavy saddles suitable for ranch work, and compete in rodeos that highlight practical ranching skills like roping, steering, and outwitting cattle. English riders dress like landed gentry, ride in light little saddles designed for getting over obstacles during a hunt, and compete in shows that include jumping and dressage, sometimes referred to as "horse ballet."

My new place of employment catered to the latter and contained about thirteen thousand square feet of imported, high-tech materials cut, molded, and engineered into saddles, tack, and clothes as chiseled and honed to their specific purposes as tools on an architect's drawing table. Among the bits, of which there were thousands, one could choose between a German-made, wide-port Weymouth constructed of high-oxidizing copper, silicone, and zinc for horses with flat palatial arches to a double-jointed, two-ring elevator bit covered with apple-scented polymers for those horses who didn't like the taste or smell of metal. Blankets were designed for warming or cooling horses in heated stalls or drafty trailers, for winding up or winding down from workouts, or for standing in rain, frost, wind, or snow with designations made according to fill weight, fabric strength, and breathability. Bridles weren't made, they were constructed. Breeches weren't sewn, but designed. One didn't come to the store to buy a helmet, one came to the store to be properly fitted for head gear by staffers trained in the art of skull shape, injury statistics, impact strengths, and style.

The defining piece of equipment was the saddle. There were specific saddles for dressage riders, hunters, jumpers, and cross-country eventers, and they were so finely tuned to their respective styles, they required a professional saddle fitter to decipher them. When clients needed a new saddle, they first came to the store for a consultation in which everything on their bodies, from their heads to their feet, was measured down to the half-centimeter. Then saddle fitters went to the stable and measured the horses for the same finite details, which if misinterpreted could mean disaster for riders who had spent thousands of dollars and hours preparing for a show.

A dressage horse, for example, is judged in a show on the fluidity of its movements across an arena. Every step it takes and every muscle needed to make it is scrutinized, so if the saddle doesn't accommodate a wide back or a higher-than-normal wither, the movements suffer in the eyes of the judges. A saddle's weight, its length, its width, its curvature, the very suppleness and origins of its leather make all the difference in the world, and saddles are rarely put on professional horses "as is." They're widened or tightened and adjusted and reflocked until they fit the horses' shoulders and backs like a well-tailored politician's jacket.

The horses themselves—Thoroughbreds, Trakehners, Hanoverians, and Westphalians—are masterpieces of genetic engineering, with papered lineages as complicated and tightly controlled as tax records. For the most part they're bred with the light bones, long legs, and personalities of temperamental runway models, and among their more serious owners, everything from what they eat to which of their muscles should be exercised on any given day is calculated and weighed down to the ounce and dime.

They are watched over and pampered in the fashion of royal heirs. Their coats are bathed with rosewater shampoo, hooves polished with tea tree oil, and manes and tails glossed with citronella-scented silicone spray until they sparkle as if studded with stars. Swollen legs are wrapped, sore hooves are soaked, dry skin is moisturized. Temperatures and heartbeats are monitored by groomers and trainers who know more about the physiology of horses than they do about themselves, and equine doctors, dentists, eye specialists, and chiropractors are on every cell phone's speed dial.

The customers of the store—the owners, trainers, and groomers—shopped with a tutored purpose and fingered the fabrics, sniffed the leather, and read the labels with senses alert for quality. Among them were bluebloods and immigrants, college students and Saudi princes, celebrities, schoolteachers, and CEOs. They came from the cities, suburbs, and country estates of North America, South America, Europe, and the Middle East in search of the perfect saddle, the strongest shipping boot, the worthiest lunge line. No seam was too exact, no spur too polished. It didn't matter if they made a living with the sport or used it as a part-time escape; they all searched and studied and fingered and sniffed for the most flawless products on the planet created for the planet's most flawless horses.

None of whom included wild mustangs.

• • •

I was late more often than not during the first month of the new job, because some animal always seemed to get loose or into some kind of trouble first thing in the morning. One day the sheep escaped when the pony kicked out a new hole in the fence. Another day I found a goose entangled in barbed wire. On another day someone didn't bolt the Mustang's stall, and I found him pacing in the front yard.

When I arrived late one morning because of a particularly nasty rooster fight that took a rake, a pair of pliers, and a full half an hour of my time to break up, I snuck in through the warehouse at the back of the store, hoping no one would notice me. My first intimidating hurdle was Irene, the warehouse manager. She was a stern defender of efficiency, and her drill-sergeant objections to slackness or ineptitude rang at times from the back of the warehouse to the front of the store. When I saw her up on a ladder organizing stacks of out-of-season fly masks, I calculated my success at slipping past her at about 99 percent. In case she glanced down, though, I walked quickly so I appeared busy rather than late. But just when I thought I made it beyond her field of vision, her voice rang out from the altitude of the ladder like a fiery, six-winged seraph proclaiming holy justice from on high.

"You know, you've got chicken feathers sticking out of the back of your hair."

The heifers, Miss 11
and Miss 12

The goats

Rooster

Even in the worst weather, the Mustang won't seek shelter in the barn.

Three-month-old chicks raised
in the guest bathroom

One of the rams (who immediataly
rammed the author after the
camera shutter clicked)

Two of the lambs and their mothers

The white horse, Studley

The lambs with Davis Nickolyn
and Alex's daughter

One of the scarecrows

These days: Christine and Cassius at Diamond Acres Farm

The two-year-old, Cassius

These days: The Mustang

These days: Irene and the Mustang

The Mustang's tattoo

The Mustang spends hours staring out into the open fields.

I spun around as my hand automatically shot to my head. I pulled out several white quills, and because I didn't want to explain the rooster fight—I felt silly just saying the word *rooster* let alone admitting that I had any—I looked at them in my hand as though I'd never seen such things before and couldn't imagine how they had gotten there. Irene chuckled and came down the clattery metal ladder.

"So, you've got chickens too?"

We'd never really had a conversation before, so the word *too* meant she'd heard about the horses. I braced myself against the sentence for having a wild mustang stallion and now roosters on my property and said, "They're not mine," to clear my name right away. As soon as I said it, though, I felt guilty, as if I'd betrayed a friend somehow, and I questioned why after so many years of being an adult, I still knelt in the presence of peer pressure.

"Yeah, I heard," she said and dusted her hands off on her thighs as she walked toward me. "Your neighbor's barn burned down or something?"

"Right, and all of them are going home when he gets his insurance money and builds a new barn in the spring."

"I heard one of the horses is a mustang," she said. I expected another look that didn't try hard enough to conceal the disdain, so I nodded and clenched down on my jaw. "I also heard he's a stallion. You know, the BLM is supposed to geld those guys when they're rounded up. How did he stay a stallion?"

Still fresh on my knowledge quest about mustangs, I replied, "I don't know. What's the BLM?"

"The Bureau of Land Management," she said. "That's the federal agency that rounds them up from public lands. He's got one of those white freeze brands, right?"

I nodded quickly. "On his neck."

"Yeah, so he was definitely captured from the wild by the BLM, and by law, they're supposed to be gelded."

This surprised me, not because of the law but because she knew about it. I got the sense from the other women in the store that they didn't know anything about mustangs, only that they didn't own them and neither did any of their customers.

"How did you know that?" I asked.

She laughed with a hue of pride. "I ride Western. I own a quarter horse."

I didn't make the connection and raised my eyebrows. She laughed again.

"Usually the only people who adopt mustangs from the BLM are Western riders. You know, cowboy types who like the challenge. Have you ever seen the Mustang Challenge? I did once, and it was a-*mazing*."

Before I could ask her what the Mustang Challenge was, my cell phone rang. It was Dustin, and his name blinked on and off like a DANGER AHEAD road sign. I considered ignoring it, and the thought crossed my mind that my new job might depend on ignoring it, but he wouldn't be calling unless it was an emergency.

"Melinda?" As usual he sounded panicky and out of breath. "You have to come home. It's the sheep."

Relief that he called about loose sheep instead of loose horses competed with irritability that he called me at work about something he could handle himself.

"What about the sheep? Are they loose again?"

Instead of answering me, he coughed heavily and said, "Oh, man," and then coughed again and then gagged.

I suddenly pictured one of the rams standing over Dustin's prostrated body stabbing him in the neck with his horns.

"Dustin, are you OK? What's going on?"

He cleared his throat. "Oh, man," he said again. "You gotta come home. I'm down in the barn, and I can't find Alex, and the sheep are having babies."

Up until that point, I'd been so focused on the Mustang and the two-year-old, I hadn't thought much about the pregnant ewes. "Babies?" I said as my brain connected the dots between pregnancy and offspring. "They're actually having babies?"

"Yeah, they're having babies all over the place," he said and then gagged again. "And I think they're *eating* some of them."

"They're *eating* their babies?" It sounded too awful to do anything but repeat.

"Please," he said. "Just get home as fast as you can."

I hung up, rebuttoned my coat, and asked Irene to tell Frances there was an emergency. "Tell her I *had* to go home and that I'll work Saturday to make up for it," I said.

I ran toward the warehouse door, yanked it open, and as the cold air from the parking lot hit my face, I heard Irene call, "You have *sheep* too?" and then slammed the door shut behind me.

• • •

Chapter Sixteen

For the record, sheep do not eat their young. What Dustin saw was the ewe eating the expelled afterbirths of her triplet lambs to keep predators from sniffing around. The afterbirth is a big blob of bloody placenta covered with semitransparent membranes, and since the lambs kept popping out, each followed by their own placentas, the ewe spent a lot of time eating.

That part was over by the time I got home and found Alex standing at the sheep's stall door and Dustin sitting on a bale of straw at the opposite end of the barn, pale and shaking and barely able to speak. I told him to go to bed, and when he nodded and stood up, he swayed and rested his hand on a pole for support.

Inside the stall, the three lambs wobbled around on legs twice as long as the rest of their bodies. They were wet, and the ewe licked them dry as they took turns punching their button noses at her udder, which was as swollen as a balloon full of water. One of the lambs toppled over, and the ewe nudged him until he stood back up, and when he bleated and she bleated something back, an unavoidable, high-pitched, baby talk, "Aaaaawwww," escaped my mouth before I could quell it.

The lamb looked up at me. His brown eyes blinked, and the motion disrupted his focus from his balance. He rocked, then his legs folded underneath him like the ribs of a paper fan, and he tumbled back down into the straw. I put my hand on the stall's door latch to go in, but Alex shook his head.

"We should leave them alone for a while," he said. "It is important they get the first milk. It makes them strong."

As I would learn from the stacks of books about sheep and lambs I borrowed from the library and ordered online during the next several weeks, the "first milk" was colostrum, sometimes referred to as "liquid gold," because it was thick and yellow and rich with concentrated vitamin A, vitamin E, iron, and antibodies without which a lamb couldn't survive more than a few hours.

I would also learn from the books, which included *Raising Sheep the Modern Way* and *The Beginning Shepherd's Manual*, that cold was the number one killer of newborn lambs. In the natural state of things, ewes wouldn't breed until winter, so their lambs were born in the warmth of spring. These sheep, however, were so confused by domestication, they had the instinctual IQs of gerbils. It was February in the upper Midwest, when wind chills averaged zero, and the books warned with capital letters that even the slightest of drafts could chill their little bodies to such an extent they'd die overnight of hypothermia.

So when the second ewe delivered her own set of triplets a few days after the first, and one of them shook uncontrollably for more than a few hours, I convinced Alex to move them all up to the henhouse, which was smaller and less drafty than the barn. There was no way six of the cutest damn things on Earth would die under my watch, I warned him, and then headed out to Farm & Fleet with a bulleted shopping list in my hand.

• • •

Bob looked at me over the top of his glasses that slipped below the bridge of his nose. His eyes bulged beyond their lids like he was in pain, but when I asked him if he was all right, he didn't answer, so I shrugged and went back to reading from my list.

"... and six infrared heat lamps, six 175-watt bulbs, a bunch of extension cords, a veterinary digital thermometer, Vaseline, lamb electrolytes, a nasal syringe, udder balm, latex gloves, and lamb sweaters."

I looked up. Bob hadn't moved and didn't say anything, so I shoved the list in his direction. "I'll just follow you," I said and made a forward pushing motion with my cart to get him going.

He took the list, pushed his glasses back up his nose, and looked at it, then he turned and shuffled down the aisle. He seemed about as eager to accommodate me as a petrified corpse, so I babbled about the lambs to keep him awake and pushed the cart close on his heels to keep him moving.

"We have three girls and three boys," I said to his back. "Missy, Sissy, Prissy, Popcorn, Butterball, and Geronimo."

He kept moving.

"I'll also need things that aren't on the list like toys and treats, maybe some collars with little bells if you have them."

He rounded a corner and quickened his pace.

"Do they make beds for lambs, you know, like they do for dogs?"

When we got to the livestock section, he pulled the items off the shelves one by one and placed them slowly in the cart. When he got to the bottom of the list, he sighed, looked at me over the top of his glasses again, and announced that the store didn't carry lamb sweaters.

"But the books say that if it is cold I should put sweaters on them," I said.

He raised his arm, "Probably meant baby sweaters," he said and pointed toward the clothing section behind me. "There are ladies over there that will help you."

"And what about treats and toys, you don't have them either?"

"No."

"No collars?"

"No."

His finger, still in the air, jabbed at the clothing section again. "Baby sweaters," he said. "Thata way."

• • •

The lambs got a heat lamp and three sweaters each. I scrubbed the chicken house, the ewes' udders, and the lambs' fuzzy butts clean. I put half a foot of fresh straw down and nailed pink insulation I found in the barn along the walls to keep out drafts. Following pictures in one of the books, I took each lamb's temperature rectally at least once a day, and in the evenings, when I got home from work and the chores were done, I lay on the soft straw under the warmth of the heat lamps and watched them play.

At three weeks of age, the lambs were like toddlers on roller skates. They had the will to move in a straight direction and understood the logistics of getting from one place to another, but their legs were so long and their muscles so floppy, they couldn't coordinate the two to get there. As a result their games lacked rules and usually consisted of leaping straight up into the air. A lamb could get two feet off the ground from a complete standstill. If they got a running start, they might make three feet or more, and vague winners and losers were determined by whether they made eye contact with the chickens who glared back at them from lofty roosts.

A more sophisticated game involved head butting. If two lambs resting at opposite sides of the shed made eye contact, something invisible twinkled between them, and they stood, teetered until they found their balance, and then charged like drunken cherubs in the general direction of the other. They rarely made contact, but when they did, they bounced off each other, fell to the ground, and then bleated for their mothers to come save them. The first one to reach a teat was the winner.

One of the lambs, a little guy from the second batch, didn't like to play. He was smaller than the rest and preferred nuzzling his nose into the crook of my neck as we lay under the heat lamps in the evenings. He smelled like the fabric softener I used on their sweaters, and when he fell asleep, his breath shuffled in warm puffs in and out of my ear. When I'd finally get up and pull him away from my neck, he'd *bah*, which sounded like *ma-aa-aa*, until his mother came and took over.

One night, though, I noticed he smelled funny, kind of sour, and his nose felt cold against my neck. His breath sounded snuffy too, and when I sat up to see what was wrong, he rolled away in a bundle of limp compliance.

"What's going on," I said as pulled him up onto my lap. He lifted his head, looked up at me with eyes milky with fever, and then dropped his nose to his chest.

When I tried to stand him up to take his temperature, his legs collapsed beneath him. I tried again and again to get him to stand, but his body sagged with dead weight in my hands. I finally laid him down, tore off my coat and covered him, and ran to the house to call Alex.

• • •

"Where is he?" the veterinarian said as she walked through the front door of the house and took off her coat. I pointed to the laundry basket in front of the fire. Behind the vet, two young interns came in and stepped over the coat that she dropped behind her on the floor.

"How old is he?"

There was such urgency in her voice that I panicked, couldn't think, and turned to where Dustin, Alex, and Maracella and their five kids and three visiting cousins from Mexico stood in a tight huddle by the couch. The cousins, in their thirties, spoke no English and whispered questions to Alex in Spanish when I looked over at him.

"Three weeks," Alex said.

The vet knelt down at the side of the laundry basket. Beside her, one of the interns opened a medical case and snapped on latex gloves. The other intern grabbed a table lamp and held it up over the basket, so the light pooled in a circle, focused over the back of the vet's bent head. She unfolded the blankets, pulled the lamb up, and said, "Let's just see what's going with you, little guy." But his eyes were closed, and his head rolled to his shoulders.

I gasped from where I hovered in the shadows behind the intern with the lamp. Less than an hour before, when I'd run into the house to call Alex, the lamb looked weak but was still awake. After Alex told me he didn't know what to do for the lamb but that he'd be right up, and I immediately dialed the first veterinarian in the phone book who made house calls, the lamb was still moving around. Even after Alex, his family, and their cousins arrived and we brought the lamb into the house and put a pot of water on the stove in preparation for the vet, he was still alive.

But now, in less time than it took to boil the water, he looked as lifeless as soggy stuffed toy.

"Is he . . . OK?" I asked knowing as I looked down at his unmoving body that he wasn't.

The vet lifted the lamb's eyelids, but they slowly closed shut. She put the end of her stethoscope to his chest and concentrated her gaze on the fire as she listened. Then, after less than a minute, she pulled the plugs of the stethoscope out of her ears, wrapped the ends slowly around her neck, and knelt back on her heels away from the basket.

"Is he dead?" Alex's daughter, Estella, whimpered from the other end of the room where eleven people braced themselves as they stared at the limp little body in the circle of light in the basket.

The vet looked up, first at me and then to the eleven pairs of eyes by the couch. Estella whimpered again, and Alex reached over, put his arm around her shoulder, and pulled her close to his side.

The vet said nothing, just stared up at the people in the room around her. Then, as if facing an impossible barrier she knew she had to cross, she puffed out her cheeks, shrugged at her interns, and said, "Well, OK, let's give it a try."

The room cranked into high gear. "We'll need a heating blanket, a bowl of warm water, and more lights," the vet said. I turned to Dustin and told him to get the heating pad from the bottom drawer in my bathroom. Then I turned to Alex and told him to gather more lamps. Then I turned to Maracella and said, "*Agua por favor.*" She nodded and headed for the kitchen.

"He's hypothermic," the vet told her interns as she hung a plastic bag of fluid from the arm of a floor lamp Alex brought over. "That means an intraperitoneal injection of a warm, 20 percent dextrose solution at a dose of four to five milliliters per pound of body weight. . ."

Dustin came down with the heating pad. Maracella brought the water. Alex lined up lamps in a ring around the vet and her interns until they were bathed in an amphitheater of light. As she worked, the vet catalogued every move for the interns, ". . . inject two centimeters below and one centimeter to the side of the navel . . ." Sweat simmered in beads on their foreheads.

They worked for more than hour. They tore open packages, unwound plastic tubes, checked and rechecked their watches, the thermometer, the level of fluid in the bag. They changed their gloves and wiped sweat from their faces. They repositioned the lights. They called out to us for more water, towels, and blankets, and they rubbed and wiped and stroked the lamb's body as the vet whispered, "Come on, little guy, come on."

But eventually a kind of tired surrender took hold of the vet. She didn't stop rubbing the lamb in his basket, but she slowed a little bit, and the look of sharp and focused concentration in her face thinned to something soft and watered down. Something sad and silent passed between the interns too, and as they watched their mentor's purpose give way bit by bit, they slowly put down the tubes and syringes in their hands.

After a while, the vet leaned away from the basket, but she stared at it a long time before she looked up. I wanted to assure her, to thank her, to tell her we knew she'd done everything she could, because I couldn't stand to see this woman of science and exactitude grapple with a guilt that wasn't hers. She finally looked up and smiled at us as if to assure us the worst was over, and I wondered if grace under pressure and remorse was something they taught in vet school. Then, as she inhaled to apologize and say the words no one wanted to hear, the blankets in the basket moved.

At first I thought I imagined it, but when they moved again and Estella gasped and pointed and said, "Look," the lamb's head pushed and worked its way up out of the blankets like a slow-motion germinating seed. We stared. Even the vet and her interns stared as if seeing something supernatural or cosmic or miraculous that they knew they couldn't believe. The lamb swiveled his head, took a good look around, and then in a weak but recognizable voice bleated an imploring "*Ma-aaa-aaa.*"

To this day I've never heard a cheer as impulsive and shared as the one that exploded in that room that night. It was as if fifteen people of different ages and from different places rode down the crest of a shared crashing wave and yelled out with the same thrilling sense of relief. Alex pumped his hands in the air. The vet and her interns slapped high fives. Dustin, Maracella, and the three cousins hugged one another as Estella and her siblings danced in place.

But the cheers of joy terrified the lamb, and he screamed and burrowed back under the blankets.

• • •

Later, when I walked the veterinarian out to her truck, she told me there'd be no charge.

"For all intents and purposes that lamb was dead when we got here," she said. "Normally, I wouldn't have tried to revive him, but with all of you staring at me like that . . . well . . . I felt like I had to do *something*."

"I still want to pay you. You saved that lamb's life."

She shook her head. "My interns learned something worth more than money. They probably learned the most valuable lesson of their professional lives tonight."

"What's that?"

She looked over at the two women packing up the back of the truck. They'd turned it on to warm it up, and the rear lights shone up into their young faces. "That there are times when you shouldn't give up."

After they left, I stood on the porch and watched their rear lights disappear down the road. Inside, the lamps still burned, and I heard Maracella washing out the pots in the sink and the children laughing in the kitchen around her. In the living room I heard Dustin trying to explain hypothermia to one of the cousins.

Alex came out onto the porch then, and we stood side by side in silence at the railing. I sensed he wanted to tell me something and assumed it was concern about the vet bill.

"She didn't charge us," I said to alleviate his worry right away.

He smiled, but it was distracted, so I knew there was something else.

"I got a letter from the insurance company today," he finally said and then stood there and stared down at his boots.

"Did you get your check for the barn?"

He shook his head and pushed his hands into the front pockets of his jeans. "No. They told me they are not going to pay."

I said, "What?" to give myself time to absorb the information.

"They said they are not going to pay for a new barn. They said it was an electrical fire. They said they are not responsible for paying."

I looked away from his face and back down toward the road. Alex did the same, and we stood there a long time without speaking.

• • •

Chapter Seventeen

For several weeks Alex and I didn't discuss the animals' future. We rode out the last of the winter storms feeding and mucking in silence. For my part, I didn't want the responsibility of worrying about it, and I sensed Alex felt the same way. But they were his animals, so after a while, when the first day of above-freezing temperatures came in early March, I asked him what he planned to do.

He was scooping up shovelfuls of watery manure that bled away from the large muck pile when it started to thaw. Around us, the ground frozen solid for so many months was now a quagmire of mud, manure, and melted snow that sucked up horse hooves, boots, and whatever one dropped with the resolve of hungry quicksand. Slices of melting snow slid down the barn roof, and icicles dripped from the eaves into pools of mire and mess. Alex stopped shoveling, stood upright, and looked over the soupy paddock to the mare, the pony, and the white horse covered ear to tail in mud as he wiped sweat and mud with the back of his coat sleeve away from his forehead.

"I can't take them back without a barn," he said as he watched the mare nudge the pony away from her pile of hay. "They can't run loose. The coyotes, they will eat the sheep, and the foxes, they will eat the chickens. The horses, they need a barn for the summer when it gets too hot and in storms when there's hail or lightning and in the winter when it gets too cold."

The pony flattened his ears and went back for more of the mare's hay. "I have been trying to find new homes for them. But I am having no luck." The mare pushed the pony away with more force this time, and he turned and bucked his back legs in her direction. "I may have to take them to the auction."

"To the auction? What auction?"

He shrugged. "No one has work right now. The economy, it is bad. No one can afford to feed them. I cannot even give them away for free."

I shrugged back at Alex as if the answer was obvious, because I thought it was: "They can stay here until you find them new homes."

Alex looked at me and smiled. Then he looked back at the horses. The pony now plodded through the mud to the other side of the mare as if he hoped she wouldn't notice him coming from a different direction. When he stuck his head down under her neck toward the hay, her ears went back immediately, and she squealed and nipped at the top of his head. He backed away from the reprimand as best as he could in the mud and then clumped with ears extended sideways in a sulk toward the white horse and his pile.

"My fencing work will be picking up soon, very soon, and when it does, I won't have time to come down here and take care of them anymore," Alex said. "But I think the auction, it is OK. Many of my friends take their animals there."

I wanted to ask him why people would pay for horses at an auction when they could get them for free, but he turned back to the muck pile and resumed shoveling. I watched him and listened as the white horse squealed at the pony, a flock of geese honked north overhead, and the icicles dripped in staccato from the barn eaves behind me like amplified ticking clocks.

• • •

Irene stared in at the Mustang through the wire mesh on his stall door. Once his leg had mended, he had started his pacing circles again, and now Irene, seeing him for the first time, shook her head at the sight of it.

"Does he *ever* get out?" she asked.

"In the mornings for about half an hour when Alex cleans out his stall."

She shook her head again. "That horse is going to lose his mind in there."

At the store Irene had asked me a couple of times about the Mustang, so I invited her to come out and meet him. Her own horse, O-B, was twenty-two years old, and while she once used him for amateur teampenning contests, he was now too old for anything but gentle trail rides. I originally hoped she might take the Mustang, but when I asked her one day before she came out, she responded with a resounding, "Hell no." With anyone else I would have pushed the point, but the tone of warning in her voice and the look of blunt certainty on her face made me back off right away.

Now, as she stared at the Mustang through the wire mesh in the stall door, the same look of sureness crossed her face.

"He's too thin," she said. "Look at his ribs. Does he eat?"

I nodded. "He eats hay. I give him candy too."

"*Can*-dy?" She said it as if it was something illegal, like I'd told her I'd given him a joint. "You can't give this horse *can*-dy. Jeez, what are you thinking? This horse needs grain, at least two scoops a day, and not that crap that's full of molasses and corn. Candy. Jeez."

She said it like she said everything, with a brusqueness that some people at work took as bossiness, but which I recognized as a directness that didn't waste time on small talk, fine points, or euphemisms. She would have made a good lobbyist. Or a good matron of an Arizona dude ranch. Instead she lived in the suburbs and was wife to her high school sweetheart "Big Art," a mother who doted on their six-foot-tall high-school-aged son "Little Art," and an experienced rider of both horses and motorcycles who could pull a loose horseshoe or change a bad spark plug as easily as she fried eggs for "the boys" every morning.

While the owner of the store referred to the women who worked there as the "girls," she referred to Irene as a "gal." Since political correctness still shadowed me, I took private offense at the term, but when Irene pulled up that morning straddling a small motorcycle in my driveway like a cowgirl, dressed in a jean jacket and black-fringed leather chaps, and said, "Howdy," when she turned off the engine, I let the moniker stand.

Before I could tell her how much the Mustang liked the candy, she moved to the two-year-old's stall and peered in.

"Now that," she said as she put her hands on her hips, "is a good-looking little horse. Look at those muscles. It's the Mustang's son? You can tell. Short legs, big neck, thick mane and tail. Who's the mare?"

I pointed out the barn door to where Mamacita, the pony, and the white horse lounged in the morning sun. Irene walked to the door, looked out, and put her hands on hips again.

"She's a Haflinger. No wonder he's so stout."

"She's a what?"

"Haflinger. It's a breed of horse. They all have that same light coloring and white manes, and they all have those same broad chests and strong hocks. They're little but strong, and the military used to use them as pack-horses. Wow, what a combination: Mustang and Haflinger. He's going to be a handful."

"He already is," I said and told her how he'd kicked down the wall between the two stalls. She raised her eyebrows as if to ask, "What did you expect?" and probably would have, but the white horse outside suddenly squealed at the pony, who'd nipped his side in an attempt to get the big horse to play.

"That black-and-white horse, he's a paint," Irene said. "That's a horse who's predominately white with splashes of color. They're usually crosses between Thoroughbreds and Quarter Horses. Wow, he has two blue eyes. They usually have only one."

"What's the pony?" I asked.

She shook her head and waved her hand at him. "He's just a muddy little shit. So, tell me again," she said as she turned back to the Mustang's stall. "What's the deal with these guys?"

Inside, the Mustang stopped pacing and looked at Irene. His ears went back, his head bobbed up and down, and when he realized his threat had no purpose, he went back to circling again.

"They belong to my neighbor Alex, whose barn burned down. His insurance company won't pay to build a new one, so now he's trying to find them homes. He says if he can't pretty soon, he's going to take them to the auction."

"To *auc*-tion?" She said it like she'd said *can*-dy.

I shrugged and nodded. "He says a lot of people he knows take their horses to auction. What I don't understand is, why would people pay for a horse that no one else wants for free?"

"Why?" she asked and looked at me as if she couldn't believe I asked. "Don't you know about kill buyers?"

"Kill . . . buyers? I thought horse slaughter was illegal."

"Yeah." Her look softened as she realized I really didn't understand what she was talking about. "Horse slaughter *is* illegal in the United States but not in Canada or Mexico. What is *legal* is for kill buyers to get horses at an auction here and then ship them over the border to the slaughtering plants. It's how a lot of people make their living. It's done all the time. I just figured everybody knew that."

• • •

By design, horse slaughter is a secretive business. Poll after poll shows that a majority of Americans have no tolerance for the practice, especially when it comes to wild horses. The main goal of the Wild Horse Annie Act of 1971 was to protect American mustangs from more slaughter, and it was passed unanimously in both the Senate and the House of Representatives and signed quickly by President Richard Nixon.

"Wild horses and burros merit man's protection historically," Nixon wrote, "for they are a living link with the days of the conquistadors, through the heroic times of the Western Indians and the pioneers, to our own day when the tonic of wildness seems all too scarce. More than that, they merit it as a matter of ecological right—as anyone knows who has ever stood awed at the indomitable spirit and sheer energy of a mustang running free."

That's what the public wanted, and their congressmen and senators agreed unanimously and voted accordingly.

In 1971, though, horse slaughter itself was still legal within the United States. While horsemeat couldn't be used for dog food anymore, and the wild horses were protected from any more roundups, domesticated horses were still butchered and shipped overseas. In 1990 there were sixteen horse slaughterhouses in the United States, but very few people knew they existed.

Things started to change, however, as word got out. In 1998, California voters passed a proposition that banned the slaughter of horses, donkeys, and burros for human consumption. This brought the issue out of the closet for the rest of the country to see, and it ignited a storm of protests that closed down thirteen of the sixteen remaining slaughterhouses.

The public's outrage over horse slaughter was why Montana Senator Conrad Burns, late on the night before Congress's Thanksgiving break in 2004, secretly slipped in a one-page amendment he'd just written into a 3,300-page Omnibus Appropriations Bill the night before the bill's filing deadline. Burns, a former cattle auctioneer for the Billings Livestock Commission, knew his amendment would receive no committee hearings and no debate, and that neither the public nor his fellow lawmakers would know anything about it until it was too late. Once it was secretly inserted, it couldn't be removed by a vote.

The amendment gutted the intent of the Wild Horse Annie Act and allowed wild horses gathered by the Bureau of Land Management (BLM) to be sold for slaughter. It stated that "excess animals" who were more than ten years old or who were unsuccessfully put up for adoption by the BLM at least three times could be "made available for sale without limitation." It added: "Any excess animal sold under this provision shall no longer be considered to be a wild free-roaming horse or burro for purposes of this Act."

Throughout his controversial political career between 1988 and 2006, Burns at one time or another publically called Arabs "ragheads" and African Americans "niggers," and when asked about his position on exploding prescription drug prices, told the *Washington Post* that senior citizens went to doctors to have "somebody to visit with. There's nothing wrong with them." In 2006, *Time* magazine selected Burns as one of the Five Worst Senators in America, calling him "serially offensive." Citizens for Responsibility and Ethics in Washington labeled him "one of the most corrupt members in Congress."

He was, however, loved by the ranching industry, which depended on public lands to support their sheep and cattle herds and wanted the wild horses out. The agribusiness sector, which includes the American Sheep Industry Association, the Livestock Marketing Association, and the National Cattlemen's Beef Association, donated more than $1.3 million to Burns during the course of his senatorial career. It also gave him a lobbying job when he was eventually tossed out of office.

When asked by a *Vanity Fair* reporter why he sponsored the amendment, especially since there were only 153 living wild mustangs left in the state of Montana, a spokesman for Burns responded with, "He did it because other people asked him to."

When the amendment became law by default, the backlash was immediate. "The thing that is so damaging about this Conrad Burns's amendment is that he passed it on an appropriations bill that no one knew about," said fellow Republican, Representative Ed Whitfield of Kentucky. "I've not talked to one senator who knew about it. And I certainly know that nobody in the House knew about it. I don't know his motivations, but more than likely he was protecting the ranchers who have leased those lands."

Even would-be supporters of Burns, like large-game hunting groups, were appalled. "The state made famous for its wanton slaughter of Yellowstone National Park's bison as they struggle to reach winter range now has a senator who wants to feed enduring symbols of the Wild West to Frenchmen," stated a senior blogger for *On Your Own Adventures*, a popular hunting television show.

Five months after the amendment slipped by and was approved, the House of Representatives passed a bipartisan bill that repealed it. On the Senate side, however, the bill was blocked in the subcommittee for the Department of the Interior, of which Burns was the chairman.

In a 2007 backlash to the Burns Amendment, Congress banned horse slaughter in the United States, and the last three slaughter plants shut down. But the new law, despite its best intentions, did not ban people from buying horses at auctions and shipping them to Canada and Mexico, and horse slaughter actually increased nearly fivefold. In 2010 nearly 138,000 horses were shipped to Canada for slaughter, nearly the same number before domestic slaughter ceased.

To this day the BLM states on its website: "The BLM, despite the unrestricted sales authority of the Burns Amendment, has not been selling any wild horses or burros to slaughterhouses or to 'killer buyers.'" The BLM requires anyone who purchases a wild horse to sign a contract saying that he or she will "not knowingly sell or transfer ownership of any listed wild horse and or burro to any person or organization with an intention to resell, trade, or give away the animal for processing into commercial products." But there are no compliance checks by the BLM after a sale, and thousands of mustangs have slipped through the cracks and ended up on the killing floors in Canada and Mexico.

One such kill buyer, a man named Tom Davis, purchased seventeen hundred wild horses at ten dollars a head from the BLM between

2009 and 2012. Davis, a neighbor of Ken Salazar, the current head of the Department of the Interior, which oversees the BLM, told the agency that he used the horses for "movies in Mexico." But when *ProPublica,* an independent, nonprofit newsroom of investigative journalists, dug into the story, it found that when Davis applied for the horses via e-mail, he stated that he didn't care what types of horses he received, "so long as they were big."

Davis agreed to an interview with *ProPublica,* and while he never admitted he sold the horses to Mexican slaughterhouses, he did tell them he was in the process of finding investors for a slaughterhouse of his own. "Hell, some of the finest meat you will ever eat is a fat yearling colt. What is wrong with taking all those BLM horses they got all fat and shiny and setting up a kill plant?" he said.

When the reporter asked him if the BLM ever checked up on where he took the horses, Davis said, "They never question me too hard. It makes 'em look good if they're movin' these horses, see? Every horse I take from them saves them a lot of money. I'm doing them a favor. I'm doing the American people a favor."

• • •

As Irene and I stood at the Mustang's stall and watched him pace, the left side of my brain reminded me that the horse didn't belong to me. None of them did; they weren't my responsibility. I'd moved here to clear my head and write a novel, and I was so far behind schedule on both accounts, I'd run out of money before I saw either. Worrying about the fate of someone else's horse could no longer inhabit the agenda, because doing so up until this point had only put greater distance between me and my goals. I had to be sensible about this, and if sending the animals to auction was the only solution, who was I to argue? They weren't my animals, and maybe someone nice would buy them anyway.

Then the right side of my brain whimpered, "But . . ." And it only took a few forward flashes of the Mustang in an auction pit, frantic and terrified by the ricochet of bids all around him, to turn back to Irene and ask for help.

"What, you want help finding homes for these guys?" she said.

"You know a lot of people, and I thought maybe . . ."

She shook her head. "You've got an unregistered pregnant mare, and you don't know who the sire is. No one will want her."

"Yeah, but . . ."

"Then you've got an unregistered paint horse with two blue eyes. Most people are superstitious about two blue eyes, because they think it indicates genetic problems including craziness."

"OK, but . . ."

"And *then* you've got a two-year-old Haflinger/mustang cross who is already certified as crazy and a mustang stallion who was," she held up one finger, "rounded up from the wild as an adult," she held up a second finger, "then abused by people," she held up a third finger, "and is now confined to a stall." She waved the three upheld fingers back and forth across her chest. "There's no way you're going to find anyone to take *him*."

She looked back into his stall and shook her head as she watched him pace. "No way."

• • •

Chapter Eighteen

Chickens and eggs: It never occurred to me to seriously question the circular causality of which came first until one morning in late March when I found twelve tiny chicks running across the chicken yard, and I stood there a long time trying to figure out how they got there.

I really had no idea how the egg thing worked. I knew that chicks hatched from eggs, but I never worked out the mechanics. Later, when I checked out poultry-care books from the library by the armful, I learned every stage of the egg's development and to this day can detail exactly when and where in the assembly line of the hen's reproductive system the rooster's sperm fertilizes the ova. But that morning as I stared open mouthed at twelve chicks that hadn't been there the day before, it was still a little up in the air. Had someone dropped them off in the middle of the night? Had they fallen out of a tree? It took several minutes of staring at the adults, the roosters who were boys and the hens who were girls, before I made the connection.

My immediate question was who was supposed to take care of them.

When I called Alex, he was busy on a new fencing job and told me with what sounded like unfamiliar irritation not to worry. "The mother, she will take care of them," he said. But as I watched the chicks follow one of the hens around, I questioned her maternal ability. She didn't seem emotionally attached to her babies and spent most of the time pecking the ground for her own food as they followed her around crying.

Indignant about the hen's lack of attention, I bent down and picked one up. Immediately, the hen jerked her head up, pinned her beady, bullet eyes on me holding her chick, and then let out a scream and attacked me. She flew at my face with the spread wings and talons of an avenging eagle, and it happened so fast and took me so off guard, I forgot to put down the chick. I stumbled back in the mud and tried to protect my face from the hen with one hand as the baby chick screeched for help in the other. The hen was relentless, flew at my face and stabbed at my skin with the force of a pneumatic drill, and it wasn't until I fell facedown into the mud that it dawned on me to put the chick down.

I had two long gashes on the back of my hand and one across my forehead as a result of the hen's attack, and as I learned throughout the course of the next two weeks—as eighteen more chicks appeared out of nowhere—mother hens will fight to their own deaths to protect their young from predators. It got to the point where feeding the chickens every morning became a contest of duck and cover, and I went to work with heavy makeup on my hands and face to hide all the scratches of defeat.

Despite the hens' protective skills, several weeks later the chicks started disappearing. There were so many of them, and they scurried in such chaos around the chicken yard, that I didn't notice it right away, but one morning I realized that one of the mothers who'd hatched three chicks the week before had none following her around anymore. Over the next two weeks, a total of ten more babies vanished, and despite my searches into the deepest crevices of the henhouse and yard, I couldn't figure out where they'd gone. There was a solid six-foot wire fence around the chicken yard, and even if a stray cat or raccoon made it over the barrier somehow, I doubted they'd make it past a mother hen with their skulls still attached to their bodies.

When Alex came to do chores one morning and I asked him about it, his eyes wandered listlessly across the enclosure, and he shrugged.

"Maybe it is coyotes," he said as his eyes drifted away from the yard and out over the backfields to a distance I couldn't follow, because he wasn't looking for coyotes but for answers to things that were private.

"Can coyotes climb fences?" I said to pull him back into focus.

He shrugged. "I don't know." And he stared out at the fields some more.

For the past several weeks, he'd told me he had been so busy with new work he had trouble keeping up, and I'd noticed a shade of distraction in his voice whenever I phoned about new chick losses. "I don't know what happened to them," he'd say and then tell me he'd call me back later when he had more time, even though he never did.

Now that I had him in person, I wanted him to solve the mystery of the disappearing chicks before he got away again, but his face was so closed as he looked out over the fields, I sensed there was a much bigger problem that needed solving. I waited for him to tell me what it was, but we stood there a long time without speaking.

Finally I asked, "Is everything OK?" He jerked his head toward me as if I'd startled him. Then he jerked his head back toward the fields.

"I am getting busy with work," he said with a dull defeat I'd never heard in his voice before. "And when summer comes, I will have no time at all."

I followed his gaze out to the horizon. "And you're worried about the animals?" I said as much to finish his thought as to avoid having to wait for it.

He nodded. "There is a big auction in June."

Then something in the sky caught his attention. He squinted and moved his hand to his forehead to shade his eyes. I looked out but didn't see anything until he pointed up to the silhouette of a large bird that arced in silent circles over the fields.

"It's a hawk," he said.

The bird coasted on a swell of air and curved in a clockwise direction. He dipped and rose without moving his wings as if held by a string from above. Then he stalled as if something suddenly occurred to him, and his wings snapped tight against his body. He banked to the right and then dove in a fast-sweeping arc toward the earth. He didn't stop when he met the horizon but swept up something with his claws and then rose back up to finish the arc under wings that pumped in slow motion.

I gasped. "Did he just . . . ?" but Alex motioned me to be quiet as the bird flew toward us with its prey. As it neared, the small body he carried came into focus, and I saw it struggle to break itself free. The hawk flew directly over us, circled around, came back, and hovered over a large spruce in the corner of the chicken yard. Then he descended prey first into a nest the size of a kiddie pool, where another hawk sat waiting.

"That," Alex said as the heads of both hawks disappeared under the rim of the nest, "is where the chicks have gone." And then he laughed, apparently impressed by their ingenuity.

• • •

"I need something to make hawks go away."

Bob pushed his glasses up on his nose. He no longer spoke to me, and I knew now that when he turned away, it meant I was supposed to follow. These days, though, I didn't feel so out of place in the aisles as I squished after him in my muddy new galoshes.

We ended up in the section of wire cages and traps, and Bob pointed up to a row of plastic owls perched side by side on the shelf. The sign below them stated, MOUNT THIS GREAT HORNED OWL TO SCARE HAWKS AWAY. THE LARGE EYES AND REALISTIC FEATURES WILL KEEP PESTS FROM COMING AROUND. FILL WITH SAND TO STABILIZE. TURN FREQUENTLY TO IMITATE LIFE.

I reread the last sentence. "To imitate life?" I said and turned around, but Bob was already gone.

• • •

The three fake owls I bought and stabilized with sand and turned every day didn't work. The chicks kept disappearing, and the diameter and height of the hawks' nest increased every day.

I went back to Farm & Fleet and bought a four-thousand-foot roll of bright orange bailing twine. I spent the weekend stringing it from one fence post to another until the strings of twine covered the entire chicken yard in a big orange web of protection. It was intricate and tedious work, but when the twine ran out, there were still big gaps, so I tore a white sheet into strips and tied them at every junction in the network to act as flags of warning.

The next morning, though, two more chicks were gone, and I spent that night reading blog posts about hawks and how to keep them from killing chickens. While most suggested fake owls or even scarecrows, others swore that creating loud noise worked best. Hawks didn't like commotion near their nests, and since they probably hadn't laid their eggs yet, I read that if I put up scarecrows in addition to the owls and then shot a rifle into the air every morning, they'd probably leave for a safer neighborhood.

I went to the thrift shop in town and bought a billowing wedding dress, a high-saturation Snow White Halloween costume, and a man's old suit. I stuffed straw into the clothes and into pillowcases for their heads and attached them together with staples. I found three metal fence posts in the barn, pounded them into the ground so they stuck up through holes in the web, and shoved the scarecrows down on them.

Then I stood at the base of the tree and banged two metal trash can lids together. When Dustin got home from work, I made him do the same thing, and every morning and every night we stood for intervals of ten minutes each and banged the lids up at the hawks.

But even that didn't work, and by the end of March, there were only six chicks left. One morning as I looked out the kitchen window, I saw one of the hawks dive down from the tree and through a small hole in the web as easily as a needle through burlap. Before I could even register what was going on, he flew back up through the same hole with a screaming little chick in his claws.

It was one thing for the chicks to disappear without a trace, it was another to actually see why. And it was too much, like witnessing a murder, so I disinfected the downstairs bathroom, filled it with straw, and brought the last five chicks inside. I didn't know what else to do.

Alex told me that whenever I found a hen sitting on eggs, I should collect them so there wouldn't be any more babies, but sticking one's hand under a broody hen is like sticking it in the mouth of a lion. It also seemed a little cruel. A hen sits on her eggs for twenty-one days and barely even moves for food or water. She just sits there staring and watching and warming the eggs until she's thin and her feathers fall out. At this stage the eggs are her only reason for being, and if a hand or a rat or a raccoon tries to snatch them away, she uses whatever reserved energy she can find to defend them.

So I let them be. And when the eggs hatched, I brought the chicks inside.

By early April two dozen chicks inhabited not only the downstairs bathroom, but the sunporch and dining room as well. I used the lambs' heat lamps to keep them warm and bought special chick food, feeders, and waterers. They ate and they drank and they thrived, and the more they thrived, the more they ate and drank, and soon the house sounded and smelled like a backwater island rookery.

Meanwhile, the hawks hunted back in the fields, and eventually when one of them stopped leaving the nest, I knew the eggs had been laid.

· · ·

I wasn't that surprised when Dustin told me he was moving out. He was apologetic, as if he was leaving me behind wounded to go find help we both knew wasn't there, but I understood and didn't blame him for saving his own skin. He was a kid in his twenties who lived a thousand miles away from his friends and in constant fear of loose rams, rampaging geese, wild horses, and increasingly aggressive juvenile chickens who could now leap over the baby gates of their rooms and roam the house like microraptors pretty much at will.

He moved in with my son, Jacob, two hours away near Chicago, and even with the chickens still in the house, the rooms seemed quiet and lonely when he left. If Alex's work hadn't picked up, which led me to spend ever-increasing amounts of time caring for the animals, I would have spent my free time at work or visiting the kids. But now I was here morning and night, which left me with hours of time on my hands. I tried getting back to the novel, but after six months of not writing a word, there wasn't much of a novel to get back to. I subscribed to basic cable and bought a TV, but programs on the Discovery Channel, National Geographic, and Animal Planet were boring compared to my daily life, and reruns of *The West Wing* and *Desperate Housewives* left me feeling isolated, hickish, and out of touch.

With the weather warming up, I spent more time outside playing with the lambs, cleaning up the barn, and talking to the Mustang in his stall. But I couldn't shake the feeling of being alone and had to remind myself frequently that was why I moved here in the first place.

But I felt *too* alone. It wasn't as if Dustin had been a small child who needed my care or an old friend whose conversation I missed. It was that he escaped with all the good reasons and left me behind scrounging for leftovers to stay. It all felt off, and as the days wore on, increasingly like a mistake.

One morning as I raked up weeds in the chicken yard, I found a dead baby hawk at the base of the spruce tree. It was about the size of a robin and still had down instead of feathers, which meant it was only a few weeks old. It must have fallen, and when I looked up at the nest so carefully built and guarded for this one little thing, I saw that the parents were gone.

As I stared up, a light breeze rustled a strip of white sheet woven into the side of the nest, which they must have picked off at some point from the netted twine. I wondered about the baby hawk's death: Had the parents seen her fall and then watched helplessly as she died, or had they thought she'd just disappeared? Either way they hadn't stuck around, and I figured as I stared up at the abandoned nest that when the doing of a thing lost purpose, it was probably best to cut losses and move on.

• • •

Chapter Nineteen

I sat at the computer and reread the e-mail I'd sent to the Bureau of Land Management (BLM) the previous week: "To Whom it May Concern: This is the *second* e-mail I am sending you about my request that you help me find a new home for a wild mustang stallion on my property. I sent my initial e-mail to you a week ago, but haven't heard anything back. I am assuming it was an oversight . . ."

The first e-mail to the BLM went out after I told Irene that Alex was sending the animals to auction in June, which at the time was still six weeks away. Irene suggested the agency might be able to help me find a home for the Mustang through its adoption program. "I don't know anything about the BLM," she said, "but they're the ones who round them up, so you'd think they'd be able to find him a place to go."

I changed the date on the e-mail on the screen, deleted the text, and wrote: "To Whom it May Concern: This is the THIRD e-mail I am sending you about a wild mustang on my property who needs to find a home, and I am afraid if I do not hear back from someone in your office soon, I will have to contact my congressman."

I hit "send." Nothing got bureaucrats moving faster than telling them you were about to call the boss, which in this case was Congress, which funded the Department of the Interior, which in turn funded the BLM. Because the congressman I worked for at one time represented an urban district, I never dealt with the Interior Department or knew anyone in the BLM, but I still knew people who knew other people who did, and if no one responded from the agency within the next twenty-four hours, I'd give those people a call.

I wondered if I still had their numbers. Then I wondered if they'd even remember me. It was more than five years since I worked for the

House of Representatives, and in five years of federal political time, a lot of the scenery could change. There was a new president, new elected officials, new staffers, and new department heads with new staff of their own. The congressman I worked for still held office, but I had no idea if the staff stayed the same, and even if it did, I wasn't important, wasn't part of the scenery anymore, and once I really thought about it, couldn't imagine them taking time off from dealing with declining health care, increasing homelessness, urban decay, civil rights abuses, drug laws, prison overcrowding, terrorist threats, gun control, and corporate tax increment financing issues to help me find a home for a horse.

I sat back in my chair and stared at the screen: "Your message has been sent." I was a civilian now, and with .com after my e-mail address instead of .gov, I suspected the e-mail went straight to the junk bin.

Even if the BLM got back to me about the Mustang in time, it wouldn't solve the problem of finding homes for everyone else. Alex told me he'd build a small shed for the sheep, but the others—the mare, the pony, the white horse, the two-year-old, and all of the chickens, geese, and ducks—had to have a proper barn.

"They have to go," he said.

Before this, when Alex first brought the animals to the farm and throughout the fall and winter, I had a hard time understanding the ease of his devotion to them or how he could laugh all the time at the trouble they caused. He was open and unembarrassed about keeping them as pets, even in front of his father, and if a lamb got loose or a duck fell in a window well, he rescued them with the soft, smiling attentions of a parent.

Now I couldn't understand the unyielding hardness in his voice or the look of resolution in his eyes. Everything about him seemed opaque. When he came to do chores, he didn't look at the animals, just mucked and fed and watered. And when I reiterated that they could stay in my barn until he found them homes, he didn't look at me when he said that he didn't have time. It was as if he was putting a deliberate and physical distance between himself and the animals, weaning himself from affection that might haunt him later when they were gone.

"I have a new baby coming and five kids still in school," he had said just that morning after I pestered him again about sending them away. "I have to work as much as I can in the summer so I have enough money for the winter. We almost didn't make it through this last winter, so I don't have any choice. It is as if I am, how do you say," he nodded his head toward the Mustang pacing in his stall, "in a pen?"

"Trapped?"

"Yes," he nodded. "Trapped."

And that I understood. He didn't mean that he felt trapped by his responsibilities to his family but by the decisions he had to make to live up to them. He felt hemmed in by pressures of time and circumstance that dictated what he did, when he did it, who he was, and who, he thought, his children would be some day. It was really no different from my own career that had started for all the good reasons but ended under the weight of them. After a while the policies and the paperwork took precedence, and the reasons just got in the way. There was no give and take in that, no room for anything else, and the pressures to get the paperwork done turned stronger than the original purpose. The motivation was no longer about inspiration or fulfillment but about meeting the deadline and keeping the job. For Alex, it didn't matter anymore why he originally took on the animals, it just mattered that he had them, and now they were in the way. They took up too much space in his head, and I understood that too.

I just wished I didn't. I didn't want the responsibility of worrying about the animals any more than I wanted responsibilities that would *keep* me from worrying about them. The farm was an escape from pressure, but because I didn't have any pressures *not* to worry about the animals, I did so by default—especially about the Mustang, who for reasons I still didn't fully understand took up most of my worrying.

I closed down the e-mail and Googled "BLM wild horse roundups." I thought maybe if I found the name of a specific person on staff who was responsible for the roundups, I could target him, pull him away from the safety of group anonymity, and get a quicker response about the adoption program.

What I didn't realize was that the BLM used the word *gather* in place of the word *roundup,* and that by typing in the "wrong" word, the search engine pulled up 17,400,000 results from wild horse welfare organizations other than the BLM, none of which I'd seen before. As I scrolled down the page, something told me to stop, to shut down the computer and go watch *Desperate Housewives* instead, but by the time I reached the bottom of the screen where the links of videos lived, it was too late.

• • •

The black stallion ran full speed out of a gulley in the foothills of the Black Rock Mountains in northwest Nevada and into the frame of a video camera. A second later a hard-breathing mare followed him into the picture, then their two-year-old son, then another mare, then a twenty-six-year-old matriarch glistening with sweat, then three young mares with their three weanling foals, and then sparks of midwinter sun that flashed off the blades of a helicopter rising up in the gulley behind them.

The eleven horses ran hard. They followed the stallion down the slopes of the canyon onto a flat, broad plain of sagebrush and snow. One of the foals dropped behind, and his mother slowed until he caught up. This put her last in the line and directly under the helicopter that swerved left and right to keep her moving forward.

At the front of the line, the stallion stopped, and as he searched the canyon floor for the best route of escape, the others caught up and surrounded him. The helicopter moved over them and hovered trying to get them to move, and they soon disappeared from the video frame behind a wall of dry snow whipped up by the rotating blades. Then suddenly the stallion saw a lone horse running across the plain ahead of them, and he shot out of the snow cloud to follow. The rest of the family ran after him.

An hour earlier they'd been feeding in their winter range at the lower elevations of the mountains, but like 75 percent of the other horse bands in the 550,000 acres that made up the Calico Mountains Complex, the BLM slated this family for removal, and Conrad Burns's legislative sleight of hand and its ripple effect now allow the BLM to do it with helicopters.

The BLM determined that the appropriate management level for the half-million acre Calico Mountains Complex was about six hundred horses, which meant nearly two thousand had to be "gathered." Once they were gathered, the horses in this family would be separated according to sex and age and then hauled in a stock truck to facilities where they'd either be adopted out to private individuals or housed in government holding pens in the Midwest for the rest of their lives.

The lone horse the stallion saw running across the canyon floor belonged to a contractor hired by the BLM to round up the excess wild horses from the Calico Mountains between December 2009 and January 2010. The horse, called a Judas Horse, was trained specifically to lead panicking wild horses through a funnel of netted gates that fed into a series of holding pens. Once the black stallion and his family followed the trained horse into the funnel, men hiding behind the nets jumped out with white flags, drove the band forward into the corral, and then shut the gates closed behind them.

All in all it was a fairly easy process, especially with the helicopter, and the contractor—in this case Cattoor Livestock Roundup Inc.—received several hundred dollars for each horse captured.

Meanwhile, members of the press and wild horse advocates watched the "roundup" on the sidelines. Public viewing of the Calico roundups was limited to Mondays, Wednesdays, and Saturdays, and ten people at a time—preapproved by the BLM—were allowed to watch on any given day. Many of those present that day complained about the BLM's restricted public access to the roundups, and while the BLM claimed it was to keep the gathers safe, advocates claimed it was to hide the agency's roundup methods, which were hazardous, cruel, and unnecessary.

It wasn't a new argument. Since the passage of the Wild Horse Annie Act, the BLM gathers came under fire not only for the way they were conducted but for the reasons behind them in the first place. The BLM manages 245 million acres of public land—roughly the size of Texas and New Mexico combined—and according to its mission statement must balance "the health, diversity, and productivity of America's public lands for the use and enjoyment of present and future generations." While the BLM's current responsibilities include energy development, public recreation, timber harvesting, and natural, cultural, and historical resources, the agency was originally created to manage livestock grazing on public lands. With that as the foundation, and with many ranchers serving as bureau leaders, including Ken Salazar, many felt over the years that the BLM was more accountable to the livestock industry than it was to the public.

The general perception of the BLM was based in large part on the agency's increasing allocations of public lands for livestock grazing while at the same time removing wild horses in the name of protecting natural resources on the range. But a General Accounting Office (GAO) investigation gave life to that assertion, and noted that there was no evidence that the removal of wild horses improved rangeland conditions at all—and furthermore that rangeland degradation was caused by grazing livestock.

Despite the GAO investigation, which included sixty-two pages of scolding and recommendations, the BLM continued to round up wild horses and burros, and by 2007 at least 267,000 had been removed, and the 53.5 million acres of public lands allotted them in 1971 had been reduced to about 34 million acres. In the meantime, the agency increased the number of permits it issued for cattle and sheep grazing, which meant that at the end of all the number crunching, approximately 567,000 head of cattle and sheep grazed on 160 million acres of public lands, compared to 33,000 wild horses and burros on 34 million acres.

While the numbers hung in the backdrop of the Calico roundup that day, the more immediate concern of the people watching on the sidelines was the fate of this one small band of eleven horses. Report after report issued by the general press and wild horse advocates portrayed the round-ups as dangerous for the horses both during and after, and graphic images of frightened, suffering, and dead animals flooded the Internet.

The horses were first subjected to a terrifying chase by a helicopter for up to ten miles, and many of them died along the way or were in such bad shape by the time they reached the holding pens, they had to be euthanized. Foals were particularly vulnerable to "hoof slough," which occurred when they were run so hard and over such a long distance they literally ran their hooves off and had to be killed as a result.

Once the survivors were corralled, the families were immediately broken up for easier handling—foals from mares and mares from stallions—and herded onto stock trucks by yelling cowboys, waving flags, and electric prods. Many deaths occurred at this stage of the gather, because the horses panicked when separated from their bands, and they reared and ran in wild circles and tried to jump the six-foot fences around them and either broke their necks or fractured their legs or fell under the stampeding horses around them.

In one video of a roundup made public, a stallion, his mare, and their weanling foal were taped running into a trap pen where the foal was immediately separated from his parents and placed in his own small holding pen. The foal, who'd never been alone in his life, whirled in circles and cried out for the mare and stallion as he rammed senselessly against the gates of his pen. The stallion, still in his enclosure barely big enough for him and the mare to stand, charged the fence in an attempt to get out but fell and broke his neck. He didn't die right away, though. He stood up and wobbled first against the fence and then against the mare until several minutes later his legs finally buckled and he collapsed. The mare stood with him for almost twenty minutes as she split her attention between his body on the ground and her screaming foal in the other pen.

Soon after that, wranglers drove her into a chute, which led to the open back door of a stock trailer. Once she was onboard, they put a tarp over the stallion's body, dragged it through the chute, and put it on the trailer with the mare. Then the trailer took off. The foal, left behind and alone, continued his frantic cries, and the mare's return calls to her foal echoed long after the truck disappeared down the road.

For the people watching the capture of the eleven-horse family at the Calico Complex roundup that morning, they felt their video cameras were the best way to document whatever might happen. In the end, 86 of the 1,922 horses gathered from the Calico Mountains would die as a result of the roundups, and 40 mares would spontaneously abort their fetuses. But on this morning, all the onlookers knew was that 11 horses in this one family were at risk, and the footage they recorded, which I now watched, caught it all on tape.

Once the eleven horses were corralled in a small pen, wranglers immediately separated the black stallion from the rest of the family and placed him in his own small enclosure. Then they pulled out the two-year-old. Then they separated the three foals from the mares.

In his pen the stallion paced for less than a minute, taking in the scene before he reared up against the six-foot fence that separated him from one of the frantic mares. He was a strong horse, stocky and well muscled, and when his front legs lunged over the top of the fence and got caught, he nearly pulled the fence back down over him as he twirled his head and strained his neck in order to yank away.

"He's caught up. He's caught up," a voice in the background said as the horse pulled back one more time. And then, "He's falling, oh, God," as the stallion plunged backward to the ground.

The stallion immediately got up and paced to the far end of the enclosure. He didn't seem hurt and turned toward another panel of the stock fence that separated him from open land. He collected himself, pulled up his shoulder muscles and arched his neck, and then took off full speed directly at it. The person holding the video camera, fearing the worst, gasped as he neared the fence. Then the stallion jumped.

And he cleared the fence and took off running toward the range.

Several strides after the jump, he plunged straight through a three-strand barbed-wire fence, pulling it and several fence posts down and along with him as he headed back toward the mountains.

The person holding the video camera took fast, uncontrolled breaths as the stallion got smaller in the distance. Then another voice in the background said, "Wow, what an amazing horse." The person filming choked.

Whoever it was, though, had enough presence of mind to pan back to the holding pens where one of the stallion's mares stood at the fence and watched him disappear on the horizon.

• • •

I stared at the computer screen. Then my hand slowly reached for the cell phone and dialed Alex. I couldn't take my eyes away from the last frame of the video—a still photograph of the mare behind bars watching her stallion fade away—and as I waited for Alex to pick up, I wondered what happened to her in the end.

"Hello?"

And then I wondered what happened to the stallion. He was free, but could a horse ever recover from something like that, or would he spend the rest of his life obsessed about what happened to his family?

"Hello?"

Could the mare ever forget? Could the foals? I looked over the top of the computer and out the window to the barn. Could any of them?

"Hello, Melinda, is that you?"

"Don't take the horses to auction," I said. "I'll keep them."

• • •

Chapter Twenty

I didn't wake up the next morning with a hangover of regret. My first thought wasn't, "What have I done?" or "How did this happen?" And I felt no more a victim of impulse than I did if I had a gun to my head. There wasn't the slightest sense of sudden or overwhelming responsibility, no feeling of entrapment, no anger or dread or wailing repentance.

That would all come later.

Instead I woke up still under the influence of what I'd seen and learned the day before, and my first thought, which must have simmered all night in my brain until it thickened into a solid and concentrated objective, was that I had to get the Mustang out of his stall.

• • •

"You *what?*" Irene looked at me with eyes that almost crossed in disbelief. She said it so loudly that her assistant looked up from taping boxes with flight response twitching all over her face.

I shook my head. "It's not what you think. I'm only keeping the animals until I find them homes. But that's not important right now. I need your help with something else . . ."

Irene's head jerked backward from the top of her neck as if I'd tossed sand at her face. "Not important? Not *important?*" Then her head shot back forward until her eyes were only a few inches from mine, and the force of her indictment hit me like a slap. "You told Alex you'd keep all the animals, and you think that's not *important?*"

I could almost see the left side of Irene's brain bulge through her forehead as it flexed its muscles until buttons popped, while mine, relegated over the past several months to near atrophy, whimpered somewhere near the soles of my feet. I could hear it, though. I knew how illogical the situation seemed, but there was something so illogical about the reasons for the situation in the first place that common sense didn't seem important to the moment at all.

What sense was there in how the Mustang was taken from the wild, severed from everything he knew including his family, adopted by someone who abused him, and now existed with no purpose, no challenges, and no connections to a herd, a range, or a reason for being save pacing a circular path in a twelve-by-twelve-foot space in my barn? I couldn't make sense of that, and I didn't want to understand how anyone could. My head just wasn't able to go there, because it was so busy trying *not* to think about the overall horror of it all.

And besides, the sheep were going back to Alex's in a few weeks when the shed was done, and I would find homes for everyone else somehow. Maybe I'd ask Irene to help me . . . In the meantime, Alex's son would come up every day after school to lend a hand.

But there was no time to explain all of that to Irene whose eyes, face, and body were winding up to make a point. She raised an index finger and opened her mouth to voice the central theme of my incompetence, but I interrupted before she got anything out.

"I have to get the Mustang out of his stall. Can you help me?"

Her eyes softened immediately. The muscles in her face loosened and her shoulders dropped. It was like watching ice melt in a microwave, and as the thought of opening the stall door thawed out and her right brain tiptoed in over the puddle, she slowly, inch by inch, lowered her finger.

• • •

"You . . . *what?*" Bob asked when I went to Farm & Fleet to buy barbed wire and told him about my decision to take the animals. They were the first words I'd heard him speak in months, and the stress that he placed on the word *what* was the first real emotion I'd ever seen him express. I wasn't sure what the emotion was—if it signified disbelief at my stupidity or pain at the thought of me coming to the store even more—but at least it was an emotion, which meant our relationship was moving forward.

"Yes, and I need barbed wire, lots of it, to make a big fence in the pasture to keep the horses apart."

He shook his head, and I braced myself for another lecture, but he went back into his silent mode and shuffled off toward the Fencing section.

The barbed wire came in 12.5-gauge or 15.5-gauge rolls of two points per five inches or four points per five inches with either single, double, or traditional twists. It hadn't occurred to me to measure the pasture, so I didn't know how many of the 1,320-foot rolls I'd need, but as I stared down at the violent-looking spools of prickly galvanized steel, it did occur to me that I didn't want to touch the stuff.

Barbed wire was invented in the late 1800s as a cost-effective way for ranchers to keep their cattle and sheep within their newly claimed lands and to ensure predators, including other ranchers, stayed out. Prior to its invention, ranchers used either flat, thin wire, which didn't contain cattle very well, or thick, thorny bushes that took years to grow. Once the razor-sharp strands of barbed wire crisscrossed the American West in an ever-expanding grid, however, intensive animal husbandry was born, and barbed wire is still credited with the meteoritic rise, prosperity, and influence of the livestock industry in the United States.

I bent down, put the tip of my finger on one of the barbs, and then yanked it away in pain. Just that one touch drew blood, and as I put my finger to my mouth, a picture of the wild stallion who'd ripped through the barbed wire to escape captivity flashed in my head. Rumors about the horse spread across the country after his escape. Some reported he'd been recaptured by the Bureau of Land Management (BLM) during the Calico roundups, while others testified they'd seen him patrolling the capture area looking for his family long after the trucks hauled them away. I pinned my hope on the latter. The BLM cut the Calico gathers short after many of the wild herds in the mountain complex took flight to areas beyond the roundup's domain, and I liked to imagine the stallion ran back to the mountains to warn them all to get the hell out.

• • •

"You *what?*" Lenny said when I told him why I needed his help running the low-watt electric tape I'd bought instead of barbed wire across the borders of the pastures.

• • •

Irene slid the latch of the Mustang's stall sideways and then looked around her before she opened the door. We'd already put the mare, the pony, and the white horse in one section of the pasture and the two-year-old in another, but she double-checked instinctively just to make sure.

When she'd opened the two-year-old's stall earlier, he'd bolted out and run into the paddock before she could stop him. Then she had to let him buck it out for half an hour in his new freedom before she could get near enough to snap a lead rope on his halter. She led him easily enough to his new digs in the northwestern field, but the second she unlatched the rope, he tore off running and bucking and twirling in the air, all as if trying to learn how to fly.

When he reached the back end of the pasture, he stopped and composed himself just enough to look around with eyes wide and ears as erect as soldiers, but then he seemed to lose control and took off bucking again. He covered every inch of the field, ran from one end of the expanse to the other, and Irene chuckled when he stopped at the electric tape and shook his head angrily at the thing after he touched it.

Now that it was the Mustang's turn, she seemed nervous. Except for the few minutes every day he spent in a tiny enclosure when his stall was cleaned, he hadn't seen daylight or run loose for almost six months. She'd called it a crime earlier and said anyone who did this to a horse, especially a wild one, should be shot, but now that the time came to let him out, she hesitated as she looked one more time around her.

"He'll probably explode, so stay clear," she said as she mapped out her own escape route with her eyes and then stepped aside and let the door swing open.

Whenever Alex took him out of the stall, he clipped a lead rope to his halter and led him with no leeway in the rope to the little pen. Now that the door was open without anyone to escort him out, the Mustang didn't seem to understand what he was supposed to do. His nose came out first and then the rest of his head, but instead of bolting forward, his eyes turned to Irene and me, and he stood there and looked at us a long time.

"Go on, buddy," Irene said and pointed her finger to the open door.

The Mustang seemed to understand, and he turned his head until the sun streaming in from the open door caught in his eyes and reflected the sky from the lenses. He took a step forward, and I saw that his legs shook and his ribs jutted through his skin like the hull of an abandoned boat. When Irene gasped and said, "Jeez-us, look how weak he is," I realized I hadn't noticed how thin he'd become. I felt sick. This whole time I'd imagined him like the stallions I saw in the videos, shiny and strong, with muscles like chiseled stone, as he was when I first saw him. But I'd been so busy feeling sorry for myself over the past several weeks, I hadn't seen him become this creature who could barely walk out of his stall.

He took a few more shaky steps toward the door. He stopped and looked out and then back at Irene and me again.

"Go on," Irene said. "It's okay." And he seemed to understand this too and walked forward. When his body cleared the door, and Irene and I stepped out of the stall we'd been hiding in across the aisle, he stopped again and looked up at the sky. Irene and I stopped too. His legs trembled, and he lowered his head, and then in slow motion he bent his knees and dropped in a gradual slump to the ground.

I rushed forward, but Irene grabbed my arm and pulled me back. "Leave him alone" she said without taking her eyes from the horse whose body collapsed on its side.

"But . . ."

"Just let him be."

I turned back toward him. His head moved back and forth on the ground in the quiver of a seizure. I panicked. Letting him out of the stall was too much strain on his weak body, and as he fell and convulsed and died, we just stood there watching.

"Irene, he's . . ."

She held her hand up to silence me.

The Mustang's nostrils fluttered and then suddenly blew hard, and dust puffed up around him. Then he let out a low, slow grunt and turned over onto his back. His legs flung up into the air and fell to the opposite side. Then his legs came back up into the air, and the movement repeated itself again and again until I realized that he wasn't moving in surrender to death but to the sheer joy of rolling on the grass in the sun.

• • •

Several weeks later I received an e-mail from the BLM, which included apologies from a "Wild Horse and Burro Specialist" for taking so long to get back to me. Because I'd copied down and sent the brand symbols on the Mustang's neck in my earlier e-mails, the specialist was able to determine that the horse was "titled," which meant he'd been adopted for more than a year since being captured, so by law he was considered "personal property" and no longer under the jurisdiction of the BLM.

"Thank God for that," I said out loud as I read the e-mail.

From the brand symbols, the specialist determined the Mustang was born in Nevada and gathered when he was about six years old, which meant he was twelve years old now. He'd spent half of his life as a wild horse and half as "personal property," which explained everything I needed to know about why he was so afraid of people. And then I wondered if horses felt hate.

When I was done reading the e-mail, I hit "reply" and asked the specialist to send me the Mustang's title. I assumed given the history that I wouldn't hear from the agency again for several months, but the title and a letter from the US Department of the Interior arrived in my mailbox less than two weeks later.

I tore it open and read it as I walked from the mailbox up the driveway along the Mustang's paddock.

Dear Ms. Roth:

By way of this letter, I certify to you and anyone else that this may concern, that the wild horse with the U.S. Government freezemark 9756 9866 . . . is a titled horse and no longer has 'wild' status under the Wild Horse and Burro Act of 1971.

I stopped and reread the last sentence. That one sentence typed on one piece of paper by one federal bureaucrat in an office one million miles away designated the wild horse in my paddock as no longer wild. Because he was no longer officially wild didn't make him a domesticated horse, though. And if he wasn't a wild horse or domesticated one, what was he, just my "personal property"?

"Jerks," I said as I shoved the title back into its envelope and looked over the fence to where the Mustang stood, where he always stood these days: as far away from me as possible, staring out over the fields.

• • •

Robert called that night. The legislature was in full swing, so I hadn't talked to him in several weeks, but spring break was just around the corner, and he wanted me to visit him for a few days.

"I need a break," he said with an exhaustion I'd never heard in his voice before. "And I haven't seen you for, what, a year or something now?"

I counted backward, but what seemed like more than year turned out to be only six months.

"Come on," he said. "We'll get in my car and take a road trip. We'll just get in the car and drive."

I thought about his car and about the heated leather seats and about how its German engineering muffled all sounds from the outside while its high-end surround sound system played music with the fidelity of a concert hall so that watching the landscape stream by was like watching a beautiful movie from the safety of a warm cocoon.

"I can't right now," I said with a regret that was as true as it was unexpected. Then I explained why, told him in one long babbling sentence about the wild horse roundups and the stallion who broke his neck and the mare who stayed trapped behind. And then I told him that I needed a month or two to find homes for the animals and that then I'd be coming home.

"Wait a minute," he said. "Why do *you* need to find homes for the animals?"

So I told him, and there was a long silence from his end, which he finally broke with a jeer of disbelief and anger.

"You *what?*"

• • •

Chapter Twenty-One

The 400-pound woman in her fifties lumbered out of the backseat of the car with the help of her 135-pound son in his twenties. She wore an orange housecoat that billowed over her body, and he wore a skintight camouflage T-shirt that clung to arms as thin as fishing poles. She had on white slippers that seemed too small to hold her up, while he had black army boots that seemed six sizes too big for his frame. After he helped balance his mother against the side of the car, she leaned back and gasped for air as he leaned into the backseat and pulled out a metal walker.

"Here we go," he said as he maneuvered the woman away from the side of the car and into the opening between the walker's side braces. "You're all set."

I tried not to look at the woman who huffed for air from the exertion of moving from the car to the walker, but she was so . . . corpulent, that it was hard to pull my eyes away from the white flowers and curlicues that grew lushly on the orange acres of her robe. She laughed in a way that indicated she was used to gawkers and then pushed the walker forward several inches, raised one of her white slippers, and took a step.

When she caught her breath again, she said "Hello" and told me her name, while her son walked quickly down the hill toward the paddock without a word. With an effort I thought might kill her, the woman lifted the front end of the walker off the ground, plunked it down facing the paddock, and then hauled her body into position behind it.

"Is that him?" she called down to her son.

The woman was one of a handful of responses to a Free-to-Good-Home ad I had placed for the horses in an online equine magazine Irene told me about. So far I'd rejected each one of them. One woman wanted the pony for her pony-ride business that traveled to carnivals and birthday parties, because as she told me, "We go through them pretty quick." One man wanted the Mustang for a "little backyard rodeo," and another man called and said he'd take the horses off my hands for "a fee." When this woman called and said she was looking for a gentle horse to take out on occasional trail rides, I nearly offered her the entire contents of my savings account to come out and meet the white horse.

Now that she was here, I realized I'd misunderstood. She must have meant that her son wanted a horse for occasional trail rides, and while I had no objection to that on the surface, I didn't like the way he walked straight down to the Mustang's paddock without even asking if he was the right horse. I also didn't like some of the foul things he yelled out when he touched the electric tape or the way he then yanked open the gate in anger at being zapped.

I cupped my hands around my mouth and called, "That's not the right horse." But the guy with his back still toward me, waved his hand impatiently in the air as if I'd been rude to him by interrupting his important and procedural appraisal.

"Does he handle horses well?" I asked his mother as the Mustang at the opposite end of the paddock pointed his ears at the strange man suddenly walking toward him.

"Never been around one," the woman said and laughed. "But he's darn good with animals, and he'll be able to tell if a horse is gentle enough for me to ride."

My head snapped away from the paddock to the woman standing beside me in her walker. "The horse is for *you?*"

She laughed again. "I know I'm a little out of shape," she said. "But I heard horseback riding is a good workout and will help me lose weight. God knows I tried everything else."

I instinctually looked around for a hidden camera, for some indication that I was the subject of a new reality TV show that played tricks on unwary bystanders. Then the thought occurred to me that I might really be in a straightjacket in a padded facility talking to a make-believe person on an invented farm as doctors and nurses asked my parents and my children what stresses or incidents might have triggered the psychotic breakdown. Certainly no one in the real world would think they could lose weight riding a horse, when they couldn't get on the horse without a crane in the first place.

The woman chuckled as if she read my thoughts. "Don't worry," she said. "I'm having a GBS at the end of the month."

"A what?"

"Gastric bypass surgery. It's where they staple up part of my stomach to make two pouches that they connect to my intestines ..."

Suddenly the Mustang let out one of his warning snorts that reached us all the way at the top of the hill. The man walked toward him quickly, which to a wild horse is an implied and impolite threat. The stallion snorted again, pawed the ground, and lowered his head and shook it. I thought about running down and saving the man's life but turned instead to his mother and told her the white horse was no longer available. Then I turned back to the paddock and watched a young man learn a hard, pants-wetting life lesson about the consequences of rude behavior.

• • •

The number of mustang rescue organizations surprised me. When I Googled the term, I got 111 million hits and found groups and individuals in every state of the country, but when I started writing and calling the ones closest to me, I either got voice mails that were full or automatic e-mail responses that said, "We cannot take in any more horses at this point ..."

I did get through on the phone to one woman in Southern Illinois who told me there were just too many mustangs in need of help. "People like the idea of owning a wild mustang," she said. "But when they adopt them, they have no idea what they're getting into. We can only take the worst cases now, so the fact that your horse has food, water, and shelter pretty much disqualifies him for any help from us. I'm sorry."

As I would learn, for many if not most of the people who run the mustang rescue centers, the Bureau of Land Management's (BLM's) continuing roundups of about ten thousand horses a year—despite the forty-one thousand already in government long-term holding pens who can't find homes because adoptions have declined drastically—threatens the quality of their own adoption efforts, because there are so many more mustangs who need their help every year.

And wild mustangs aren't like other horses. They are hard to find good homes for. They are like Apple computers or Saabs: When they work they are the best in their class on Earth, but when they don't, they are expensive and hard to maintain.

Later I would meet Chad Kelly, a man from southwestern Missouri who used to train wild horses as a contractor for the BLM to ease adoptions. Under his contract with the agency, he took in mustangs straight off the truck after roundups and spent several months working with each one to gentle them enough to adopt out.

"The problem is, most of the people who adopt these horses don't have the patience for them," he said. "I can train a wild horse straight off the truck to be ridden in less than a week, but it takes a *long* time for trust to build up between you, and most people don't have the patience to follow through."

Kelly, a former chemical engineer with four degrees under his belt, worked his way through college breaking colts and then, after ten years making batteries for a company that supplied NASA, went back to the horses full-time. He said he never really valued his professional success and its eighty-hour workweeks, but the horses he understood, and within several years of working with the mustangs, he'd trained more than anyone else in the country.

"Some of the horses that come off that truck are very fearful," Kelly said. "And when a horse is scared or hot, he quits thinking and just reacts. I learned right away that if they're blinking their eyes, they're thinking. But if they're not blinking, if they're just staring, then they're scared, not thinking, and they'll run, just run, and they'll run through *anything*.

"I'll work with a horse for three months or more until he trusts me. I can ride him and pet him, and he's more trusting than a domesticated horse. But what happens a lot of the time is that someone will adopt him, take him home, and then not work with him for a week. And within that one week, the horse turns wild again, and he'll turn any other horses around him wild too."

Kelly said it is actually easier to work with a wild horse just off the range who's never been around people, than it is to work with a domesticated horse who's been around people all of his life but was handled poorly or abused.

"With a domesticated horse, you get incremental stages of trust. You can ride him for years and never fully trust him, because you don't know what bad experiences he's had. But with a mustang, it's 0 to 100 percent if you can get him to trust you."

The problem with trust that is either 0 or 100 percent is that if abuse or mismanagement is a wild horse's first experience with human beings, it is easy for him to stay in the 0 range for the rest of his life.

• • •

I'd avoided putting up a flyer on the bulletin board at work about the horses, because while Irene knew about them, I didn't want the others to realize how "ill bred" they were, and I was pretty sure none of the customers who came to the store would want them anyway. I wasn't even sure if I'd be allowed to put up a flyer for a FREE wild mustang stallion with issues, a pregnant Haflinger mare (father unknown), a scruffy pony, a paint with two blue eyes, and a two-year-old bulldozer of miscellaneous heritage, none of whom had any formal training and, as far as I could tell, only spoke Spanish on a board full of ten-thousand-dollar well-titled, well-trained aristocrats.

But it was three weeks since I'd taken them on without one prospect of finding them homes, and desperation drove me to believe that maybe one of the peers of the equestrian realm would take pity and shed their grace upon me. I decided the best way to approach it was through an appeal to their sense of charitable duty:

Barn Fire Orphans Need Loving Homes
Beautiful Haflinger mare with potential as hunter pony (once she foals)
Darling little pony with sweet disposition (not gelded yet)
Tall, handsome black & white potential jumper or dressage horse (not gelded yet)
Well-built two-year-old, small but strong, with enormous potential (not gelded yet)
Mustang with the spirit of the Great American West (not gelded yet)

I brought the flyer to work and waited until I thought no one would see me pin it on the bulletin board. I didn't put my name on it, just my phone number, and figured if no one saw me put it up, no one would know it was mine. I had confiscated a tack earlier, so it was ready to go when the way was clear, and the plan was to walk quickly to the bulletin board, pin the flyer up in one covert movement as I passed by, and then head for the bathroom just around the corner. It would happen so fast and with such stealth, no one would see me do it.

What I didn't anticipate was that someone would come around the corner just as my fingers pushed the tack in.

"Whatcha got there?"

It was Karen, a woman my age who'd worked at the store for several years and had a solid but unassuming sense of herself and an easy, perceptive smile. Because she didn't ride herself, but had a daughter in her twenties who did, we'd become friends in the way people do who share professional inadequacies, kids of the same age, and a lunchroom. Up until this point, though, I'd told her nothing about my recent past, about why I lived on the farm, or about the zoological loose ends that lived there with me, and she, sensing underground issues, never asked.

Now, however, I was caught with my fingers pushing a pin into the evidence. I didn't even have time to pull my hand away before she came up on it and read it out loud, word for word, as if it was an official notice everyone in the store should know about. When she got to the last line about the Mustang, she read it twice.

"The spirit of the Great American West?" She laughed, nudged me conspiratorially, and looked around to see if anyone could hear. "You know, you should probably change that one. It just makes him sound crazy."

"He *is*," I blurted with a sudden and overwhelming need to confess everything in as loud and shrill a way as possible. I needed to tell someone how ridiculous the situation was and how ill equipped I was to manage it. I had to tell someone about the growing regret of moving to the farm and about how none of this—not the animals, not the job in a saddle shop, not the calluses on my hands—were ever part of the plan.

Most of all, though, and this was something new: I wanted to admit to someone how . . . lonely . . . I was and how every morning I woke up now with the realization that if I died in my sleep, no one would even know. The kids and my sister came out to the farm when they could, but it was a long drive, a trip they had to plan rather than a spur-of-the-moment visit, and with Dustin gone and neighbors who minded their own business, no one would know I was dead until they found me several weeks later all decomposed and gross and half eaten by mice. It was as if my hard-won solitude was a disqualification from the human race. I could have lived on a spaceship orbiting Earth with a broken radio and not been more alone.

And so I waxed dramatically in my head until I felt the heat of tears in my eyes and had to look up at the ceiling to keep them from revealing things best left unrevealed. When I got control, I waited a beat and then lowered my voice, "He is as crazy as they come."

The smile on Karen's face disappeared and she nodded. "I know. Irene told me about him." She looked back up at the flyer. "Listen, why don't I send my daughter, Christine, out to see them. She's trained her own horses, and she knows a lot of people. Maybe she can help you find them homes."

I bobbed my head up and down, afraid that if I spoke, my voice would crack and the tears would erupt again. It was a nice gesture on her part, and I appreciated it, but I knew that like everything else that had happened so far in my Great Escape it was one big waste of time.

• • •

Chapter Twenty-Two

Christine held her hand on the bulge of the mare's side and smiled. "I can feel the foal moving," she said and then took my hand and moved it to the mare's warm belly where I touched a tiny knee or nose or hoof that rolled just underneath the skin. Since I hadn't been on petting terms with the horses, I hadn't thought much about the baby before, and I grinned and pressed my palm a little firmer against the gentle rise and fall.

Christine looked over to the fence where her boyfriend, Jimmy, lounged over the top rail squinting against smoke from a cigarette that dangled from his lips. "Come here and feel it," she called, but he shook his head, pinched the cigarette between his index finger and thumb, and then flicked it away into the grass.

"He's not crazy about horses," she said. "I mean, he tries to like them, because he knows how important they are to me, but I think they scare him, and he doesn't want to admit it."

I understood that, but I couldn't understand the relationship between the girl next to me and the kid draped across the fence. Christine was beautiful, with deep, wide-set eyes and long, thick, curly black hair that that blew in the wind across a face as white as polished bone. Jimmy, on the other hand, had no hair. He'd shaved himself bald presumably to accommodate the tattoo across the back of his skull, and his skin had the pastiness of someone who slept in a coffin during the day. Christine rode horses most of her life and hoped to make a living training them someday. I presumed from Jimmy's tattoos, body piercings, and heavy chain links he wore around his neck that he'd spent most of his life in detention centers and hoped to make a living avoiding prison, a stake through the heart, or both someday. She wore tight breeches and tall strict black riding boots; he wore droopy crack-revealing pants and tall unlaced red sneakers. When they first arrived, she smiled and shook my hand while he glowered at the sun and refused to make eye contact. They seemed as different as strangers on a bus, and even after she spent an hour inventorying the horses, I couldn't build a plausible connection between the two.

"How long have you known him?" I asked as I put my ear against the mare's side hoping I might hear secrets from the womb, but the foal's knee or nose or hoof suddenly jabbed out at the side of my head, and I jerked away.

Christine laughed and patted the mare's neck. "A while. We want to get married, but I'm going to take classes in the fall to become a vet tech, which will take a couple of years, so we're waiting until Jimmy gets a job."

I looked over at him as he leaned away from the fence rail, lit another cigarette, swiped angrily at a fly near his face, then leaned back in. She'd wait a long time, I thought, and then put my hand back on the mare's side.

Christine sighed. Then she took a deep breath, stretched out her arms, and turned in a slow circle. "I want to live on a place just like this," she said. "I've *always* wanted to live somewhere where I can look out my window every morning and see my horse."

"You still live at home?"

She nodded. "I have to board my horse, Mocha, at a stable, and it's really expensive, so I'm living with my parents to save money."

I nodded then, but not with appreciation of her sacrifice for her horse but with appreciation for a series of problems and answers that floated loose in my head—then slowly came together and locked with precision into place like puzzle pieces: She wanted to live on a farm with her horse but couldn't afford it, while I lived on a farm and could. It would take a while for me to find homes for everyone, and she had all the time in the world as she waited for Jimmy to get a job. I needed help taking care of the animals, and she loved animals. If I died in my sleep, there'd be someone here to find me . . .

"I have an idea," I said so suddenly that Christine and the mare both flinched. "Why don't you stay here for a while? You can live rent free in exchange for chores and bring your horse." I pointed up to the house. "Look, there's a bedroom you can have that looks right out over the pastures."

Christine's eyes widened and followed my hand up the hill. Then they moved out over the fields and eventually came back to my face, which she scanned for complications. When she found none, her smile of disbelief slowly turned into a long, drawn-out grin of collusion, and on the spot we came to a silent agreement and shook invisible hands.

"I think it would be a relief to my parents," she finally said after she looked back up at the house and then out over the pastures again.

"A relief?"

She nodded and looked over at Jimmy. "He's been staying with us for a while now, and it's been hard on them. They don't really understand him. They can't see past how he looks to how sweet he really is, so I think they'll be relieved when he's gone."

"When he's gone?"

She smiled, because she didn't understand that I didn't understand. "Yeah. I think Jimmy and I moving here would solve a lot of problems." She patted the mare's neck one more time. "I can't wait to tell him." Then she took off running—almost skipping—across the field toward her sweet vampire on the fence.

• • •

On the farm were two tall concrete silos and the round base of a third, which had never been built. The base was a rusty concrete eyesore about twelve feet in diameter that stood four feet up from the ground and was covered with a rusty metal disk. Despite its lack of practical purpose, it served well as a place of safety from a pissed-off horse, and I came to know every crack and fissure on the metal cover's surface, because I'd been sitting on it for more than an hour.

After Christine left, I was agitated to distraction about the thought of retracting my offer to her. I couldn't imagine living with Jimmy, there was just no way, and in my state of agitation, I forgot to latch the gate of the two-year-old's pasture. Before I even climbed the hill up to the house, I saw him push through the gate, tear across the mare's field, jump a small wire panel, and then run full force toward the fence surrounding the Mustang's paddock where he came to a sliding halt.

It happened quickly and with such determined precision on the two-year-old's part that it was only in retrospect that I realized he was on a single-minded course of attack. His chest rammed up against the fence, and when it cracked, the Mustang's head shot up from grazing. Before I even made a move to stop the inevitable, it happened: The Mustang charged toward the fence, the two stallions reared up, and then they lunged for each other's throats over the cracked top rail.

I ran down and screamed and waved my arms at them from a distance of about twenty feet, but rage blinded them, and their own screams drowned out mine. Their front legs batted at each other over the top of the fence, and when their hooves came down in unison on the top rail, it broke and split open like an eggshell.

The gap gave them more room, and they dove at each other with extra momentum. The two-year-old gnashed his teeth at whatever was in front of him. At one point he made contact with the Mustang's upper lip and clamped down, and as blood shot out and scattered up into the air, he pulled back and ripped a chunk off.

Then their front legs pounded on the next rail down, and I knew if I didn't stop them, they'd break completely through. I ran to the barn. I grabbed a shovel and a two-by-four with no clear plan of how I'd use them. By the time I got back to the horses, they'd broken through the second rail.

I waved the shovel in one hand and the two-by-four in the other, but the stallions paid no attention. They squealed and plunged with renewed energy through the widened gap, and there was no way to get close enough to whack either with the weapons.

Then I thought about how Alex used the lasso. Just waving it above his head was usually enough to scare them. But I didn't have a lasso, and the only rope I could think of was one I used to tie the door of the henhouse shut at night, and it would take me several minutes to go get it. I didn't know if I had several minutes before the third and last rail cracked, but when I threw the shovel at the two-year-old and it landed three feet short of him and then threw the two-by-four, which sailed straight over his back, I realized I didn't have any choice.

I ran up the hill scattering chickens and ducks in my way. When I reached their house, I couldn't breathe, couldn't see through the sweat in my eyes, and couldn't untie the rope on the door, because my hands shook and because time and moisture had tightened the knots into balls of cement. I heard the horses squeal from down the hill. I pulled on any loose end of rope I could find, but it wouldn't budge. They squealed again, and I scratched at the knots until my fingernails splintered, and then I bent forward and tried using my teeth.

Nothing worked. Not one inch of the rope dislodged, and I turned around, spit dirt from my mouth, and skimmed the chicken yard for a strong pointed stick or a sliver of anything I could use to wedge the knots open. Right away my eyes landed on the scarecrows, the hideous, billowing effigies of Halloween celebrities, a bride, and several old men, and without a glance back at the rope, I ran and uprooted Snow White.

Together we flew back down the hill.

• • •

From where I sat on the silo base, I watched with some satisfaction as the wind snapped Snow White's yellow skirt like a high-surf warning flag. My tactic had worked, but it worked so well, I now sat trapped by its effectiveness.

I dug my cell phone out of my pocket, flipped it open, and stared at the time and date. It was late afternoon on a Saturday in May, and I'd been trapped for almost an hour, which meant if I didn't work up the courage to call 911 soon, night would come, I'd die of exposure, and someone would find me several weeks later with crows plucking breakfast from my body. But at least I'd already be dead, which was better than being eaten alive by a horse.

I looked at the two-year-old, who grazed smugly several feet away from the silo. When I'd run to the fence earlier waving Snow White above my head, he hadn't looked so self-assured. Both he and the Mustang took one look at the lunatic rushing toward them with a flamboyant missing link flailing overhead, and primordial fear superseded their rage and they ran like hell. I hadn't seen the Mustang for almost an hour.

The two-year-old, however, ran wide-eyed to the back of the field, but when he saw me propping the scarecrow up on the fence, he came back for a second look. I heard him snort behind me. I whirled around. He stamped his foot and snorted again, and I took off for the silo.

For the record: An angry adolescent horse with injured pride is probably the most intimidating animal there is. A hungry lion, a poisonous snake, a gnashing alligator, none of them come close to a two-year-old stallion whose first attempt at real aggression was just upstaged by a fake Disney character stuffed with straw.

Also for the record: I've invented a new word, *snircle,* which is a verb used to describe a horse snorting and circling a silo for an extended period of time. It can also be an adverb, and as I sat there being snircled, watching the sun sink slowly in the west, a whole raft of new descriptors drifted into my head, which I applied with clear conscience not only to the two-year-old, but to Alex's insurance company, Dustin, the chicken species as a whole, the vampire, the Bureau of Land Management, the Department of the Interior, and the rest of the US government since I was in the territory.

I stared at my phone. I couldn't call 911 and tell them I was trapped on a silo by a horse. I couldn't call Alex, because he was at work, and when I dialed Lenny, I got a message that said his voice mail was full. Anyone else I could think of was at least two hours away and would only tell me he or she told me so. So I sat there and glared at the horse and contemplated what solitude really meant. When I was done with that, I played Sudoku on my phone. When I was done with that, I called Christine, told her I couldn't wait for her and Jimmy to move in, and then asked her to come rescue me.

• • •

Chapter Twenty-Three

Twenty minutes after Jimmy moved in, I plotted ways to make him leave. I designated him caretaker of the chickens, ducks, and geese, told him he wasn't allowed to smoke in the house, and had the cable package disconnected. But he wouldn't take care of the birds because it upset his asthma, smoked in his room and claimed he didn't, and played video games and watched movies from his extensive collection of DVDs. I caught a glimpse of his "sweet" side when he said I could borrow his DVDs anytime I wanted, then added that since they were mostly about martial arts and guerilla warfare, I probably wouldn't want to.

"I've got *The Sound of Music*," he said as he pulled it out of his DVD stack and handed it to me. "You can keep that one."

For her part Christine spent most of her time outside with the horses, the two-year-old in particular, who charmed her somehow into thinking he was as gentle and good-natured as he was attractive. She gave him a name—Cassius—and when I reminded her that Cassius murdered Caesar and that as a result Dante named him, along with Brutus and Judas Iscariot, as worthy of spending eternity in the center of hell being chewed on by Satan, she smiled matter-of-factly and said, "I know."

What was it about nice girls and bad boys? Probably the challenge of making them good boys, I thought, or some maternal instinct that told them that if they didn't love the troubled male, no one else would. Since Christine's horse, Mocha, was old, blind in one eye, and retired from showing, I figured that with Cassius it was the former and that with Jimmy, the latter.

Christine put Mocha in the "normal" pasture with the mare, the pony, and the white horse, where he fit right in. As the herd boss, the mare approached him first, took one good look at his blind eye and aging frame, and then nipped at him to see how he'd react. When he just stood there and took it like a fallen general thrust among the plebs, she deemed him acceptable and then whirled around, kicked out a back leg that fell just short of hitting him, and trotted away with her nose high in the air.

At first Christine spent time with each horse assessing its potential. There was, she said, a small market for Haflingers like the mare, and she knew someone who might be interested in her for breeding. She also had a friend looking for a horse to train as a hunter/jumper, and the white horse was big, strong, and compliant enough to qualify. The pony was a little shyster, she said, but his cuteness would probably override his temperament, and she'd spend a little time teaching him manners.

The other two, however, were about as appealing as bottled lightning.

"They need to be gelded," she said. "No one I know wants stallions, because they're too hard to handle, and gelding gets rid of the testosterone that makes them that way."

Since Cassius had never been abused, he didn't carry excess emotional baggage, so once he was gelded, Christine said it would just be a matter of training him adoptable, which would take time but was doable. His father, though, was such a different story, she didn't know if she had the tools to even try.

• • •

Christine was a student of "natural horsemanship," which meant she didn't train horses through any physical aggression but through a series of techniques that mimic how horses communicate with each other in the wild. Horses weren't broken into submission by a trainer who jumped on their backs and let them buck it out until they were physically and mentally exhausted; instead they were gentled over time into accepting the trainer as their herd leader.

Christine told me that herd behavior was the foundation of natural horsemanship, and even though it took a lot longer than the more traditional method of breaking a horse's will through physical antagonism, it built a stronger trust between horse and human, because it was something the horse instinctually understood.

She showed me how it worked with Cassius. "It's a matter of pressure and release," she said as she walked toward him in his pasture with a lead rope, and I followed a safe distance behind. When the young stallion saw us coming, he picked up his ears, snorted, and trotted our way with his tail high in the air. I lunged forward and grabbed Christine's sleeve to pull her back to the fence, but she laughed as if being attacked by a teenage stallion was as threatening as being attacked by a caterpillar.

"Don't worry, he's just curious," she said and then held out her hand palm up as the two-year-old got near. "Just don't look at him in the eye."

I immediately looked him in the eye, and I saw vengeance, a lust for human blood, and a reflection of her mother's face when I told her that her daughter's body couldn't be viewed at the wake because there were hoofprints embedded all over her head. But when Cassius reached Christine's upheld hand, he stopped, sniffed it, and then tossed his head and trotted away.

"Now is when I start applying pressure," she said.

"Now is when *you* start applying pressure," I said as I steadied myself from the dizziness of not breathing and headed back for the fence.

In a wild herd every individual has a place in the hierarchy, and those higher up assert and cement their authority using body language to *move* the other horses with pressure and release. If a young mare grazes too close to an older mare, for example, the older horse applies pressure by pinning her ears and cocking a leg to warn the other to back off. If the younger horse complies, the older mare's ears move forward, her leg drops, and the pressure is released. If the younger mare doesn't move, the warning pressure turns more serious, and the older horse might show her teeth or snap out until the other horse submits and steps away. Once pressure is released, a fight has been avoided. In fact, fights rarely if ever occur within a wild horse band, because horses understand the signals of pressure and release like people understand the signals of a stoplight.

Christine's goal, then, was to move Cassius where she wanted him to go, which was to come up to her hand again. She assumed a nonthreatening pose of shoulders and head down and walked toward the stallion in a slow but deliberate way. She kept her eyes averted, because predators such as mountain lions stare directly at their prey just before they attack, and she talked indirectly to him as much to acclimate him to the sound of her voice as to hide the sound of any fear she might have betrayed by a rapid heartbeat.

When Cassius saw her coming, he trotted off to a far corner of the pasture, turned, and looked back at her. She kept coming, and he took off again. Christine followed him with the same pose, applying unthreatening pressure to get him to move, until he finally stopped in a far corner of the field and faced her with questioning, pointed ears. She immediately stopped too, releasing the pressure, and then turned her back to him to remove any perceived last remains of force.

The stallion took a few steps toward her. She kept her back to him and continued talking until he inched close enough for her to feel his breath on her shoulder. Slowly, almost imperceptibly, she turned around, raised her hand to his nose and stroked it, and then clipped the lead rope to his halter and led him around the pasture like a lamb on a silk ribbon. From that point, in what seemed to me like bio-spiritual hocus-pocus, she was the leader and he was an obedient, dewy-eyed devotee. All in all, it took about ten minutes.

When she later tried the same thing with the Mustang, he ran for almost an hour. Unlike Cassius, who merely trotted away from Christine as if it was a game, the Mustang ran full speed from her in fear. Cassius never dropped his ears or his tail, and his eyes stayed wide with a sort of curious amusement, but the Mustang ran with his ears cocked halfway back and his tail low between his hind legs. And when he passed by me where I stood at the fence, his eyes were dull and narrow with a weary dread as if he'd been chased too many times before, as if he was tired of running but too afraid to stop.

At first I wanted Christine to back off and just let him be. I wanted to tell her that he'd already been chased by the worst—helicopters, wranglers with electric prods, owners unable to accept his past—and that a young girl would never be able to erase that from his memory no matter how good her intentions. It was habit now to run away, and if forced, he'd run forever.

When he passed by me at the fence a second time, he looked at me, and I wondered for that one moment if he looked at me for help. Once he passed, though, I reminded myself that he was as afraid of me as he was everyone else. When he reached the end of the fence line, though, he doubled back instead of moving on, and as he approached me for the third time, his eyes darted from me to Christine and back to me again and then stayed fixed on my face until he ran past. As he doubled back a fourth time, and then a fifth, each time looking for my eyes, I wanted his fear to end.

But as much as I wanted Christine to stop pushing him, I wanted him to stop running and give in. If he let her approach him, let her stroke his nose, let her take the responsibilities of leadership off his shoulders, then maybe he'd understand that he didn't have to run anymore. So I let it go on, and Christine kept on pushing, and he kept on running, and the only time he stopped for that entire hour was to pause at a far corner to catch his breath.

...

Several weeks after she moved in, Christine found a home for the mare and the pony. A friend with acreage and a small barn had always wanted a foal to train, so she'd take the pregnant mare and the pony to keep her company.

I was ecstatic. It would be a good home, and two of the herd would stay together. That alone almost made up for having Jimmy in the house. And when a week later Christine announced that another friend wanted the white horse to train as a hunter, I almost came close to hugging him.

As relieved as I was, the breakup of the little band in the back pasture was harder than I expected. The mare and the pony were picked up one day while I was at work, and when I got home, not only did the back pasture seem too empty without them, but the white horse, left behind, ran in worried circles calling out for them. By nightfall he was inconsolable, experiencing what Christine called "equine separation anxiety disorder," which meant he suffered from a normal response to losing his herd, which meant to me that it wasn't a disorder at all.

He called for them all night. By morning his grieving spread to Mocha and Cassius like a virus, and the placid old general nearly foamed at the mouth as the two-year-old ran frantic serpentines in his pasture next door. For the next two days, until the white horse left for his new home, the three wouldn't eat, wouldn't sleep, and wouldn't stop looking for the mare and pony. It was as if they thought the two were lost somewhere in the pasture and that if they just kept searching and calling out, the missing pair would eventually be found.

The only one who didn't seem upset was the Mustang. He stood at his fence and stared out at the three other horses, his eyes dull and worn-out with experience.

Once the white horse left, Christine suggested we reshuffle the remaining three so they could at least see one another from their respective pastures. It was cruel, she said, to isolate horses from other horses, and while they couldn't physically be together as a herd, visual contact would alleviate some of their stress.

We moved Mocha up one field so he was adjacent to the Mustang's paddock, and then moved Cassius into Mocha's old digs, which meant the three boys in their three contiguous fields could socialize over their fences. As it turned out, however, the two stallions were still more interested in killing each other than in socializing and spent almost every waking hour of their days pacing back and forth along their fence lines calling out insults over Mocha's back. For the stallions, the old gelding was a barrier that kept them from settling their scores, and I knew it was only a matter of time before one or both of them broke through.

• • •

Chapter Twenty-Four

Testosterone, at its most measurable level, is a tetracyclic molecule that consists of carbon, hydrogen, and oxygen atoms bonded together in a chain, which by chemical standards is heavy and stable. As it flows through the bloodstream, testosterone is fairly nonchalant, sort of like fuel with no trigger, and when it locks into hormone receptors on certain tissues, those tissues respond accordingly and bones become denser, muscles stronger, and voices deeper. While the physical results of testosterone don't alone cause trouble on the domestic front, when the fuel reaches the brain, sparks fly, and if mixed with adrenalin, such as when two stallions face off, it ignites aggressive behavior potent enough to send a spaceship to the moon.

For this reason, most people who have horses don't keep stallions. Those who do sometimes go to extreme measures to keep them under control by isolating them in stalls where they have absolutely no contact with other horses for most of their lives. Others try to emulate wild horse herds and let their stallions run in pastures with a group of mares, but this poses all kinds of logistical problems for professional breeders who must know to the minute when a mare is ready to conceive. The state of nature and the state of business don't mix well, and for this reason, most domestic stallions live solitary lives.

In the wild, horses move up to twenty miles a day within the social context of a herd, so stallions kept in stalls have no mental way to cope with immobilized seclusion. In addition to behavioral problems such as cribbing (grasping an object with the incisors and sucking in wind), weaving (standing in one spot for hours as the body moves side to side), geophagia (eating dirt), coprophagia (eating feces), excessive head shaking, pawing, stall circling, anorexia, and self-mutilation, segregated stallions can turn into raging lunatics at the drop of a hat that even the most seasoned horse handler can't control.

One livestock veterinarian, Dr. Glen Lehr of Harvard, Illinois, told me that the only difference between a bull and a stallion is how they kill a person: "A bull will crush you," he said. "But a stallion will strike out and chew on you." He knew this because the near-death experiences he had during the forty-nine years he spent as a large-animal vet were split evenly between defending himself from the two.

"Breaking up two stallions is the most dangerous thing. They just go nuts. I've seen a stallion pick up a man by the back of the neck and throw him like a rag doll.

"Once, I literally had hoofprints on my back for six weeks after a stallion came after me. When the owner asked if I was OK, I said, 'Just take me to a tavern, so I can get a few shots of blackberry brandy, then I'll be okay.' But once I got to the tavern, someone took me to the hospital. I had three broken ribs and damage to my left kidney and ended up staying there for five days."

While some stallions are calm and manageable, professional horse handlers know they can never be trusted completely. A trainer, Jodi Funk, told me one of the most dangerous aspects of her job is walking a "well-mannered" stallion on a lead rope.

"You have to keep them focused," she said. "You can't let your guard down for a second. If you walk with a gelding or a mare, you can let them look around, but with a stallion, you can't let him lock his eyes on anything. If two stallions lock their eyes on each other, it's over."

The testosterone that fuels the aggressive behavior in stallions is produced in his testicles. About every ninety minutes, the pituitary gland in the brain releases a hormone that surges down to the testes through the bloodstream and binds with special receptor cells, which sets off a chain reaction of events that eventually produces testosterone molecules. While some equine professionals use chemical castration to inhibit the production of testosterone in stallions, most do something first done by the ancient Scythians back in 800 BC, which was simply to slice the testicles off.

• • •

I arranged for Christine's veterinarian to do the castrations, called "gelding" by horse people presumably because the word *castration* is a little too much for most cowboys to take. The vet told me on the phone that he'd need water, some rope, and at least two strong people per horse. Because gelding the Mustang and Cassius had become my single-strongest focus—one that determined whether the horses got adopted or not—I coordinated the schedules of any strong male I could find to make sure the job got done. Included in the list were some of Jimmy's friends, my kids, my sister, and Alex, his family, and several men who worked for him.

All in all about twenty people showed up. While the women in the group stood on the lawn in eager anticipation of a festive social gathering—Maracella brought beer and a Crock-Pot of Mexican stew, and I supplied more beer and dessert—the men in the group shuffled their feet and refused to make eye contact as if attending a formal wake. The vet was late, so as we waited on the lawn, Maracella turned on a portable radio that blared Latin music, and we doled out beer to the uneasy men and food to oblivious children who, paper plates in hand, chased chickens and ducks across the grass. The only thing missing, I thought, was a mariachi band and a priest to conduct Requiem Mass.

Down in their paddocks, the Mustang and Cassius ran back and forth along their respective fence lines. The commotion of the people on the lawn either excited or agitated them; I couldn't tell which. And by the time the vet pulled up in the driveway, the horses were running and bucking on one side of his truck, while women and children danced to music and men saluted him solemnly with cans of beer on the other. Because I was at the top of the hill, I couldn't hear what he said when he climbed out of his truck, but I saw his mouth first form the word, "Wow," and then, "No thanks," when Alex ambled down and offered him a beer.

The vet decided the lawn would be the best place to conduct the gelding. Because he had to get the two stallions in one place at the same time, he sedated Cassius in his paddock first as Christine held him by a lead rope and then the Mustang in his paddock after Alex lassoed him. Before the anesthesia completely took hold, Christine and Alex led the two horses to the lawn, where they stood weaving back and forth and glaring at one another through a drunken, limb-numbing haze. They wanted to have a go at each other, and the Mustang found the energy to pin his ears back for a second or two, but as the drugs took hold and convinced them all was right in the world, their ears fell sideways, their lips relaxed until they drooled, and their eyes turned shiny with bliss.

Cassius was the first to go down. The vet staged men on either side of the horses to help them down when they dropped, but when Cassius's legs stiffened and he fell sideways like a rigid marble statue, one of Jimmy's friends said, "Whoa dude," and one of Alex's men said something equally alarming in Spanish, and they jumped away from the falling horse without apology or embarrassment. Once Cassius landed, the vet put a towel over his face to keep sunlight from waking him up too soon. Then he tied a rope around the horse's uppermost back leg, pulled it back to expose the testicles, and told my son-in-law to hold it taught.

Meanwhile the Mustang held his ground. As the vet went to work laying out his tools and cleaning Cassius's testicles, the Mustang looked on as best he could through drooping eyelids. His legs shook and his tongue hung out of the side of his mouth, but despite the inevitable power of the drugs, he remained upright as if intent on remaining a stallion. Alex held him by the rope around his neck, and I took the opportunity to pet him.

"No worries," I whispered as my palm ran down the length of his nose, which ended at the soft, thin skin of his muzzle, where drool clung like dew on his whiskers. He breathed in the smell of my hand and exhaled a velvety puff of warm air that I wanted to hold on to and remember. Even when he became docile once the testosterone left his bloodstream, I'd already seen the worst in him and doubted I'd ever find the courage to pet him like this again.

I let my hand wander down to the dense muscles of his chest. There were scars there, some new and still scabbed over from the fights with Cassius, others old and now permanent accessories from fights in a distant past. As my palm moved over them, I wondered if any of them were the result of his capture by the Bureau of Land Management (BLM).

In every video of the roundups I'd seen, the stallions fought their captivity with all of the testosterone they had. For them the helicopters, chutes, flags and electric prods were the ultimate enemy, and they reared up in their enclosures and struck out at the metal bars in what for them must have been the ultimate fight. Only it wasn't a fair fight. While their testosterone gave them the strength and courage to fight off other stallions, chase mountain lions away from foals, and even upbraid the boss mare when necessary, it couldn't compete with the fear produced by other hormones in their brains when the helicopters first appeared on the horizon.

If horses believed in gods, a helicopter must have looked like one. When it suddenly appeared out of nowhere, it triggered a surge of adrenalin and cortisol into the horses' bloodstreams that directed all available energy away from nonessential functions into those needed to survive the moment: muscles for running; bronchial tubes for increased oxygen intake; blood vessels for the accelerated output of blood. Even though testosterone bellowed for the stallions to stand their ground and fight, it was like trying to command order in a crowded theater after someone has shouted, "Fire!" Flight and fear became something the horse couldn't control.

BLM contractors count on this fear, and old-fashioned methods of herding on horseback hold none of the fright factor of a helicopter. The pilots are trained to manipulate a herd's collective flight zone, the distance within which a predator can approach before the horses move. A skilled pilot can push into perimeters of the flight zone and push the herd into the trap site.

According to BLM operating procedures, the roundup contractors are expected to ensure the "safe, effective and humane handling and treatment of wild horses during gather operations," but after watching video after video both by wild horse advocacy groups and the BLM itself, I wondered what definition the government applied to "humane" other than it had something to do with humans, which wasn't saying a whole lot under the circumstances and made me feel ashamed.

The horses, running at full speed from the helicopters for up to ten miles, arrive at the trap site exhausted, battered from the run, and soaked and steaming with sweat despite the frigid air. Those hardest hit include the old ones, whose hearts and lungs can't keep up, and the young ones, whose hooves are too soft to withstand the violent run. The horses are so afraid of the helicopters that they run blindly and often leave foals and seniors behind without realizing it. Those who fall behind are harassed by the pilots who descend on them and sometimes jab at their flanks and rumps with the skids until the horses either pick up their pace or collapse and die from exhaustion.

But sometimes a stallion's testosterone pushes through the chaotic mob of fear hormones and makes its way to the brain, and when that happens, even a helicopter, even a god, can't control a stallion whose family is threatened.

Photographer Carol Walker took pictures of wild horses in McCullough Peaks, near Cody, Wyoming, which includes more than one hundred thousand acres of colorful cold desert mountains, canyons, and badlands that served as the perfect backdrop for the horses—bays, grays, chestnuts, palominos, and buckskins—who lived there. These horses descended from heavy draft horses like Percherons mixed with the original Spanish breeds, so they were big and strong as far as wild horses go, and Walker spent five years out on the range trying to capture their beauty on film.

She'd gotten to know many of the members of the various bands that made up the larger herd, so when the BLM announced they were scheduled for roundup, she decided with trepidation to attend and photograph the gather. (When I interviewed her later and asked how she found the strength to watch wild horses she knew lose their freedom in such a disturbing way, she told me, "Someone's got to do it. Someone's got to record what's happening.")

The helicopters drove bands into the trap site all morning. Walker's lens caught the stampedes with haunting frames of distant horses like insects under birds of prey as they ran from the helicopters down snow-covered foothills and across flat frozen land to the trap site. Most of the bands were large, with up to forty horses driven in at a time, but at one point on that first morning, one small family caught Walker's attention—a stallion, his mare, and their foal—because the pilot had a hard time driving them into the trap funnel.

With the mare leading and the stallion running protectively in the rear, the trio swerved away from the trap funnel over and over again. The pilot spent half an hour trying to push them through until finally the stallion—a dark bay who looked like the Mustang—stopped running, turned around, and faced the helicopter while the mare and foal sped away.

"It's a really brave horse who will turn and face a helicopter," Walker said. "That's what makes the roundups so incredibly inhumane: They use fear to chase them."

However afraid he was, the stallion stood his ground, and Walker caught a moment on film that defined defiance better than any words could: a small, dark horse challenging a helicopter at eye level and only a few feet away as his family escaped behind him.

What the stallion didn't know was that as he squared off against the helicopter, wranglers on horseback went after the foal and mare and chased them straight into the trap corral. When the stallion finally turned away from the helicopter and ran full speed back toward the mountains, he did so completely alone.

The next morning, on the second day of the roundup, Walker captured his image again when he returned to the trap site and circled at a distance looking for his family.

Now, as I ran my palm over the bumpy surface of the Mustang's chest, I wondered if I was about to do him even more damage by stealing what one of Jimmy's friends called "the love spuds." For some reason, castrating a domesticated horse like Cassius didn't feel like a crime nearly as much as did castrating a once-wild horse who might have challenged a god.

But it had to be done. If he wasn't gelded, he'd be a danger to any person or other horse around him, and any attempts to acclimate him into domestication would end up in further isolation and abuse. There was simply no safe or productive place in the modern world for a once-wild mustang stallion.

And so, the slicing began.

By the time the Mustang's legs finally buckled and he slumped to the ground, the vet was already at work on Cassius. He used what looked like a razor blade to cut through the scrotum, the thin filmy bag of skin that held the testicles, and then put his fingers inside to pry one of them out. For some reason I expected the testicles to be industrial-colored cylinders of steel, but they were as white and malleable as cottage cheese. When the first one popped out along with a few splashes of blood, a collective groan went up among the men who'd been naive enough to watch.

For the record: I am a female and thus do not understand exactly why the sight of razor blade on a testicle upsets the males so much. Is it because of perceived physical pain, or is it psychological grief? Either way they seem to get overly dramatic about it. When I surveyed the faces of the men around Cassius that afternoon, they either scrunched up as if to ward off blows or they streamed tears. When the vet grabbed the emasculator, a large tortuous-looking clamping device that would complete the procedure, the bellow of a tenor in a tragic opera couldn't have topped the sounds that came out of those men.

The emasculator (which is what it's really called) clamps around the spermatic cord, which supplies hormone-laced blood from the brain to the testicles. When the vet maneuvered it over Cassius's spermatic cord and squeezed the handles closed, it both crushed and cut the tissue at the same time with a sound like crunching glass. When the testicle fell off with a plop on the ground, Alex, still standing by the Mustang, moaned and sort of wobbled on the heels of his boots. He quickly dropped to rest on his hamstrings, pulled his cowboy hat off, and wiped sweat from a glistening forehead.

"Are you OK?" I asked.

"Oh, man," he said and then mumbled something in Spanish as he shook his head at the ground.

In the meantime, as the vet went to work on the other testicle, one of the chickens noticed the bloody white blob on the grass and snuck in under the vet's legs to get a better look. She pecked at the thing, liked what she tasted, and cackled to alert the others of something new and interesting. When the vet saw her under him, he picked up the testicle and tossed it away across the grass with the hen following it down the lawn. Within seconds, twenty other chickens joined the chase, and when the testicle stopped rolling, descended on it en masse.

This set the children on the lawn off into screams of delight, and before any mother could stop them, they too descended on the testicle. One of them plucked it up out of the mob of chickens, threw it, and the chickens chased it like puppies chasing a stick. Then the kids started tossing it back and forth in a game of catch. And so it went as one testicle after another plopped onto the ground until there were four love spuds being tossed around like water balloons not only by the children but by most of the mothers as well.

It was a beautiful sight.

• • •

Later, after the horses woke up and were led still fairly sedated back to their paddocks, the vet and I stood at the Mustang's fence and watched him come to terms with reality. He weaved a little at first but eventually took a few unsteady steps. Up at the top of the hill near the house, the music played again from the radio while the women and children ate dessert, the men guzzled beer, and the chickens finished off the testicles.

"Does he understand what's happened?" I asked.

The vet shook his head. "Probably not. He's sore, but I doubt he knows why."

He then explained the recovery process, which was surprisingly simple: The wounds were left open and unsutured to allow drainage, and the only thing I had to do was make sure the horses moved around as usual to encourage the drainage. Over time the wounds would heal from the outside in, all on their own, and unless the horses developed fever or excreted an excessive amount of blood, the vet didn't even have to come back out to check them.

"How long will it take before the aggressive behavior stops?" I asked.

The vet shrugged. "For the testosterone to completely leave their bloodstream can take up to six months . . ."

"Six months?" I expected him to tell me they'd be gentler within six hours.

The vet held up a palm and shook his head. "But that doesn't mean they'll settle down in six months. It only means the hormone that makes them aggressive will be gone. For some horses, and I expect this will be the case with your Mustang, the aggressive behavior never completely subsides."

I stared at him waiting for a punch line that would indicate he was kidding. When it didn't come, even after I whimpered to encourage it, I finally worked up enough sense to ask why.

"Because he's been a stallion for twelve years," the vet said. "The younger horse's behavior will probably change within the next six months or so, because he hasn't had enough time for the aggressive behavior to become habit. But with that mustang," he nodded his head to where the tattooed horse walked with stiff, slow steps to the fence of Mocha's paddock, "he's been a stallion for so long that the behavior is printed like instructions in his brain. Add to that the fact that he was a wild stallion who was expected to act aggressively for the first half of his life, and you've got a horse who might never moderate behaviorally."

From the top of the hill, we heard a screech and turned in time to see a rooster chasing one of Jimmy's friends across the lawn. His pants were so baggy, they dropped below his hips and he had to hold them up like a loose skirt as he ran. The vet laughed, but I was still numb from shock, still trying to process what he'd just told me, and I turned back to look at the Mustang who despite the surgery and lingering anesthesia, was already back to pacing along the fence of the paddock that separated him from the two-year-old.

After the vet left, I climbed the hill and headed straight for the cooler. I didn't like beer, but it was all there was, and I drank it until everyone left. When I finally climbed the stairs to go to bed, I was groggy, weepy, and so absorbed with self-pity, I forgot to close the doors of the henhouse. When I woke up the next morning, I was still groggy, weepy, and so absorbed in self-pity that it took me several cups of coffee before I realized that none of the roosters were crowing.

• • •

Chapter Twenty-Five

They were scattered all over the lawn—hens, ducks, chicks, and roosters—completely intact save their heads. It was a massacre, a dead-quiet battlefield after the battle, and as I followed headless bodies to the wide-open doors of the henhouse, I couldn't imagine what creature would cut off their heads and leave them strewn like paper plates after a picnic across the grass.

Inside the henhouse, the six geese huddled wide-eyed and silent in a corner with two remaining ducks, five hens, and one rooster. Somehow they escaped the slaughter, but around them the feathers of those who didn't carpeted the straw. I knelt down and held my hand out to the geese. Instead of honking and assaulting me as they normally would, they backed farther into the corner.

"What happened here?" I asked them as guilt clogged my throat at the sight of their terror. "Who did this?"

Hawks wouldn't indiscriminately kill dozens of chickens at a time, and they didn't hunt at night anyway. I assumed coyotes would have eaten whole bodies, and I couldn't imagine a slow-moving raccoon or skunk killing this many birds. The only thing I could think of was voodoo practitioners or vampires, but I didn't think any locals were inclined toward exotic religions, and Jimmy's friends all left before I went to bed.

"It was probably a fox."

I whirled around to the door where Christine's silhouette stood out against the morning sun. "Foxes eat the heads," she said as she stepped in and scanned the wall-to-wall feathers. "But how did it get in?"

I had to fight the first impulse to tell her I didn't know, but the sight of the carnage around us was too much for my conscience to ignore. "I think I left the door open last night," I said and stood up and pushed by her to get outside and breathe some air.

Later that afternoon when Jimmy finally woke up, I made him dig twenty-two graves for the victims under some ancient apple trees in what was once the orchard. The trees were in full bloom with pink and white flowers, so it seemed a peaceful resting place, but the next morning I found half of the graves dug up and the headless, now half-eaten bodies strewn around the orchard in the pattern of windfall.

The morning after that, I actually saw the fox. I'd just let the chickens and geese out and was getting water for them at the pump when I heard one of the geese start screaming. It didn't occur to me that the fox would hunt in the light of morning, but when I ran back to the chicken yard, I saw the small red vixen with the neck of a goose in her mouth.

It took me a second to understand what I was seeing. At first I thought she was a small dog, but her hair was an orange red unlike any dog I'd ever seen, and her tail was as black and bushy as a chimney brush. When her eyes darted toward me, there was the same vivid panic in them as in the Mustang's when he was frightened, and I realized I saw something wild.

I didn't know what to do. I felt paralyzed by both the sudden beauty of the fox and the equally sudden horror of the goose in her mouth. It was as if I'd stumbled upon something sacred and awful at the same time, and my brain couldn't decide which to address. The limp, white goose won out, and I screamed, "Drop it," as I ran toward the chicken yard waving my arms.

The fox darted out the gate with the goose still in her mouth and made it deep into the backfields before I got there.

• • •

"I need something to keep a fox away from chickens," I told Bob when I found him stacking fifty-pound bags of calf milk replacer in a section of the store that had housed horse blankets all winter.

The whole store seemed new with planting, calving, foaling, and lawn-care equipment replacing shoveling, deicing, and heating supplies. Bailing gear took the place of snow fencing, wagons supplanted sleds, and seed packets and fertilizers stood where snow blowers and antifreeze stood for the past seven months.

The centerpiece of the new seasonal display was the double row of tubs filled with two-day-old hatchlings who'd arrived for Farm & Fleet's annual Chick Days. They'd been shipped in from a northern hatchery and included ducklings, turkey poults, goslings, and chicks who'd grow into layers, meat producers, and backyard pets. Some were exotic species like Araucanas chickens, who laid blue eggs, or Mille Fleur Bantams, who grew beards and feathered feet. Others were considered standard breeds—Rhode Island Reds, Giant White Turkeys, and Jumbo Pekin Ducks—whose handwritten signs indicated whether they'd lay white eggs, brown eggs, big eggs, or many eggs or whether they'd be fat, juicy, and ready for the fryer by the holidays. Regardless of their talent, their chirping could be heard throughout the store and drew even the hard-core customers in the Large Engine Parts aisles over to take a look and smile down at them.

Bob, however, seemed oblivious to the community gathering around the nursery, which was in sight of where he stacked bags, and didn't look even up at me when I asked him about the fox. He just kept pulling bags from a cart and throwing them onto the pile and told me to either board up the windows of my henhouse or purchase a shotgun.

• • •

"Yeah," Jimmy said as he tried pounding what would be his third nail into a board over one of the chicken house windows. "I know all about tools and stuff."

He said it with a tone of nonchalant defense after I'd asked him if he'd ever done any manual work before. He seemed to have trouble hitting the nails in such a way that they didn't bend, and while the question was innocent on my part, it seemed to strike him as condescending.

Outside, Christine worked with Cassius in the back pasture, while Irene worked with the Mustang in his paddock. It had only been a week since the gelding, and neither horse seemed any calmer, but while Christine was able to teach Cassius his first ground manners—following her calmly on a lead rope, letting her pick up his feet, and standing still while she groomed him—Irene was still trying to coax the Mustang out of his corner.

"I worked for my dad one summer roofing houses," he said. "But it was, you know," the nail under his hammer crooked sideways, "not my thing."

I bent down, picked another nail out of the box, and handed it to him. "What is your thing?" I asked.

He took the nail, wetted it between his lips, and placed its tip against the board with deep concentration. "Not sure yet," he said as he raised the hammer behind his head, drove it forward, and landed it just to the right of the nail. He stood back and shook his arms as if to loosen them from great strain and then leaned back in toward the board, zeroed in on a spot, and pinned the nail back on. "But not this."

Outside I heard Christine praise Cassius, "Good boy," and I walked to the door and looked out. The henhouse was at the top of the hill, and from my vantage point, I could see not only the back pasture and the front paddock, but the farm fields that extended in every direction as far as I could see, newly planted with corn, soybeans, and alfalfa whose pattern and colors demanded attention like the skirts of a multitiered ball gown.

I could also see the barn, and as Jimmy resumed his pounding, I thought about something the real estate agent had told me when I first came to look at the place ten months before. We'd been standing at the top of the hill, and he'd pointed down to the barn where wind rattled the plastic-covered windows and crows flew in and out of the cupola perched on the roof like an abandoned dollhouse.

"Used to be dairy," he'd said. "They used to make a go of the place. A real good go at one time."

Even to someone like me who knew nothing about barns, the building's ruin was obvious, and we stared at it and clucked our tongues like we would at the news of a neighbor's divorce or the downfall of a once-great leader.

"Should have been taken down years ago, but . . ." He shrugged and stared at the obvious. "There's nails in that barn come all the way from Cork, Ireland. Came in a box with the man who built the place back when nails were hard to come by, real hard to come by, along with just about everything else, including food. When he decided to come to America, he burned down the family's farm—built up by his father and his father before that—burned everything to the ground and then picked up all the nails to bring with him."

At the time I hadn't cared about the barn's history or its nails, but now as Jimmy destroyed one after the other, I felt a pang of guilt and gluttony. I was just one more person in a hundred-plus years' worth of people who had lived here and who had cared increasingly less. What once stood as an icon of America's strength, the hard-won, prosperous family farm, was now nothing more than a rundown halfway house for societal expatriates, vampires, and unwanted horses.

I looked over at Christine. She'd snapped a long nylon lunge line on Cassius's halter and kissed at the air to get him to move. He didn't understand yet that she wanted him to circle around her, but he'd learned so much in such a short period of time, I knew it wouldn't be long before he trotted in smooth, level rings from her lunge line.

Then my eyes turned down to the front paddock where Irene stood several yards away from another of the country's icons: the American mustang. She held out her hand to him, and I saw her lips move with words meant to calm him, but the second she took a step forward, he flinched as if she'd struck him, and then he trotted away.

• • •

It was still chilly in the mornings, and as I sipped my first cup of coffee on the front porch the next day and pulled my sweater close around me, I surveyed the henhouse now boarded up with scraps of wood that crisscrossed the windows in off-kilter Xs. Along with the two remaining scarecrows impaled on their sticks and now tattered and headless from the wind, it looked like a scene from the Blair Witch woods.

But then something in the front paddock caught my eye, and when I looked down the hill, I saw three little foxes running in circles on top of the Mustang's muck pile. They were exact miniatures of the fox who'd stolen the goose, and when I saw her watching on at the edge of their playground, I realized they were her babies.

One of the pups scampered down the steepest side of the muck pile, veered around his mother, and then hightailed it back up when she nipped at the air behind him. The other two on top of the pile played like kittens: One stalked another and then pounced; they rolled in a tight embrace down the side of the pile; and, when one broke free and ran back up, she stopped and waited for the other to chase her. Soon all three dashed back and forth across the top of their little mountain in a wild-eyed frenzy as if they'd just been let loose from a kennel.

Meanwhile the mother stood guard. Her head twitched side to side, and she must have been on high alert, because when I moved to rest my coffee cup on the porch railing, her head shot toward me, and she turned and ran with the pups close behind her before the bottom of the cup even landed.

I saw them disappear in a thicket of vine-meshed bushes that grew on the old foundation of a long-gone outbuilding. When I went down to investigate, I found a hole about the size of a wagon wheel formed between cracks in the foundation. Tiny paw prints indented the mud around the hole along with piles of gnawed bones and whole chicken feet, which they presumably didn't like, and I realized as I stared down at their little compost pile that it was the opening to their den.

Two things occurred to me in rapid succession: One was that the most mesmerizing little things I'd ever seen had been living right under my nose, and the other was that I'd just cut off their food supply.

That afternoon I went to the grocery store in town and bought a frozen chicken. That night I thawed it out in the sink, and the next morning I put it on a plate and took it down to the den. It was gone by the time I got home from work, not so much as a bone was left, so I went back to the store and bought as many frozen chickens as my freezer would hold.

While I knew that the store-bought chickens were just as much victims as the live ones the mama fox caught, at least they were already dead. And besides, they weren't *my* chickens, which as I'd learn in the weeks to come would turn into a weighty distinction.

• • •

Chapter Twenty-Six

I didn't realize until he called me late one night in June that I hadn't talked to Robert in almost two months. I'd been so consumed with the demands of the farm that I hadn't even thought about him, and I felt a twinge of something close to guilt when I heard his voice. I was pretty sure, however, that during the weeks just before and after the close of the legislative session in May, when the Capitol building turned into a pressure cooker of all-night meetings, eleventh-hour amendments, and exhausted, jittery, undernourished, overly caffeinated lobbyists, lawmakers, and aides making desperate, final sprints to the passages of bills, that he hadn't thought about me either.

"How'd you do?" I asked, not sure if I knew or if he'd even told me what bills he'd been responsible for passing or killing. There'd been a time when I knew everything on his agenda, knew every "whereas" and "therefore" of every bill, resolution, amendment, and provision in his hands. I knew what carrots he dangled, whose money he shuffled, and what information he awarded or withheld and why. But now I had no idea what he'd worked on this session, though I thought I remembered him mentioning a tax increment proposal back in the fall . . .

"Like pissing on electric wire, baby. Fried to the balls. Listen, are you done with the great American novel yet?"

"The book?" That was another thing I hadn't thought about in months.

"Yeah," he said. "Is it finished?"

"Finished?" I hadn't even started. The novel I'd set out to write during my year in the country didn't have a title, a plot, or even a genre upon which to perch. There were no character sketches, because no characters existed. There were no scenes, not even in my head, because I had no idea what the book was about. I never had. I'd come here believing solitude and fresh air would inspire me somehow, but instead . . .

"It's getting there. Why?"

"Because, my dear," he said, "I need another lobbyist."

"What does that have to do with . . ."

"I want *you* to be that lobbyist. I want you to wrap things up and get back down here."

"Me?"

"Soon as possible."

"But . . ."

"Listen, I didn't even have to think about it. In fact, I didn't think about it, Jim did, and he was right, you're perfect for the job. You know the issues. You know the people. You write a kick-ass speech. Besides, sweetheart, who are you kidding? You're not cut out to be a country girl eating beef jerky and making birdhouses out of gourds or whatever it is folks do up there in McHick County. When's the last time you had a latte? Any Starbucks up there? So finish up the damn book, and come back and work for me. Either that or come back, and we'll get married. I don't care which. Your choice."

I was still trying to process the job offer—lucrative political work that most only dreamed of—so when Robert threw in "marriage," my brain shut down from the overload. We'd never talked about marriage before, and for him to toss it into the bid like loose change almost as an afterthought, took me completely off guard.

"Uh . . ."

But that's what Robert was good at: talking fast and getting to the point. People didn't know what hit them. The result was usually a knee-jerk response in Robert's favor made by people pressured to keep up with the conversation. If there was any hesitation, any semblance of contemplation on their part, Robert just picked up the pace, which left even the most independent thinkers worried about falling behind.

"Listen, sweetheart," he said. "If you don't stop this recluse gig pretty soon, you're going to grow whiskers and lose your teeth, know what I mean? You're already dropping your Gs and hoarding animals. You know as well as I do that you can't stay holed up there forever, so come back now, before it's too late."

If only he knew how late it already was. I had calluses on my hands, the fingernails that weren't bitten down were ragged and split, my hair was orange from the rusty well water, and everything I wore, including my nicest work clothes, came from Farm & Fleet. I had a small scar on my face courtesy of the mama chicken and numerous other scars on my arms and legs from roosters, burr plants, poison ivy, barbed wire, and one hundred years' worth of protruding nails. My skin was damaged from the sun, wind, and dirt I could never completely wash off, and I'd stopped trying to hide it all with makeup months ago. If Robert saw me now, I doubted he'd recognize me.

"I know how much you want to be around your kids, but you won't be on a strict clock and can take time off pretty much whenever you want to go see them."

"Time off from a job or being married?"

He didn't seem to notice the sarcasm and said, "Either," without missing a beat.

"I've got a contract that's going to take me to DC a lot in the next year. Jim can take over my regular contracts here, Tony can juggle Jim's old clients, but I need someone able to step in and take over Tony's work without having to learn a whole new alphabet. You know the alphabet forward and backward. It's right up your alley. And if you don't want the job, you can stay at home, drink lattes, and write all the books you want. Go visit your kids whenever you want. We can adopt a dog or something . . ."

"Robert . . ."

"No kidding, a dog. It's the American Dream. What do you say?"

This was Robert at his most affectionate, and despite the abruptness, it felt like sliding my feet into a pair of warm old slippers with a good book in one hand and a latte in the other.

"I haven't had a latte since I moved here," I said.

"So that's a yes?"

And I could always get my hair fixed and put on some makeup. It occurred to me to ask myself questions like: Do I really love him enough to marry him? Would I be happy living so far away from the kids again? But outside I heard a rumble of thunder and remembered a storm was coming in, which meant I'd be dodging lightning and sloshing around in manure and mud in the morning when Christine and I did chores. I wasn't cut out to be a country girl, on that count Robert was right. And there was no room for considering long-term emotional issues when the mere thought of the near term—pulling muddy goulashes off my feet, burrs out of my hair, and hay out of my bra—suddenly made me want to weep.

"I need a little time," I said. "I have to find homes for the horses."

"You still have those things?" he said as if he'd forgotten I had them in the first place and substantiated how far our worlds had spun away from one another.

"It's not as easy as you'd think."

"Tell me," he said. "What's so hard about it?"

Robert wouldn't have the patience to hear the entire story through to the end if it included too many subplots and details. Somehow I had to explain equine standards to someone who'd probably never seen a real horse, then incorporate the dynamics of herd behavior, archaic federal legislation, the power of helicopters, and more than three hundred years' worth of American history to boot. I couldn't very well start out with "It all began with Columbus," and expect him to stay awake, so I said, "It's complicated," and hoped it was enough.

"How complicated could it be? Look, here's what you do: You put an ad on Craigslist for the horses, you give them a high price tag so people think they're worth something, then you use all the money you get and rent yourself a U-Haul to get your stuff down here."

I closed my eyes. Maybe I could skip the Columbus part and jump right to horse slaughter for the drama factor. Or maybe if I threw in stuff about how cunningly Senator Burns slipped his amendment into an appropriations bill late at night, it might hold his attention for tactic's sake if nothing else.

"It's not that easy," I said. "I might be able to pull that off with the younger horse, but not with the Mustang. Nobody decent wants a horse like him, and he's been through so much . . ."

I could hear an "Oh, jeez" in the sigh Robert let out when I treaded too close to sentimentality, so I backed away and let him interrupt.

"Can't you just take the damn horse back to where he came from?"

"No," I said, indignation slithering over my skin like a draft. "Even if the Bureau of Land Management would take him back, I couldn't consider it."

"Why not?"

Because, I thought, the BLM had no business taking care of wild horses. Because the agency had so mismanaged its responsibilities, there were now more captured horses living in federal long-term holding facilities than there were left in the wild. Because the BLM claimed that the 26.9 million acres of public land available wasn't enough to support the remaining wild horses even though it equated to 721 acres of per animal, and so the roundups would continue.

But that was too much information wrapped up in too much of my own emotions, albeit the same emotions shared by most of the American public who knew about it. But it was still too much for Robert's fleeting attention span, so I fell back on, "It's complicated," and hoped once again it was enough.

"What's so complicated? If the BLM won't take him back, and I can grease the skids on that if you want, then just take him back to Montana or Nevada or wherever he came from. Just put him in a trailer, drive out to where the buffalo roam, and set him loose. Simple."

It *was* simple. It was beautifully simple. It was so simple, I hadn't even thought of it until now.

After we hung up I spent two hours on the computer and every spare minute I could find in the following week mapping out a road trip to Nevada.

• • •

Chapter Twenty-Seven

I asked Irene to come out the following weekend so I could tell her about my plan to return the Mustang to Nevada and to ask if could borrow her horse trailer. In addition to her consent, I counted on her offering to go with me, because I would make it clear that I had no idea how to load a horse onto a trailer, how to unload a horse from a trailer, or how to drive a horse trailer in the first place.

I stood in the Mustang's paddock while I waited for her and coaxed him toward me with an iced oatmeal cookie. Irene didn't use treats when she worked with him, because she said trust, not bribery, was the key to gentling a horse. But I was pretty sure the Mustang would never trust anyone, so I settled for just making him happy. Cookies made him happy, or as close to happy as he could get, and when he saw me hold it up in the air, his ears shot forward like antennas, and he stepped slowly closer, inch by inch.

When he got to within a foot of my hand, I lifted the cookie out toward him. He flinched at the movement and backed away but only enough to get clear of petting distance. He knew I'd try to pet him once he took the treat, so he kept his front hooves about three feet away while he stretched his neck forward as far as it would go, followed by his nose, and finally his lips, which he extended about five inches from the rim of his mouth like a pair of elongated bulbous tweezers. I knew the second they made contact with the cookie, the lips would pluck it out of my fingers and then spring back with the nose and neck faster than my eyes could follow. Then he'd trot away.

Today, however, I had things to tell him, so when the lips reached forward for the cookie, I pulled it back toward my chest. He yanked his head back and stared at me. I figured that while he wouldn't come closer to get the cookie, he also wouldn't trot away without it. Not when it was iced.

"I've got news," I said and took a small bite of the cookie to keep him a little worried and attentive.

"First of all, Christine wants to keep Cassius as her own horse."

He stared at the damaged cookie.

"She asked me yesterday if she could have him. Mocha's too old for her to show anymore, and she thinks Cassius has great potential as a cross-country jumper. So we don't have to worry about finding him a new home.

"Then I called Alex and asked him if he'd consider building a little house on his property next to the new sheep shed for the chickens who are left. He said he would, when he has time, which means we won't have to worry about them either."

I took another nip at the cookie's edge and savored the resolutions that had lined up so perfectly during the previous week. I now fully believed in astrology.

At first, when Christine asked me if she could keep Cassius, she misunderstood my stunned silence as a rejection of the idea and babbled on about how much she'd come to love him, how well she'd take care of him, and how happy he'd be in a big stable with other horses.

"You're going to . . . take him away?" I asked, still dazed from good news.

"I could keep him here if you want," she said quickly to ease the misgivings she thought I had. "But it would be easier for me and better for him if I boarded him at a training barn where they have indoor arenas and jumps and other trainers who can help me, and he'd be turned out to pasture every day, and he'd be well fed, and . . . ," she paused to catch her breath. "You could come see him whenever you want."

"Whenever I want?" I said, just to give my brain time to pull alongside the concept that not only did someone *want* the increasingly assertive little delinquent in the backyard but that she wanted to take him *away*. It was too good to be true, and as I searched for caveats I figured had to be there, Christine placed her hand on my shoulder and looked deep into my eyes to assure me.

"When*ever* you want."

I took another bite of the cookie as I stared at the Mustang.

"The best news," I said as a column of drool dropped from the Mustang's lips, "is that you are going home. I've got it all planned out. We're going to put you in a trailer and drive for two days to Antelope Valley in Nevada. There are horse herds there, maybe some of them you know, and we're going to let you run off and find them."

His eyes followed the arc of the cookie as I brought it back up to my mouth.

"Now pay attention while I explain this," I said and let my teeth take one more small bite. "You're going to be scared during the trip there, because you won't understand what's going on, but .. "

He suddenly snorted. I stiffened in alarm and stopped chewing as his eyes narrowed to slits that bored into the cookie like drill bits. He shook his head. Then he lifted his front hoof and stamped it once on the ground. I jerked back, and when he stepped toward me, I threw the cookie at him, turned, and ran for my life.

• • •

Irene stared at me with the same dumbfounded look I gave Christine when she asked if she could keep Cassius. We stood at the Mustang's fence, and my announcement that he was going back to the range where he belonged struck her as so brilliant, her eyes snapped back and forth between him and me, and for once she had nothing to say. I felt satisfied to the point of smugness, so I admitted with false modesty that it wasn't really my idea but Robert's.

"Who's Robert?" she said and suddenly jammed her hands on her hips.

"A friend. A lobbyist I know."

"A lob-by-ist?" she said as she thrust her head toward me and spit out the syllables as if pepper coated. "A lob-by-*ist?* What in the hell does a lob-by-ist know about horses?"

I pulled away in surprise. "Nothing. He knows nothing about . . . I mean, he just mentioned it . . . it was a joke really, and . . ."

She pulled her head back and rolled her eyes. "Some joke. For a minute there, I thought you were serious." Then she laughed as if relieved.

I didn't understand, not at first, but as she laughed and relief bobbed in her eyes like buoys, I realized she actually thought I was kidding.

I cocked my head and smiled with her. "It's not a joke. I want to borrow your trailer, drive him out to Nevada, and set him free."

She stopped laughing slowly. I expected her to widen her eyes as she took this in and then to nod at the serious ingenuity. Instead her eyes softened like they would at the whimsical proclamation of a naive child as her head moved back and forth with pity.

"You were serious."

"Why wouldn't I be?" I felt threatened by her sudden and apologetic sympathy. "He originally came from public lands in Nevada, and since I'm part of the public who believes he shouldn't have been rounded up in the first place, I think I have every right to take him back and set him free. It's the only place for him. It's the only thing that makes sense, and it would be a happy ending for everyone."

Irene shook her head slowly at every word I said.

"Maybe for you it would be a happy ending, but not for him," she said.

Irene had to help me. I had to talk her into this. There was no way this couldn't happen.

For the past week I'd imagined over and over again how it would feel to drive the sixteen hundred miles to Nevada, unlatch the back of the trailer door, and watch the Mustang step out, look all around him around, and blink at the brightness of a sun he hadn't seen in more than six years. For seven days, I watched him stand in the middle of the Great Basin where he was born and slowly come to understand: First, he'd smell something familiar, maybe windswept sagebrush pollen or the recent passage of a herd; then, he'd hear things he remembered, air currents through salt desert shrubs, the yip of a distant coyote, the cry of a circling hawk; and then, as a dry breeze swept the mane away from his eyes, he'd see the miles of empty, fenceless land that stretched out before him, and then the foothills beyond, and then the mountains beyond that, and finally, he'd understand.

And then, he'd run. And he'd run as fast as he'd ever run in his life, but not from helicopters or electric prods or lassos but to memories of a herd in the mountains he once knew, and he'd run until he got there, until he was a speck on the horizon, until Irene and I were hoarse from whooping and crying and cheering him on until he disappeared forever.

It had to happen. It had to.

"You can't just turn him loose," Irene said. "He can't ever be wild again."

Panic set in, and I shook my head as I sensed a wall going up brick by brick that would completely block off the mountains. "Of course he can. Of *course* he can. Why not? You could help me. I'll pay for the whole trip. He's healthy and sound. There's no reason he can't go back. He deserves this. We owe him this ..."

"What you owe him is as safe and comfortable a life as you can give him. What's happened has happened."

"We can change that. Make it all better ..."

"You'll never make it better," Irene said in a tone that switched from soft and sympathetic to stern and firmly severe. "For one thing, he'd probably be rounded up again by the Bureau of Land Management eventually, only this time you'd have no control over where he went. He'd either end up in a long-term holding pen, or end up with another yahoo cowboy wannabe who can't control him, and the beating would start all over again. Either way, it's not fair."

It wouldn't be fair. None of it was fair, and I wanted to stamp my foot on the ground and scream out loud how shamefully, appallingly unfair it was.

"For another thing, it's illegal to turn a privately owned horse loose on public lands. He's branded. And the brand indicates he's yours, so if he was rounded up, you'd be charged with a federal crime."

My eyes wandered across the paddock to the white symbols on the Mustang's neck. The characters, a series of angles and symbols, indicated what year the Mustang was born, in what state he was captured, and by what entity he was registered, in this case, the US government.

Shortly after the BLM captured the Mustang, he was herded into a narrow, sturdy metal chute, then pushed farther into a padded "squeeze chute" to hold him upright for the branding. The process was frightening but painless: electric clippers shaved away a swath of hair from the left side of his neck; rubbing alcohol was applied on the newly naked skin;

and the branding iron, chilled in liquid nitrogen, was applied to the spot for about twenty seconds to kill pigment cells in the hair follicles, which eventually grew back completely white.

Each brand is unique, unalterable, and permanent—a fixed accessory of identification, which for the rest of the horse's life classifies him as "once wild." Even returning to the range wouldn't alter his status in the eyes of the government: Once the mark was made, the Mustang became "property." And by default, he was mine. The symbols on his neck told whomever could translate them that he was legally my property, that I "owned" him, a designation I didn't want, because I didn't understand how ownership extended to something that I felt was stolen in the first place.

"And lastly," Irene said, "he's not a stallion anymore, he's a gelding. He couldn't form his own herd, because he can't breed, and he couldn't join a bachelor group, because they wouldn't accept him. He'd be alone for the rest of his life, and lone horses in the wilderness don't live long."

I'd done that to him. I couldn't blame the helicopters or the lassos or his previous owners for taking away the most important aspect of his survival or for the fact that there was no natural place in the world for a physically maimed, emotionally troubled, once-wild horse.

I looked up at the sky for a solution that wasn't there and then down at the manure that was quickly drying like cement on my boots.

• • •

Chapter Twenty-Eight

I sat on the front porch steps tossing Cheerios to the geese when Alex called to tell me he couldn't take back the chickens and why.

"What do you mean you're moving to the suburbs?" I said as I quickly stood up, and the geese honked at the change in my height.

"Maracella, she doesn't want to live in the country anymore, not with the new baby."

Ricardo was born several weeks before, just after the horses were gelded. Alex and Maracella threw him a party, which I attended, but they never once mentioned moving away. In fact, after my idea to free the Mustang bottomed out, I'd planned on offering to pay for the construction of a small barn on their property. I only had a little savings left, but if spending it meant leaving the Mustang in good hands, it was an investment I thought well worth making.

"But you *can't* move," I said and then grasped for the first thing I saw. "What about the sheep?"

The geese, now ignored, stabbed at the front of my shins for their Cheerios. When I waved the cereal box to scare them away, they wailed at the abuse and doubled their efforts to gore me. I kicked at them with my boot, but I missed and spun into a graceless pirouette.

"I found someone to take them. Once we sell the house, my cousin's friend, his wife, she will take them. She loves sheep."

"Does she love horses too?"

Alex chuckled. "They have too many already. I've been thinking, though, if you don't want to keep the Mustang, I found a place maybe he can go."

The geese doubled back from their flight from my boot and blared at it with riotous fury. I put my hand over my free ear. "What place? Where?"

"I met a guy last week. He has races every Sunday. He said he'd take the horse."

"Races?"

"Mexican horse races. Every Sunday in the next town over. He says he is always looking for horses. They take good care of them. You can go with us next Sunday and see."

My first thought, lulled by the sentence, "They take good care of them," reasoned that if Alex suggested it, it had to be OK and that maybe the Mustang would be happy running all the time. My second thought, though, told me to stop grasping at thin air. The Mustang had already been run enough, and there was no justification for making a sport out of it.

Then, like an insulted hero, my third thought shoved its way into the fray and flung the first two off to the sides: This was not my fate. *I* was the one supposed to move to the suburbs, not Alex.

• • •

Less than a week later, I came home from work and found the white horse grazing in the middle paddock with Mocha. I'd just rounded the first bend in the driveway and slammed on my brakes when I saw him.

"What are you *doing* here?" I yelled out the window. The two horses looked up from browsing. Grass poked out of the sides of their mouths as they stopped chewing and stared at the car. When they were satisfied they weren't being attacked, not that the two pampered domesticates actually understood the concept, they finished chewing what was in their mouths and went back to grazing again.

There were only two possible explanations for the white horse's presence on the farm: Either we were babysitting for the weekend, which seemed unlikely because he lived at a staffed stable, or he'd run away from his new home and found his way back here, which seemed even more unlikely, as most horses stay put wherever they are fed. In fact, if you put a lifetime's worth of hay and grain in front of a horse, he'd probably never move.

A third possibility, that I was imagining what I saw, took flight when I saw the look on Christine's face as she walked down the driveway toward my car. Before she even reached the door, her look warned me to reverse the car, back down the driveway, speed away as fast as I could, and never come back again.

"What," I demanded, "is *he* doing here?"

"Hi," Christine said as she put her hand on the windowsill and turned and looked at the two horses in the paddock. "Guess what?"

"What."

"He's a gelding now too."

"That's great," I said and tried to keep my voice steady and away from an octave that might shatter the windshield. "And what is he doing here?"

"Uh," she looked at the ground and tapped the sides of her boots back and forth against each other. "He's got fused hocks."

"Fused hocks."

She nodded, still avoiding eye contact.

"What are fused hocks, and what does that have to do with him being here?"

She took a deep breath and explained that sometimes a horse's hocks—the elbows on his back legs—develop a kind of arthritis, where the cartilage between the upper and lower bones deteriorate until the bones rub together. It is painful, she said, and until the two bones fuse together, which could take up to six months, the horse couldn't be cantered or jumped. Since that was the reason her friend took the horse in the first place, and since she'd be paying board for a horse she couldn't ride in addition to the cost of medication he'd need for the pain, she decided to bring him back

"Bring him *back?*" I said.

"You told her to bring him back if she couldn't keep him, remember?"

"Yeah, but I didn't mean it."

"The good news," Christine said, "is that he's gelded now. And in six months, when his hocks fuse, he'll be good as new."

Six months. I couldn't wait six months. In six months I'd either be heavily medicated or wandering aimlessly through cornfields having meaningful conversations with the stalks. And besides, no job in the political world and no marriage proposal from someone who worked there stayed open for that long. It was a lifetime, half a year. Entire delegations, staffs, platforms, and affections changed in six months' time.

I slapped my palms against the steering wheel and threw my back against the seat.

"What next?"

• • •

For the record: I now believe it's bad practice to tempt fate. It's out for blood. Even when you feed it everything you've got, it turns and bites you on the ankles.

• • •

Christine was inconsolable. We sat at the kitchen table, and she wiped her nose on her sleeve as her mother, Karen, patted her hand, and I ran to the bathroom to find Kleenex. I was out, so I unfurled a few sheets of toilet paper, but when I heard Christine wail, "What am I going to do?" I disengaged the whole roll.

Jimmy was gone. He hadn't even written a note, just packed up his DVDs and left, and Christine only found out about it when a friend asked her in a text how she was handling the breakup.

"He's just a coward," I said as I handed her the toilet paper.

"He's a bum, that's what he is," Karen said.

"A lazy, bloodsucking leech," I countered.

"A useless, good for nothing, jackass," Karen re-countered

And so it went, like a word game of condolences, until we ran out of nouns and adjectives. Nothing we said, though, got through to the girl who suffered alone behind her wad of toilet paper.

I tried a different tactic. "Once when I was in college and a guy broke up with me, I went to a friend's house and drank some scotch. I'd never had scotch before, and it sort of went to my head. By the end of the night, I'd drawn pictures of the guy on pieces of paper, and my friend dug out all of the letters and pictures of her former boyfriends, and we burned them in a bowl on the coffee table as a sort of exorcism."

Christine blew her nose. Karen asked, "So, what happened?"

I shrugged. "We drank scotch and burned past mistakes until the smoke alarm went off."

Karen smirked, but Christine pulled the toilet paper away from her face and cried, "Jimmy wasn't a mistake, it was meant to be." And then she threw her head onto her folded arms on the table. "What am I going to do?"

Karen and I looked at each other knowing there was nothing she could do. Fate had sharp teeth, and the only antiseptic was time. Karen leaned over and stroked the back of her daughter's hair.

"Why don't you pack up some things and come home tonight," she said.

With her head still down, Christine nodded at the table. "OK."

Karen had to pack her clothes, because Christine couldn't face the room and Jimmy's empty drawers alone. Several days later, Karen told me at work that she couldn't face coming back to the farm at all. She'd built a fantasyland where she and Jimmy and Mocha lived in the country happily ever after, and when it exploded and her youth and inexperience couldn't understand why, she disappeared under the debris.

"This hit her harder than we thought," Karen said. "Can Mocha stay at your place for a few more days until we find a new barn?"

I nodded. "Of course. What about Cassius?"

Karen shook her head. "She says every time she'd look at him, he'd remind her of Jimmy. She says she doesn't want him anymore."

For the record: I was happy for Alex's escape to the suburbs and I was sorry for Christine's pain, but minus the mare, the pony, and the sheep, I was right back where I started. I imagined it would only be a matter of time before they showed up again too, because this had all been just a dress rehearsal for fate that was still backstage warming up.

• • •

Chapter Twenty-Nine

Summer creeps into the northern prairies on bent haunches, sniffing along, taking a step forward, and then jumping back when it thinks it smells something strange. Anywhere north of south is suspect, so it takes its time, but when it finally arrives, the trees, the crops, and the prairie grasses detonate to make up for lost time, and the landscape changes from sepia to high-fidelity color almost overnight. In town, the farmers' market opened, soccer leagues formed, and bands played on the square every Saturday night. On the outskirts, tractors muddied the back roads, U-PICK STRAWBERRIES signs went up, and swallows built nests in barn eaves.

I barely noticed that summer had turned up. I'd been too focused on what I would say to Robert, and as I sat on the front porch on the morning I decided to make the call, the only thing I noticed was how the phone trembled in my hand. That and the tic that started snapping again in my left eye.

I had to tell Robert something about when I was coming back, but despite missing the entire first act of summer as I paced through the house deciding what to say, I still wasn't ready to talk to him. I had nothing concrete to say. I didn't know when I was going back, and with no regulations or procedures to guide me, no laws to follow or amend, I was as lost as a politician without talking points.

My choices as I saw them were two: I could send the Mustang to the rodeo and the rest to auction, hope for the best, and go back right away; or, I could wait until I found them homes, which would take at least six months and effectively render my professional future null and void. Either choice seemed too final.

It was still early morning, and as I stared at the phone, I heard the fox pups play fighting out in the orchard. They were as big as beagles now and independent enough to abandon the muck pile close to their den. I'd seen them chasing each other through Cassius's pasture and once, near dusk, running across the road, but I'd never seen them come this close to the house before. I stood up, shoved the phone in my back pocket, and walked out to take a look.

The orchard, which was only five gnarled apple trees that must have been as old as the farm itself, stood near the far end of the henhouse. When I passed by, a rooster darted out and ran after me with the awkward, fast sprint of a Jurassic meat eater, so I pulled out my cell phone and threw it at him. It landed short, just in front of his feet, and he used it as a launch pad to attack me.

When roosters confront a human, they fly thigh high and propel their legs forward so the nails at the end of their toes strike first. Then, after they beat their wings and claw their way up your body, they try to peck out your eyeballs. So when I saw him lift off from the phone, I dodged right and then quickly left to throw him off balance, and he went careening into thin air.

I left the cell phone behind and made my way through knee-high bluestem grass toward the orchard where two of the fox pups whirled after each other around the base of a tree. The grass under the trees, silky and short, made good terrain for their simulated hunts and was close enough to the tall grass to provide a quick escape if they needed it. I didn't want to scare them away, so I stayed at the edge of the orchard, where tall grass met short, and watched them chase make-believe prey.

They weren't very good at it. When they charged flower petals falling from the apple trees, they'd leap up, try to grab them but miss, and then fall spread-eagle to the ground. If one pretended to be a rabbit and another stalked and pounced, they ended up scared of their own created encounter and darted away in opposite directions. They yipped at flying birds, somersaulted when they ran too fast, and crashed like out-of-control bumper cars into tree trunks, chicken tombstones, and each other.

As possessed by play as they were, they still stopped and froze when I knelt down, and they heard the crack in my knees. They stared at me with their almond-shaped eyes. I didn't move. They didn't move. And for about five seconds we shared the orchard. Then one of the pups yipped, and in unison they darted off and disappeared into the tall grass.

My eyes followed the collapsing blades as they ran for Cassius's pasture. They weren't afraid of the horses and shot across the field and almost between his legs without a glance from him as they made a beeline back to their den.

A week before, Irene had put the Mustang in the field adjacent to Cassius's pasture. She said he needed to graze on fresh grass and hoped the fence between the two fields was a strong enough barrier, even with their dwindling testosterone. So far it had worked, and they grazed quietly side by side, heads down eating clover. But when the fox pups cleared Cassius's side of the fence and zoomed into the middle of the Mustang's field, he picked up his head, followed them briefly with his eyes, and then chased them to the end zone of his territory. He couldn't keep up and didn't know they weren't running from him, but when they vanished into the thickets that hid their den, he rounded his back and shook his head as proud as if he'd chased off mountain lions.

As I watched him settle down and go back to grazing, it occurred to me that if I went back into politics as a registered lobbyist, I'd have the credentials to promote his cause. I'd be working at the state level, which didn't have anything to do with the Bureau of Land Management, but I might be able to convince Robert to let me visit DC once in awhile. For that matter, if we got married, I could spend all of my time lobbying in defense of wild horses and their right to be left alone.

The problem with that justification, though, was that there were already dozens of wild horse advocacy groups lobbying for tighter BLM controls, and no one seemed to be listening. Despite their best, most well-measured attempts at fund-raising, letter-writing campaigns, and committee testimonials, they couldn't compete with the stronger voices of the oil, natural gas, mining, and ranching industries that also needed the resources of the country's public lands and wanted the wild horses off. Wild Horse Annie spent almost her entire adult life passing the Wild Free-Roaming Horses and Burros Act of 1971 that protected mustangs as "living symbols of the historic and pioneer spirit of the West," but that was now as gutted as a dead fish.

I sat down in the tall grass, stretched my legs out into the shorter grass of the orchard, and took a last stab at kidding myself. Maybe the gains of the wild horse advocates were small, but at least wranglers weren't running herds of mustangs off cliffs anymore. Maybe one more voice, one more person crying foul could tip the scale somehow, only . . . I knew it wouldn't make any difference. In the end the only thing that mattered to elected officials was getting the most votes, and there was no voting bloc devoted to wild horses. One more person screaming about the BLM would only be one more person screaming.

And besides, it was only a watered-down attempt to validate walking away, and as I sat in the tall grass I admitted to myself that that's what I wanted to do. I wanted to walk away from the farm and the muck and the endless chores as much as I'd wanted to walk away from politics a year before. I wanted soft palms and clean fingernails. I wanted a career that made me feel important and to bask in the light of the powerful people around me regardless of how weak the radiance was. I wanted comfort. I wanted familiarity. I wanted lattes and broadband.

I lay back onto the bluestem and looked up at the sky. At this time last year, I'd been standing in a suit on the portico of the state Capitol Building sneaking a cigarette next to a thirteen-foot bronze statue of Thomas Jefferson. No one actually walked up the mile of grand marble stairway that led to the front doors of the building, they used first-floor carriage entrances instead, so it made a good place for grabbing a smoke or getting away from the noise.

Over time the portico also became my retreat from the panic attacks, which struck more and more frequently near the end. They got so bad I could barely sit through a committee hearing or a round of floor debate without having to flee to the Capitol's porch. I'd seen a doctor who thought panic attacks stemmed from depression, but even after months of taking the Prozac he prescribed, I still fought for self-control daily. I tried telling him I never felt depressed, just strangled, and the only way I could keep from passing out was to get away from wherever I was, but his response was to write out the name of a psychiatrist he knew and a prescription for another month's worth of pills.

From the height of the portico, about three stories high, I could see the spot where a Capitol guard raised and lowered the flags. For a fee constituents could contact their legislators and order a flag flown over the Capitol, and one Christmas I ordered one for my grandmother. She said it was one of the most special gifts she ever got. What she didn't know was that many flags were flown over the Capitol each day, raised and lowered one after the other to accommodate all of the orders. If twenty flags were requested on any given day, it was the guard's job to raise and lower twenty flags, none of which flew over the Capitol any longer than it took for a lawmaker or lobbyist inside the building to pop another breath mint.

And I never told her. It seemed too artificial, and I wanted her to always think I gave her one of the most special gifts she ever got.

But that's what it was all about: creating an illusion of something special, something glittering, something important. It was as if architects designed the Roman Renaissance Capitol Building to awe people into overlooking any perceived lack of strength or reason in the people who worked inside. From its noble towering marble columns, to its heroic bronze statuary, the Capitol is bigger than life, and every day I saw tourists physically shrink and feel less important as they gaped at the gilded splendor. Even I, as someone who got daily doses of the majesty, wondered at times if I actually worked for gods.

Shortly before I left, a nine-thousand-pound bronze chandelier that hung from the dome in the building's rotunda since 1918 was being lowered for cleaning when its cable snapped, and it crashed to the marble floor. It took one year and five hundred thousand dollars to fix it, and when the press questioned the cost to the cash-strapped state, officials told them the chandelier was an icon, and the only alternative was to rebuild the entire thing, which would cost four times more. And that was the end of that. Half a million dollars justified for rehanging a nine-thousand-pound illusion of grandeur.

In the end, though, it was what the people wanted. They wanted to believe in the magical value of bronze chandeliers and flags flown over the Capitol. That's what we told ourselves anyway.

I sat up and flicked an ant off my arm. In his pasture the Mustang seemed restless and paced in wide circles with his nose and tail high in the air. I thought maybe the fox pups had come back, but I couldn't stay hidden in the tall grass forever; I had to call Robert. So I walked back to the henhouse to look for the phone to make a call. But fate intervened.

• • •

I never heard the helicopter coming. It was just suddenly there, flying low over the back end of the Mustang's pasture and looked so huge and out of place, it was like something from science fiction. It was an enormous insect with beating wings that *whop-whop-whop-whop-whopped* the air with pulsations that echoed back into themselves.

It swooped lower over the pasture and then arced back up and out over the cornfield it was spraying. It was only an agricultural helicopter spreading insecticide, but for the Mustang tearing wildly back and forth across the opposite end of the pasture, it must have looked like the Angel of Death.

I ran to the pasture gate and threw it open. The Mustang, blind with terror, nearly ran me over and slammed sideways into the fence. He reared and tried to get his front legs over the top rail, but they caught, and he yanked back and pulled off the top rail with him as he fell backward.

Out in the field the helicopter reached the end of its first pass, swerved around, and headed back toward the pasture with the *whop-whop-whop-whop-whop* getting louder as it neared.

The Mustang scrambled back up and raced across the field toward the fence on the other side. He rammed straight into it with his chest, but when it didn't give way, he spun around and headed back my way. He was like a pinball being slammed between one fence and the other by something he couldn't control. Sweat drenched his coat. Foam flew from his mouth. The whites of his eyes engulfed the brown.

Whop-whop-whop. The helicopter reached the edge of the pasture. I ran toward it waving my arms to chase it away, but the pilot must have misunderstood, because he maneuvered the machine right over my head and waved back a friendly hello.

The sound was horrendous, *WHOP-WHOP-WHOP,* and the wind the wing blades created flung dirt like darts into my skin. I tried to shake my head and scream at him to go away, but there was so much turbulence, he didn't get my point and twirled the thing in circles above my head, presumably to give me a private air show.

I turned my body sideways and pointed at the Mustang who still raced back and forth trying to find a way out. The helicopter was so close, I saw the pilot smile and nod his head as if in appreciation of my very nice horse. Then he gave me a thumbs up, and I'm not too ashamed to say, I gave him back the finger. Two of them actually. And I jabbed them hard in his direction until he gave me a salute and veered the helicopter away.

It took the pilot twenty minutes to finish spraying the field, and for twenty minutes the Mustang ran his heart out. When he finally stopped running, which took almost twenty minutes more, I walked slowly toward him and held out my hand. He didn't flinch away like he usually did but stared past me out to the empty cornfield.

"It's OK," I said. "It's gone."

His eyes shifted from the cornfield to my outstretched hand.

"It's gone."

He extended his nose toward my palm, and even though there wasn't a cookie, he didn't pull back. I slid my hand up onto the side of his face and gently wiped the sweat away.

"You're safe now. Everything's going to be okay."

He stood very still as his eyes went back out to the cornfield.

• • •

Chapter Thirty

I never announced to anyone, including myself, that I was staying on the farm. I just . . . stayed. There were no grand epiphanies or climactic moments when I decided that I wouldn't go back. The truth was I just never got around to going back, because there was no time for packing, politics, or panic attacks when helicopters flew overhead and there were so many scarecrows left to build.

So I just stayed.

The drift toward just staying, or at least of not going back, began when I called Robert and told him I had to postpone my return.

"For how long?"

"I don't know. At least six months."

I readied myself for a salvo of run-on sentences offering alternatives and bribes, and while I wanted to tell him about everything—about how much of my children's future I didn't want to miss, about how threatened I felt by a superfluous profession, and about how safe I felt now being needed—I didn't, because in the silence that followed I knew his thoughts scanned what lay between the lines. It was what he did for a living, scanning between the lines.

"I'm sorry," I said.

There was another silence. Then he cleared his throat. "Don't be," he said and then followed up with a quote from a former civil rights leader we both admired, Congressman William Clay, who wrote, "In politics there are no permanent friends, no permanent enemies; just permanent interests."

Then, a diplomat to the bittersweet end, he said he was late for a meeting and told me to call him when I was ready to come home.

• • •

After that I drifted a little further toward permanent residency when Christine called and apologized for what happened with Jimmy and asked if she could still take Cassius.

"I think the best thing would be to have something to concentrate on besides myself," she said, which I thought showed incredibly mature insight into one of the thornier tenets of life that had taken me twice as long as her to understand.

She and a friend came on a Saturday to pick up Cassius with a trailer. She was taking him to a stable about an hour away where he'd train to be a professional eventing horse. Eventing horses need to be smart and tough rather than high born, because in part they compete in rigorous cross-country courses that require acumen, stubborn bravery, and stamina. As the Mustang's son, he filled the shoes well, and when they pulled out of the driveway, he pounded his back hooves against the trailer door as if to verify and sign off on his heritage. I heard him pounding all the way back to the main road.

• • •

When Cassius was gone, I moved the white horse into his old pasture next to the Mustang, where the two came to terms across the fence line. There was none of the squealing or biting over the top rail as I expected, but rather a quiet and understood truce. *I can live with this,* I thought as I drifted on, at least for a little while.

Irene still came out every weekend to work with the Mustang. While she made some headway—he now let her pet his nose as long as he smelled peppermints in her pocket—he still balked when she tried to put her hands on any other part of his body.

"This is going to be a problem," she told me one day after she spent twenty minutes stroking his nose and then joined me at the fence where I watched on. "Look at his hooves."

Even across the distance of the field, I saw how long and cracked they were. In the wild, where horses travel up to twenty miles a day over hard-packed earth and sharp lava rock, their hooves stay short and beveled at the edge from wear. In captivity, though, in stalls bedded with straw or soft shavings and in pasture cushioned with grass, a horse's hooves grow long and brittle from lack of use and need to be trimmed every six weeks or so.

As Irene pointed, however, as we stood at the fence, she said, "There's no way in *hell* a farrier's going to get anywhere near that horse."

"So, what do I do?"

Irene shook head and shrugged. "The only thing I can think of is to have a vet come out and sedate him before the farrier gets to work."

Over the next few weeks, as new chicks hatched and scurried like battery-operated toys across the front lawn and as the fox pups turned sleek and fast in the orchard, the Mustang seemed to grow listless. He spent most of his time staring blankly out over the backfields or at the ground, and he grew thin again. He didn't pace along the fences anymore, and whenever I approached him, he didn't trot away in either fear or haughty disdain but dropped his head and let me pet him as passive as an unstrung puppet.

One weekend when Irene came out, I asked her if I should call a vet. She looked him over carefully and then decided he was depressed. Now that the mare, the pony, and Cassius were gone, there was no herd and no menace to protect them from anymore and thus no real reason for being.

"He's *lonely*," Irene said as if I should have known. "Horses need other horses just like people need other people. For him especially, having grown up in a wild herd, this is like solitary frickin' confinement."

"But there's the white horse . . ."

"That's not a herd. That's two horses on either side of a fence."

And so on that afternoon in late July, we decided to open the gate between the two pastures.

Irene predicted there would be a small skirmish in which the Mustang would establish his authority with a few loud squeals and maybe a bite or two and the white horse would willingly step down to the bottom rung. I predicted the Mustang would establish his authority by scalping the white horse and then trotting around the pasture with the remains dangling from his mouth. Irene readied herself with a long whip, which I knew wouldn't do any good if a full-fledged fight broke out, while I armed myself with a shovel, which was equally useless but looked and felt more substantial in my hands and might afford some level of protection if one of the horses came after me.

When Irene opened the gate, the Mustang looked up from staring at the ground and the white horse looked up from grazing. At first neither moved, but when Irene shouted, "Let's go!" and clicked her tongue and waved her arm back and forth between the two fields, the white horse pricked his ears forward, snorted, and then took up the initiative and trotted toward us.

He stopped to see if we had any treats, and when he didn't find any and Irene clicked her tongue and whacked him on the flank, he looked over at the Mustang, who still hadn't moved, and let out a long, low nicker. The Mustang's ears shot forward with the velocity of two arrows, and he nickered back with a stronger, higher pitch. The white horse abandoned us and trotted quickly and directly toward the Mustang, who moved forward from his direction to meet him.

My hands tightened on the shovel. "I don't think this is such a good idea," I said. Irene held up a hand to hush me.

The two horses met nose to nose. They spent a full minute sniffing each other until the Mustang took a step back, arched his neck, and snorted. I winced and waited for the foot stomp and squeal. The white horse, though, stared dumbly at the Mustang, and then slowly, as if checking to see if something was hot, stretched his neck forward, nipped at the Mustang's neck, and then pulled back and stared dumbly again. The Mustang nickered. Then the white horse nickered. Then both rounded their backs, gave small bucks, and took off running side by side across the field with each taking mild swipes at the other's necks.

"Oh, jeez, what's happening?" I said as the pair rounded a bend at the far end of the pasture and headed back our way.

"Relax," Irene said and gave my arm a nudge. "They're not hurting each other; they're *playing*."

I'd never seen the Mustang play before. I'd never seen anything in him but fear and defense. It never occurred to me that he could be happy or that something as simple as opening a gate could heal, or at least help him forget for a while, half a lifetime's worth of pain. As they sped past us in a splash of bucking brown and white, it was like seeing a different horse.

And the horse I saw stood on the floor of a cold desert valley, and he stared at me as wind from the foothills blew his mane across his eyes. And behind him were mares who grazed and foals who played and two-year-olds staring questioningly off into the wilderness. And behind them were the foothills and beyond the foothills, the mountains, and beyond the mountains, a sky full of late-summer weather. And the wind blew warm. And the clouds passed in shadows over his face. And I reached out my hand and asked if he knew me.

"They've got their own little bachelor band now," Irene said and laughed and nudged me again.

And then he was gone.

"Look at them," Irene said. "They're like two young colts."

And in his place was an older horse running along fence lines with nowhere else to go.

"They're going to be sore in the morning."

And so I let the current carry me in a long, lazy drift toward the end of my first year on the farm.

• • •

Chapter Thirty-One

Near the end of summer, my sister Susan came to the farm for a week. She and her husband were considering divorce, and she wanted a quiet, neutral place to think things through. She brought the kids and the dog, who spent most of their time playing in the barn while she walked alone through the pastures.

I let her be for the first few days but decided the best thing to help her work things out would be a little good old-fashioned hard work. I showed her how to muck out stalls, feed and water the horses, and collect eggs wherever the hens tried to hide them—in buckets in the barn, in flower-pots in the garage, in shoes laid out on the front porch—so there wouldn't be any more new chicks. Then I showed her how to break the eggs open over the foxes' frozen chicken and where to place it—every other day now—at their den door.

One morning as I drove to work, the cell phone rang. I saw on caller ID that it came from my home phone. Because of Susan's hearing impairment, she used a Telecommunications Relay Service (TRS) in which she talked directly into the phone, and when the other person responded, an operator translated it into text for her onto a special screen. It was a little awkward; you couldn't talk quickly, because the operator in the middle had to convert your words to text for Susan to read, and you had to end every side of the conversation as you would on a two-way radio with "Go ahead," so the operator knew when you'd finished a complete thought.

In a normal situation, Susan would call me, I'd pick up the phone, the operator would ask if I knew how the TRS worked, I'd say I did, and then wait to hear Susan talk. Since she didn't have to speak slowly on her end, she could babble on while I was fettered to slow, simple sentences for the operator to translate. So ordinarily, the conversation went something like this:

Susan: Hello. How are you doing? I found the greatest recipe for yellow-raisin date-nut carrot cake with rum-spiced cream-cheese frosting. I'll e-mail it to you. What's the weather doing up there? It's raining here, but the flowers need it. Lots of lightning. Go ahead.

Me: Hello. Go ahead.

Susan: Just wanted to call and tell you that Nickolyn and Davis are getting straight As, Cosmo learned how to play dead when I shoot him with my finger, and we're getting a new car, but we can't decide if we want another minivan or an SUV. Go ahead.

Me: Great. Wow. SUV. Go ahead.

However on this morning after I told the operator I knew how the system worked, Susan screamed incomprehensible words into the phone of which I only caught, or thought I caught, the words *police, Taser,* and *Go ahead.*

Me: Please repeat. Go ahead.

Susan: THEY'REALLOVERTHEPLACE. Go ahead.

Me (slowing down the car): Please repeat. Go ahead.

Susan (taking a deep breath): There are police and county sheriffs here. They're all over the farm. They tased Cosmo. They tased a rooster, and I think he's dead. Now some of them are up in the attic tasing bats. (There is a long pause in which Susan pulls the phone away from her ear, yells, "Don't go near my children," and then picks up the phone again.) Go ahead.

Me (pulling the car to the side of the road): What? Go ahead.

Susan: I don't know. I was sitting on the porch with Cosmo when they came tearing up the driveway. Five squad cars with their lights flashing. When they jumped out of their cars, Cosmo ran at them and bit one of them on the shins, so they tased him with a gun thing. I couldn't understand what they were saying to me, but they fanned out all over the place and then a rooster started chasing one of them, and he got zapped too. Then they came into the house and searched all the rooms, and now they're up in the attic. Go ahead.

Me (staring open-mouthed out the front windshield): What? Go ahead.

Susan: I *told* them not to go in the attic. Go ahead.

Me (turning the car around without checking the rearview mirror, nearly getting broadsided by an SUV, and then screaming expletives into the phone): Disregard. Home in half an hour.

By the time I pulled in the driveway, the police were gone, Cosmo cowered under a bush, a stunned rooster wandered aimlessly across the lawn, and Susan paced back and forth on the porch with two things in her hand. One of them, which she thrust at me first, was a business card with the name and phone number of a county sheriff. The other thing, which she gave me next, was a citation from McHenry County Animal Control charging that one of the horses on the property had "overgrown hooves."

I stared at both of the things in my hands and then looked at my sister and shrugged, *Why?*

"I have no idea," she said and then opened the front door and yelled for the kids to get in the car. "But we're going home."

• • •

The county sheriff was apologetic. When I called him, he explained they were looking for Jimmy as a suspect in a robbery, and he'd given his parole officer the farm as his last address.

"His *parole* officer?"

The sheriff wouldn't go into details about the robbery or why Jimmy had a parole officer in the first place, but he said he was sorry for upsetting my sister and for tasing the animals.

"We didn't know your sister couldn't hear," he said. "And when we first pulled up, we told her to put the dog inside, and when she didn't, we just assumed she told him to attack us."

"But why would someone have their dog attack police?" I asked still trying to picture how events unfolded.

"Happens all the time," he said. "Especially out in the country."

The sheriff then told me that when the geese and the rooster started coming at them from all sides, the police went into a defensive mode and took aggressive measures.

"By the time we got away from the geese and that rooster, searched the downstairs of your house with your sister yelling at us the whole time, and then got up to the attic, we were kind of spooked." He paused and chuckled. "Then we got attacked by bats."

He apologized again for all of the tasing and then said in an even more contrite voice that because the dog bit one of the officers, they had to call in animal control to check for rabies.

"While the animal control officer was there, well, I guess she saw one of your horses had overgrown hooves."

It took me a second to get over the insult of being accused of not taking care of my horses properly, and when I did, a profound embarrassment settled over me.

"I can explain that," I said.

"No need," he replied.

"No, I don't want you to think ... you see ... he's a mustang, and I only moved here to write a novel, and ..."

"Not my department," he said.

But I had to tell him. I didn't care whose department it was, I wanted someone to know. So I told him the whole story despite his professional disinterest, about how the Mustang was rounded up from Nevada, about how he was abused and ended up with Alex, about the barn fire, the sheep, the fights, the BLM, herd behavior, Robert, the helicopter, all of it. It just spilled out in a double-crested wave of regret and redemption until I thought I heard myself talking to myself.

"Are you still there?" I asked after I finished the twenty-minute tirade about the entire past year of my life.

There was a silence on the other end, and I figured he'd hung up back when the lambs were born. But he hadn't, he'd listened quite attentively, and before I had the chance to apologize for the outburst and explain my level of stress, he cleared his throat and said, "Wow," and then, "Sounds like a book to me."

• • •

Epilogue

Despite any misgivings she had about the farm, Susan moved here with Nickolyn, Davis, and Cosmo soon after she and her husband decided to go through with their divorce. It was a hard time for her emotionally, but she kept busy by taking care of the animals. It turned out that she had "a way" with horses and became responsible for distracting the Mustang with cookies while a vet snuck up and lightly sedated him so the farrier could trim his hooves.

The kids named all the chickens, ducks, and geese, who continued reproducing until we had to buy a book of baby names to keep up. They also named the horses, though it was more of a group effort that included Irene, who rejected names like Snowball and Brownie claiming they just didn't work. Eventually they agreed on Studley for the white horse because of his handsome build and gentlemanly manners and Samson for the Mustang, because nothing else seemed to fit.

Irene still came out on the weekends, and eventually her husband, Art, and their son, Art, started coming out as well. They used some of the outbuildings to store and work on their various motorcycles and classic cars in exchange for their help cleaning up the farm. My kids also started coming out more frequently on the weekends to lend a hand, and we, along with any of Irene and Art's friends or my kid's friends or Susan's friends from the suburbs or my friends from work, spent many Sunday afternoons together—after long days of burning burr bushes and stacking hay—relaxing on lawn chairs facing the western fields as we sipped iced tea and watched the sun set.

Through Christine I learned that the mare had a little filly foal. She was born white, which means Studley was the father, and she recently won a grand championship for her good conformation and manners.

Christine in the meantime had trouble with Cassius. Despite his small size compared to the tall Thoroughbreds and Warmbloods at his new stable, he bullied them to the point where their owners complained, and he had to be isolated. Christine moved him to another stable and then another stable again, but the outcome was always the same: Cassius had grown up under the influence of a wild stallion and didn't know how to behave in polite society.

She eventually found a stable just a few miles south of the farm, where the owner practiced natural horsemanship based on the principles of wild horse behavior. At the stable, more appropriately called a farm because there were no stalls, horses were turned out together on fifty-plus acres of rolling pasture and woodland where they lived and worked out their differences as a herd.

On one of my many visits to the farm to see Cassius, the owner explained that practitioners of natural horsemanship use herd behavior as the foundation of their horses' training and believe that the more closely their lives mimic those of wild horses, the more grounded and steady they become as domesticated companions. For the past three million years, the instincts passed down to them from their ancestors never fully allowed them to get over the fear of standing alone in a stall, and physical and mental problems hissed constant threats as a result. When left to their own devices, however, the instincts of horses blossom and thrive within the safety of a hierarchical herd, an established and functional family where ranks, responsibilities, and purpose are understood and where there is nothing to be afraid of at all.

"But they're constantly testing each other to see who's in charge," Jodi, the farm's owner, said as we stood at the top of a hill and looked down into a shallow valley where Cassius and about thirty other horses grazed side by side. "It's like watching a soap opera. Someone's always trying to climb the ladder."

When Cassius first arrived, the herd was led by a huge Percheron, followed by various other large or older horses who jostled for the second, third, and fourth levels of command almost daily. Any confrontations usually consisted of a nip at the air in the offender's direction, or at worst, a spin followed by a kick or two with the back legs that never made any contact. Under this routine, ranks were established with symbolic, simple gestures, and no one got hurt.

When Cassius was first released into the herd, however, he ignored the lower in the chain of command and went directly after the Percheron, squealing and biting at his neck in an all-out frontal attack.

"That first night it sounded like Tyrannosaurus rex was on the loose in the pasture," Jodi said. "For almost six months he had a hard time. He was very aggressive, and every morning some new horse came limping up to the gate with bruises and bite marks. I almost thought he'd be the first horse I'd ever have to turn away. But eventually, in large part because Christine worked with him so much, he settled down and seems content now to be second in charge."

Back at my farm, the Mustang went through a short period of new-found aggression and started fighting with Studley again. While his attacks weren't nearly as violent as before, they landed the white horse on the ground a couple of times, and I ended up segregating them in side-by-side pastures again.

I worried, though, about their separate isolations, and after reading several more books about horse care, which suggested goats, llamas, or donkeys made good companions for solitary horses, I bought two pygmy goats, Eleanor and Josie, who were a mother-and-daughter team. The Mustang, however, tried to scalp them the second they stepped into his pasture, and when we put them in with Studley, he ran in terror to a far corner of his field and stayed there shaking and wide-eyed for two days.

We ended up putting Eleanor and Josie in the barn, but they didn't like living in there, and we learned within hours that stretched into long, long months that goats, no matter how small, can escape from anywhere. Thus they became "free-roaming" goats who climbed on our cars, knocked over garbage cans, and ate every bit of vegetation ornamental or otherwise within their necks' reach until the farm looked like a vast desert plain.

They also got pregnant when we babysat a neighbor's boy goat one weekend, and several months later, when three bouncing baby bucks arrived, they took up permanent residence on our front porch, where they learned that if they rammed their heads repeatedly against the bottom of the metal screen door whenever they got hungry, someone usually came out and fed them.

On my birthday later that year, my dear children, at a loss for what to give someone who had everything, presented me with two black baby "teacup" pigs. According to the person they bought the pig-ettes from, they would never weigh more than thirty pounds, were very intelligent and could be taught to do tricks, and were so clean they would never, under any circumstances, poop inside. Since it's a law of nature that one cannot refuse a gift from one's offspring, especially when the offspring think they've given one the best presents in the world, Petunia and Petal moved into our house.

Within about three months, they weighed close to fifty pounds and pooped wherever they wanted. They were also loud. And strong. And if they smelled food on the table, they rutted at the table's legs until the entire thing shuddered in convulsions as they squealed at the tops of their lungs.

We eventually tried moving them out on the front porch, but they didn't like the goats, and the goats didn't like them, and the squealing, ramming, porch-altering battles that ensued sentenced Petunia and Petal for the rest of their natural lives to the henhouse and yard where they've grown to the size of small cows.

As for the Mustang, he now lives in the ungated back pastures with Studley and a mare I'm boarding for a friend. After considering how mares ruled the roosts in wild horse herds, I invited her to stay at the farm in hopes she'd have a calming influence on the boys. And she did. The electric fences, barbed wire, and scarecrows have all been taken down, and the three have grown fat together on grass that they share.

It's not a perfect life for a horse who was once wild, but I remind him on a fairly continual basis that my life didn't go exactly as planned either. And besides, there are times when I look out the kitchen window and see the three horses running through the tall grass with the Mustang in the lead showing the others what it's like to run free, that I wonder if I ever had another life at all.

And every once in a while, when I get tired of scraping muck off my boots and dirt out of my fingernails, I see the Mustang standing on the floor of a cold desert valley, and I reach out my hand and ask if he knows me. And he bows his head slightly and doesn't run away. And it's enough for me to drift on.

• • •

Acknowledgments

My thanks to the following:

Meric, Adia, Nickolyn, and Davis, who've helped me keep things in perspective;

Nicolyn Rau, who will go to her grave "not with the intention of arriving safely but rather skidding in sideways, glass of wine in one hand and cheese in the other screaming, 'WOO-HOO, what a ride!'"

George Rau, who couldn't have done better by us if he tried;

Alicia Farag, for her constant support during this project, our long talks, her tireless dedication to our family, and her ceaseless, often stubborn visions for a better world;

Jacob Dewey, for his sense of humor and inspiring creativity that kept me going more times than he'll ever know;

Sarah Dewey, for her sweet sensitivity that when combined with her courage and determination reminds me daily that all things are possible;

Susan Roth, for her unconditional support and who despite plunging headlong into the chaos of the farm has made this all work with her optimism, steadfastness, and constant laughter;

Adam Farag, for fixing lawnmowers, chasing horses, repairing dryers, changing headlights, stacking hay, raising beautiful children, burning brush, offering much-needed advice, and serving high-fiber pizza every Friday night;

Vivien Castillo Dewey, whose full-hearted embrace of this country has been an inspiration to us all and upon whose hammock I will swing all summer;

Richard Roth, for his music and the use of his cabin in the woods;

Irene, Art, and Art Beese, who've done so much to keep the farm going it would take pages to list it all—without them none of this would have been possible;

Claudine Hanani, my oldest friend, whom I've known since high school for (bleep) years, whose support and advice have kept me afloat on more occasions than I care to mention, and whose writing, professional achievements, and tenacity for *living* have proven constant inspirations;

Suzi Feld for her stubborn zest, her great laugh, and her passion for living life to the fullest possible extent and with whom I've spent many hours crying, laughing, drinking, and playing as we pretend to be adults;

Joyce Farag, for all of the help she gave us while visiting the farm;

Karen Quenaud, for caring so damn much about those she loves and with whom I've solved all the world's problems during our daily talks on the phone as we drive to work;

Christine Quenaud, for her resilience, optimism, and uncanny ability with horses;

Dustin Avant, for his sense of humor and his patience with me and for trying so hard despite everything;

Jodi Funk, owner of Diamond Acres in Woodstock, Illinois, whose devotion to natural horsemanship and talent with horses (and patience with Cassius) should serve as a model for equestrians everywhere;

Dr. Glen Lehr, a long-time large animal veterinarian in Harvard, Illinois, who spent time sharing information with me about his medical knowledge of horses and whose experiences deserve a book of their own;

Dr. Chris Downs, an equine surgeon at Merritt & Associates Equine Hospital in Wauconda, Illinois, for sharing medical information, for his help with the paralyzed pig, and for castrating goats and miniature horses;

Dr. Debra Junkins, owner and lead veterinarian of Pet Vet in Huntley, Illinois, for her heroic and successful attempt to save our lamb;

Ashley Roberts, for her support and steady encouragements;

Rhonda and Ron, for their willingness to share their lifelong knowledge of horses, for snow plowing, and for being the best neighbors anyone could ask for;

Chris Renguso, for listening to me rant and rave, for his talent as a graphic artist, and for introducing me to his family, which I greatly admire;

Scott Iovine, for his support and understanding during the time we've taken over (i.e., invaded) his farm;

Frances Bowers, owner of Saddlers Row, who's accommodated my never-ending responsibilities to the farm and my family;

Barb, Judi, Donna, Jennifer, Pat, Erin, Lauren, Theresa, Austynne (the Literary Leopard), Anne, Kathy, Molly, Jackie, Lili, Nickki, and Sarah, who make up the herd and whom I continually count on for help—thank you, thank you, thank you all;

Norm Stephens, who gave me the nudge I needed to write the book and whose films have tackled some of this country's most emotional and volatile issues with the poise and grace of fine art;

Tom McCarthy, this book's editor, whose belief in the book and continual encouragement and high humor kept me going through the worst of it;

And, finally, Julie Castiglia, my literary agent, who's gone out on many shaky limbs for me and whose words of wisdom I keep pinned to the wall above my desk so I can read and reread them every day.

Bibliography

"1926–1943—After the Sugar—The Los Alamitos Sugar Factory and Dr. Ross." May 18, 2011. *Rossmoor Los Alamitos History Project.* http://localsports.biz/history/2011/05/18/1897-1945-the-los-alamitos-sugar-factory-from-the-clarks-to-dr-ross/.

"American War Horse." *Idaho Daily Statesman,* June 21, 1916, 4.

"Animals: Wild Horse Round-Up." *Time,* February 20, 1939, http://www.time.com/time/magazine/article/0,9171,760780,00.html#ixzz2CU5zxVr6.

The Associated Press. "Salazar: Wild horse sales to be scrutinized." *Denver Post,* December 11, 2012. http://www.denverpost.com/news/ci_22168272/salazar-wild-horse-sales-be-scrutinized.

Bacon, Perry Jr., and Massimo Calabresi. "Conrad Burns: The Shock Jock." *Time,* April 24, 2006.

Behar, Michael. "Mustang Redemption." *Mother Jones,* January–February 2010. http://www.motherjones.com/politics/2010/01/dangerous-felons-wild-horses?page=2.

"Behavioral Problems of Horses." Reviewed by Gary Landsberg, April 2012. *The Merck Veterinary Manual.* http://www.merckmanuals.com/vet/behavior/normal_social_behavior_and_behavioral_problems_of_domestic_animals/behavioral_problems_of_horses.html.

Bekoff, Marc. "Animal Emotions: Do Animals Think and Feel?" *Psychology Today,* April 6, 2012. http://www.psychologytoday.com/blog/animal-emotions/201204/horse-named-champ-rescues-drowning-filly.

Berger, J. "Ecology and Catastrophic Mortality in Wild Horses: Implications for Interpreting Fossil Assemblages." *Science* 220 (1983): 1403–1404.

Berger, Joel. "Reproductive Fates of Dispersers in a Harem-Dwelling Ungulate: The Wild Horse." *Mammalian Dispersal Patterns: The Effects of Social Structure on Population Genetics.* Edited by B. Diane Chepko-Sade and Zuleyma Tang Halpin. Chicago: University of Chicago Press, 1989.

Berger, Joel, and Carol Cunningham. "Influence of Familiarity on Frequency of Inbreeding in Wild Horses." *Evolution* 41, no. 1 (1987): 229–231.

Berger, Joel, and Rebecca Rudman. "Predation and Interactions Between Coyotes and Feral Horse Foals." *Journal of Mammology* 66 (1985): 401–402.

Bliss, Amanda. "Hormone of the Month: Testosterone." *Horse Breeders,* [n.d.] http://www.horsebreedersmagazine.com/#/testosterone/4553858107.

"BLM says it has 'no legal recourse' to stop wild horse slaughter." *Billings Gazette,* April 21, 2005. http://billingsgazette.com/news/state-and-regional/montana/blm-says-it-has-no-legal-recourse-to-stop-wild/article_ac954a21-a447-54ad-a9b2-887ffaa2f322.html#ixzz2Ew5D9wCQ.

Brungardt, Kurt. "Galloping Scared." *Vanity Fair,* November 2006.

Catlin, George. *Manners, Customs, and Conditions of the North American Indians, with Letters and Notes.* London: Henry C. Bohn, 1857.

Chapman, Arthur. "How a Cowboy-Aviator Hunts Wild Horses." *Popular Science* 17, (November 1925): 163–165. http://books.google.com/books?id=aycDAAAAMBAJ&printsec=frontcover&source=gbs_ge_summary_r&cad=0#v=onepage&q&f=false.

Clay, William L. *Just Permanent Interests.* New York: Harper Paperbacks, 2000.

Cody, Betsy A. *Wild Horse and Burro Management.* Washington DC: National Council for Science and Environment, 1997. http://cnie.org/NLE/CRSreports/biodiversity/biodv-33.cfm.

Cohen, Andrew. "Are We Leading Our Wild Horses to Slaughter?" *The Atlantic,* October 24, 2012. http://www.theatlantic.com/national/archive/2012/10/are-we-leading-our-wild-horses-to-slaughter/263948/.

"Conrad Burns Gets Horse Whipped." *On Your Own Adventures.* December 12, 2004. http://onyourownadventures.com/hunttalk/showthread.php?t=222743.

Cothran, Gus E. "Genetic Analysis of the McCullough Peaks, WY HMA." United States Bureau of Land Management. July 6, 2006. http://www.blm.gov/pgdata/etc/medialib/blm/wy/field-offices/cody/wild_horses.Par.58081.File.dat/2004genetics.pdf.

Cruise, David, and Allison Griffiths. *Wild Horse Annie and the Last of the Mustangs: The Life of Velma Johnston.* New York: Simon and Schuster, 2010.

"The Death of Braveheart (a Wild Stallion)." YouTube video, posted by Humanity Through Education, October 12, 2010, http://www.you tube.com/watch?v=gyKWBBDhkFE.

"Death Report at BLM Calico Complex Roundup." The American Wild Horse Preservation Campaign, 2010. http://wildhorse preservation.org/death-report-blm-calico-complex-roundup.

Deesing, Mark J. "Assessment of Stress during Gathering, Handling, and Transport of Wild Horses." Wild Horse Roundups. February 26, 2012. http://www.wildhorseroundups.com/report2.htm.

de Steiguer, J. Edward. *Wild Horses of the West: History and Politics of America's Mustangs.* Tuscon: University of Arizona Press, 2011.

Dodge, Richard Irving. *The Plains of the Great West and Their Inhabitants, Being a Description of the Plains, Game, Indians, &c., of the Great North American Desert.* New York: G. P. Putnam's Sons, 1876.

Ewers, John C. "The Horse in Blackfoot Indian Culture." Bureau of American Ethnology, 1955.

Fehrenbach, T. R. *Comanches: The History of a People.* New York: Anchor, 2003.

———. *Lone Star: A History of Texas and Texans.* Cambridge, MA: Da Cappo Press, 2000.

Gray, Meeghan, Jack Spencer Jr., and David Thain. "Live trapping and monitoring mountain lion movements within a feral horse population in Storey County, Nevada, 2005–2007." *Proceedings of the 23rd Vertebrate Pest Conference,* 2008, 140–144. http://naldc.nal.usda.gov/download/27918/PDF.

"Groups Work to Rescue Animals in the West from Slaughter." *Billings Gazette*, March 12, 2005. http://billingsgazette.com/news/state-and-regional/wyoming/saving-wild-horses-groups-work-to-rescue-animals-in-the/article_1429ea25-906f-57a8-ad84-f0091f33d566.html#ixzz2Ew38Pbfo.

Gwynne, S. C. *Empire of the Summer Moon*. New York: Scribner, 2010.

Hack, Mace A., and Daniel I. Rubenstein. "Horse Signals: The Sounds and Threats of Fury." *Evolutionary Ecology* 6 (1992): 254–260.

Haines, Frances. "The Northward Spread of Horses Among the Plains Indians." *American Anthropologist* 40, no. 3 (1938).

Harvey, Julie. "Saving the Wild Horse." *Estes Park-Trail Gazette*. April 12, 2012. http://www.eptrail.com/insideandout/ci_20373582/saving-wild-horse-fundraiser-april-14-estes-park.

Heffner, Rickye. "Your Horse's Hearing." *Practical Horseman*, August 2000.

"Helicopter Pushes Yearling." YouTube video, posted by Elyse Gardner, October 17, 2010, http://www.examiner.com/video/helicopter-pushes-yearling-at-twin-peaks-roundup.

Hendrickson, Kristin. "Physical & Chemical Properties of Testosterone." Livestrong.com. September 2, 2010. http://www.livestrong.com/article/216682-physical-chemical-properties-of-testosterone/.

Hoebel, E. Adamson, and Ernest Wallace. *The Comanches: Lords of the Southern Plains*. Norman: University of Oklahoma Press, 1987.

Hunhoff, Bernie. "Wild and Civilized." *South Dakota Magazine.com*. May–June 2009. http://southdakotamagazine.com/wild-and-civilized.

International Museum of the Horse. "The Spanish Return Equus to its Prehistoric Home." 2012. http://imh.org/index.php/legacy-of-the-horse-full-story/return-to-the-new-world/the-spanish-return-equus-to-its-prehistoric-home.

International Society for the Protection of Mustangs and Burros. "The Story of Wild Horse Annie." 2011. http://ispmb.org/AnniesStory.html.

"The Introduction of the Horse into the Western Hemisphere." *Hispanic American Historical Review* XXIII.4 (1943). http://pubs.usgs.gov/tm/02a09/pdf/TM2A9.pdf.

Jackson, Jaime. "Domestic vs. Wild Horse Hooves." *The Horse's Hoof,* Winter 2008.

——. *The Natural Horse: Lessons from the Wild for Domestic Horse Care.* Flagstaff, AZ: Northland Publishing, 1992.

"Judge Dismisses Suit Challenging Calico Roundup." Animal Law Coalition. May 24, 2010. http://www.animallawcoalition.com/wild-horses-and-burros/article/1119.

Kathrens, Ginger. "The Legend of Bigfoot." *Natural Horse,* September–October 2010.

Kirkpatrick, Jay F., John W. Turner Jr., and Michael L. Wolfe. "Seasonal mountain lion predation on a feral horse population." *Canadian Journal of Zoology* 70, no. 5 (1992): 929–934.

Krell, Allen. *The Devil's Rope: A Cultural History of Barbed Wire.* London: Reaktion Books, 2002.

"Lone Black Horse Avoids Capture @ Calico Roundup." YouTube video, posted by Thoughtful Now, January 10, 2010, http://www.youtube.com/watch?v=lfKXh7BwgDc.

Long, Steven. "Plenty of Water at Nevada Roundup—And Dead Horses Too!" *Horseback.* August 4, 2010. http://horsebackmagazine.com/hb/archives/1933.

Major, Clare. "Controversy on the Range." *New York Times* September 5, 2010. Video clip. http://www.nytimes.com/video/2010/09/05/us/1248068979753/controversy-on-the-range.html.

Maverick, Mary A. *Memoirs of Mary A. Maverick.* Lincoln: University of Nebraska Press, 1989. First published in 1921 by Alamo Printing Company.

McCall, Elizabeth Kaye. "Cloud: How a devoted filmaker and charasmatic Palomino put a face and personality on the movement to preserve wild horses." *Cowboys & Indians,* September 2011.

McCort, William D. "Behavior of Feral Horses and Ponies." *Journal of Animal Science* 58, no. 2 (1984): 493–499.

McDonnell, S. M., and D. S. Mills. *The Domestic Horse: The Origins, Development and Management of its Behaviour*. Cambridge: Cambridge University Press, 2005.

McDonnell, Sue. "Reproductive Behavior of the Stallion." *Veterinary Clinics of North America: Equine Practice* 2, no. 3 (December 1986): 535–555. http://research.vet.upenn.edu/Portals/49/86ReprodU.pdf.

McKinley, Jesse. "Horse Advocates Pull for Underdog in Round-ups." *New York Times*, September 5, 2010. http://www.nytimes.com/2010/09/06/us/06horses.html?pagewanted=all&_r=1&.

McNamee, Gregory. *Aelian's On the Nature of Animals*. San Antonio: Trinity University Press, 2011.

Mollhausen, Gregory. *Diary of a journey from the Mississippi to the coasts of the Pacific with a United States government expedition*. London: Longman, Brown, Green, Longmans & Roberts, 1858.

Nack, William. "They have to be free." ESPN.com. May 20, 2005. http://sports.espn.go.com/espn/news/story?id=2063939.

Nash, Ellen-Cathryn. "Use of the 'Penetrating Captive Bolt' as a Means of Rendering Equines Insensible for Slaughter Violates the 'Humane Slaughter Act of 1958'." Manes & Tails Organization, 2005. http://www.manesandtailsorganization.org/captive_bolt.htm.

National Oceanic and Atmospheric Administration's National Weather Service. June 25, 2009. http://w1.weather.gov/glossary/index.php?letter=b.

Nock, Bruce. *Wild Horses & Summer Stampedes*. Warrenton, MO: Liberated Horsemanship Press, 2010.

———. *Wild Horses: The Stress of Captivity*. Warrenton, MO: Liberated Horsemanship Press, 2010.

Oelke, Hardy. *Born Survivors on the Eve of Extinction*. Wamego, KS: Premier Publishing Equine, 1997.

Oklahoma State University. "Sorraia." 1998. www.ansi.okstate.edu/breeds/horses/sorraia/index.htm.

OpenSecrets.org: Center for Responsive Politics. "Top Industries: Conrad Burns." 2013. http://www.opensecrets.org/politicians/industries.php?cycle=Career&cid=N00004638&type=I.

"Oral History: Edward Schlesser. *History of Kenton*, 135–138. Courtesy of the Kenton Neighborhood Association." 2013. Center for Columbia River History. http://www.ccrh.org/comm/slough/oral/schlesser.php.

O'Reilly, Basha. "The People vs. Frank Litts." *Horse Connection*, September–October 2009. http://horseconnection.com/site/pdf_docs/frank_litts.pdf.

"Origin of Navy Terminology." The Navy Department Library. [n.d.] http://www.history.navy.mil/library/online/origin.htm#hor.

Ozersky, Josh. "Taste of America: The Case for Eating Horse Meat." *Time*, December 28, 2011. http://ideas.time.com/2011/12/28/the-case-for-eating-horse-meat/.

Parelli: The Natural Approach to Horse Training. "Stallion Behavior." [n.d.] http://www.parellinaturalhorsetraining.com/video/stallion-behavior/.

Philipps, Dave. "Wild Horse Buyer Under Colorado Federal Investigation." *Tucson Sentinel*, November 13, 2012. http://www.tucsonsentinel.com/nationworld/report/111312_wild_horses/wild-horse-buyer-under-colorado-federal-investigation/.

Ryden, Hope. *America's Last Wild Horses*. New York: Lyons & Burford, 1990.

———. *America's Last Wild Horses: The Classic Study of the Mustangs—Their Pivotal Role in the History of the West, Their Return to the Wild, and the Ongoing Efforts to Preserve Them*. Guilford, CT: Lyons Press, 2005.

Saslow, Carol A. "Understanding the perceptual world of horses." *Applied Animal Behaviour Science* 78 (2002): 209–224. http://www.sjsu.edu/people/steven.macramalla/courses/c2/s1/Saslow____understanding_the_percetual_world_of_horses.pdf.

Schoenecker, K. A., and F. J. Singer. *Managers' Summary—Ecological Studies of the Pryor Mountain Wild Horse Range, 1992–1997*. Fort Collins, CO: US Geological Survey, Midcontinent Ecological Science Center, [n.d.].

Simmons, Paula. *Raising Sheep the Modern Way*. North Adams, MA: Storey Publishing, LLC, 1989.

Simmons, Paula, and Carol Ekarius. *Storey's Guide to Raising Sheep: Breeds, Care, Facilities.* North Adams, MA: Storey Publishing, LLC, 2000.

Smith, Barbara. *Beginning Shepherd's Manual.* DeKalb, IL: Wiley, 1999.

Sponenberg, D. Phillip, "North American Colonial Spanish Horse Update." 2005. Arizona's Colonial Spanish Horse Project. http://www.arizonahorseproject.com/History.htm.

Steele, Rufus. "Trapping Wild Horses in Nevada." *McClure's,* November–April 1909–1910, 198–209. http://books.google.com/books?id=zIOgVSycUvkC&pg=PA199&lpg=PA199&dq=mustangers+pete+barnum&source=bl&ots=bV79mMX4ky&sig=1nHDACmgXfQsJe-ZANgTfgOk3QA&hl=en&sa=X&ei=KbG7UMr_G87s2AX3lIHABQ&ved=0CE8Q6AEwCA#v=onepage&q=mustangers%20pete%20barnum&f=false>.

Spanish Mustang: Spirit of the Black Hills. "The Rare Sorraia Mustang." 2013. http://www.spanishmustangspirit.com.

"Tragedy at Silver King: The Death of Braveheart." Video. American Wild Horse Preservation Campaign. October 27, 2010. http://www.facebook.com/video/video.php?v=1705290874646.

US Bureau of Land Management. "BLM Calico Mountains Complex Wild Horse Gather." [n.d.] http://www.blm.gov/pgdata/etc/medialib/blm/nv/field_offices/winnemucca_field_office/programs/wild_horse___burro/winnemucca_wild_horse/calico_wild_horse0.Par.64861.File.dat/calico_fact_sheet.pdf.

———. "The Bureau of Land Management: Who We Are, What We Do." January 26, 2012. http://www.blm.gov/wo/st/en/info/About_BLM.html.

———. "The Calico Complex Wild Horse Gather and the Proposed Ruby Pipeline Project." January 22, 2010. http://www.blm.gov/nv/st/en/fo/wfo/blm_programs/wild_horses_and_burros/calico_mountains_complex/media_inquiries.html.

———. "Caring for America's Wild Horses & Burros: Fundamental Reforms—an Overview." February 2011. http://www.blm.gov/pgdata/etc/medialib/blm/wo/Communications_Directorate/public_affairs/news_release_attachments.Par.4000.File.dat/WHB_Fundamental_022411.pdf.

————. "Fact Sheet on the BLM's Management of Livestock Grazing." February 5, 2013. http://www.blm.gov/wo/st/en/prog/grazing.html.

————. "Frequently Asked Questions About the Diamond Complex Wild Horse Gather." [n.d.] http://www.blm.gov/pgdata/etc/media lib/blm/nv/field_offices/battle_mountain_field/wild_horse___burro/ diamond_complex_wild.Par.95065.File.dat/FAQs%20About%20 the%20Gather%20Operations%205.pdf.

————. "How to Read a Freezemark." August 23, 2011. http://www. blm.gov/wo/st/en/prog/wild_horse_and_burro/What_We_Do/ wild_horse_and_burro0/freezemarks.html.

————. "Mustang Country: Wild Horses & Burros." Version 3. [n.d.] http://www.blm.gov/pgdata/etc/medialib/blm/nv/field_offices/ winnemucca_field_office/programs/wild_horse___burro.Par.75828 .File.dat/Mustang_Country_final070313_ver3.pdf.

————. "Preliminary Environmental Assessment, Calico Mountains Complex Wild Horse Capture Plan." October 2009. http://www. blm.gov/pgdata/etc/medialib/blm/nv/field_offices/winnemucca_ field_office/nepa/wild_horse_and_burros/calico.Par.82691.File.dat/ CC_Gather_Prelim_EA_102209.pdf.

————. "Questions and Answers about the Silver King Herd Manage-ment Area Wild Horse Gather." June 10, 2010. http://www.blm. gov/pgdata/etc/medialib/blm/nv/field_offices/ely_field_office/ wild_horse___burro/eydowhgat_silverkinghma.Par.77399.File. dat/Q&A%20for%20Silver%20King%20Wild%20Horse%20 Gather%202010.pdf.

————. "Reforming the Wild Horse & Burro Program." [n.d.] www. blm.gov/pgdata/etc/medialib/blm/wo/Planning_and_Renewable_ Resources/wild_horses_and_burros/national_page.Par.10190.File. dat/Green_Book_WHB_2011.pdf.

————. "Silver King, Lincoln County." [n.d.] http://www.blm. gov/pgdata/etc/medialib/blm/nv/field_offices/ely_field_office/ wild_horse___burro/eydowhgat_silverkinghma.Par.17693.File.dat/ FS%20Silver%20King%20HMA.pdf.

————. "The Wild Free-Roaming Horses and Burros Act of 1971."
[n.d.] Bureau of Land Management National Wild Horse and
Burro Program. http://www.wildhorseandburro.blm.gov/92-195
.htm.

US Bureau of Land Management, Idaho State Office. *The Taylor Grazing Act, 1934-1984: 50 years of progress.* 1984. http://books.google.
com/books?id=ci9HQ-_d32QC&pg=PA40&lpg=PA40&dq=1934+
Taylor+grazing+act+wild+horses&source=bl&ots=wPqzKkMBcv&si
g=7eeCVDOcqDX3HoDhKwTshNjP_RQ&hl=en&sa=X&ei=elS7
UPylCMbJqgGY5YDwAg&ved=0CEMQ6AEwAw.

US Department of the Interior, and the US Geological Survey. "Quan-
tifying Equid Behavior—A Research Ethogram for Free-Roaming
Feral Horses." [n.d.] http://pubs.usgs.gov/tm/02a09/pdf/TM2A9
.pdf.

US General Accounting Office. "Action Needed to Address Unintended
Consequences from Cessation of Domestic Slaughter." June 22,
2011. www.gao.gov/products/A96236.

————. "Report to the Secretary of the Interior: Rangeland Management: Improvements Needed in Federal Wild Horse Program."
August 1990. http://www.gao.gov/assets/150/149472.pdf.

"Velma Bronn Johnston." Wikipedia. December 5, 2012. http://
en.wikipedia.org/wiki/Velma_Bronn_Johnston.

Walker, Carol. "Wild Horses: The Roundup of the McCullough Peaks
Herd in WY." *Wild Hoofbeats* (blog). October 24, 2009. http://
wildhoofbeats.blogspot.com/2009/10/wild-horses-roundup-of-
mccullough-peaks.html.

Weil, Christa. "We Eat Horses, Don't We?" *New York Times,* March 5,
2007. http://www.nytimes.com/2007/03/05/opinion/05weil.html.

Weiskopf, Herman. "Wild West Showdown." *Sports Illustrated,* May 5,
1975.

Wild and Free-Roaming Horses and Burros: Final Report. Washington
DC: National Academy Press, 1982. http://books.google.com/books
?id=Q2IrAAAAYAAJ&printsec=frontcover#v=onepage&q&f=false.

"Wild Horse Roundup—Challis, Idaho July 2009," YouTube video, posted by Elissa Kline, August 7, 2009. http://www.youtube.com/watch?v=sJPwOs8sW4A.

"Wild Horses Escape Roundup," YouTube video, posted by Knimig, July 28, 2008, http://www.youtube.com/watch?v=yrtIfcg-MTM &feature=related.

Wyman, Walker D. *The Wild Horses of the West*. Lincoln: University of Nebraska, 1962.

Zurlo, Emily. "Comparing the Number of Mustangs in the United States to the Number of Horses That Went to Slaughter from 1998–2007." Final lab project, University of Vermont, April 2009. http://www.uvm.edu/~ezurlo/frame2.html.